Amazing Places
to Take Your kids

Hundreds of North American Adventures

Laura Sutherland

with Family Travel Forum

Publications International, Ltd.

PHOTO CREDITS

Laura Sutherland is a widely acknowledged authority on family travel and has published several books on the topic, including *Best Family Ski Vacations in North America* and *Tropical Family Vacations*. She also writes for a number of publications and Internet sites. Laura lives in Santa Cruz, California, with her husband and two children.

Family Travel Forum (www.familytravelforum.com) is a global community of families who share expert reviews, vacation tips, and travel tales through a network of Web sites.

Facts verified by **Barbara Cross** and **Marty Strasen**.

Trademark acknowledgments located on pages 319–320.

CONTENTS

New England

The Mid-Atlantic

The South

The Midwest

The Southwest

The Rockies

The Pacific

Canada and Mexico

PLAN YOUR PERFECT FAMILY ADVENTURE

For most families, life has become so hectic and full that vacations are more important than ever. The times you spend away from the demands of everyday life are to be treasured because they represent much more than just a getaway. Family vacations provide the opportunity to reconnect with your family as you discover (or rediscover) the beauty and wonder of North America.

Amazing Places to Take Your Kids presents hundreds of truly amazing, family-friendly destinations that will provide you with ideas for simple, carefree fun. They are found throughout the entire continent, from top to bottom. Some may appeal to certain families, but to others not a bit—

Grand Teton National Park, Wyoming

after all, there's no such thing as a one-size-fits-all family vacation.

This book includes something for all tastes. Families who love the excitement of a big city will find lots to choose from, as will those who are looking to do no more than relax on a quiet beach. Culture buffs and sports fans, amusement-park fanatics and history lovers will not be disappointed at the selections.

Families seeking to educate, amuse, and entertain their young travelers will find a selection of living-history sites that provide vivid portrayals of times past. Hands-on activities and reenactors add to the fun. *Amazing Places to Take Your Kids* also presents some of the finest zoos and

aquariums in North America, as well as museums and art galleries that will ignite the imagination.

If adventure is key to your vacation, you're sure to enjoy this selection of sites. Hiking, mountain climbing, camping, and kayaking—they're all highlighted in *Amazing Places to Take Your Kids*.

An exciting array of vacation ideas awaits your family. From quirky festivals and eye-popping parades to historic landmarks and majestic national parks, you'll find something that will interest and entertain your crew. Jump in your car, hop on an airplane, or gas up the camper and head for your destination—fabulous adventures lie just ahead.

New England

New England, the colonial heart of America, is the place where pilgrims and patriots crafted new ways of life. The region's cities and towns are filled with sites that bring history to life for children. Walk Boston's Freedom Trail; take the wheel of a tall ship in Mystic, Connecticut; and enjoy the fun of a pumpkin festival in Keene, New Hampshire. Kids will love visiting their favorite storybook characters at the Eric Carle Museum of Picture Book Art in Amherst, Massachusetts. Visit places of breathtaking natural beauty such as Acadia National Park and Bar Harbor in Maine, or enjoy the simple, old-fashioned fun at quaint beach towns that have been making families happy for decades.

Swan Boat, Boston's Public Garden

Acadia National Park

Acadia covers more than 47,000 scenic acres of islands and peninsulas at the northern tip of Maine. Its glacier-carved mountains, evergreen forests, inland lakes, and surf-tossed rocky shores lure nearly three million visitors annually.

The Loop Road, which encircles the eastern side of the park, is the best way for newcomers to begin exploring the park. Start at the Visitor Center in Hulls Cove to obtain maps and information. The road will take you past Sand Beach, which is protected by lifeguards in summer. It's a great place for the kids to swim in the chilly water, or for a stroll to stretch your legs. Within the confines of the park is Cadillac Mountain. At 1,530 feet it is the highest point on the Atlantic coast

north of Rio de Janeiro. Echo Lake has a sandy beach at its southern end and offers warmer swimming than the chilly ocean. On the west side of the island, Pretty Marsh is one of the best places to look for crabs, starfish, jellyfish, and clams in the tide pools.

The only full-service restaurant within the park boundary is located at Jordan Pond. There you can reserve a table for an idyllic afternoon tea on the lawn.

The spectacular scenery that is Acadia National Park includes 26 mountains. Its rugged terrain and dramatic coastline make for some memorable sights.

Ogunquit

The name *Ogunquit* means "beautiful place by the sea," and this classic New England fishing village, with three miles of clean, powdery white sand backed by grassy hills, lives up to its name. This quaint and walkable downtown has been a family favorite for more than 100 years.

There are three sections to the beach, and each has something appealing to families. Main Beach, in front of the town itself, is lively and filled with children digging in the soft sand and splashing in the waves. Dune-backed Footbridge Beach, easily accessed by a lovely arched pedestrian bridge, is a bit quieter, while North Beach offers a private, restful area to spend the day.

A trip to Ogunquit would not be complete without a walk along Marginal Way, a 1.25-mile-long oceanside pathway that

was once a trail used for herding cattle. It meanders past tide pools, tiny beaches, and windblown bluffs on its way to Perkins Cove. This small harbor has shops, art galleries, restaurants, and an unusual pedestrian drawbridge. As you walk across the cove on the bridge, you can see the lobster fleet while tour and pleasure boats

The quiet Harbor of Perkins Cove outside of Ogunquit is home to pleasure craft and fishing vessels alike. Visitors can take a cruise on an excursion boat or relax and watch the lobster fleet set out to sea.

pass beneath you. The bridge can be raised if a tall-masted sailboat travels through.

Bar Harbor

Bar Harbor, the gateway to Maine's Acadia National Park, was New England's premier summer resort in the 19th century. It continues to attract thousands of visitors, especially in the summer and during fall foliage season.

The Bar Harbor area has a terrific selection of family activities, including an oceanarium, kayak tours, nature programs, and a small museum showcasing an excellent collection of Native American artifacts. Visitors can also rent bicycles to explore the 55 miles of carriage trails that lace the area. Families can rent a canoe or kayak and explore on

their own or take boat tours in search of whales, seals, and seabirds. Plus, there are summer classics such as mini golf, rock climbing, and tide pool exploration.

Be sure to walk along Shore Path, a wide, winding trail that follows the shoreline for more than a half-mile along a public right-of-way. The pathway passes many elegant summer homes and inns, offering a superb view of the area's Victorian architecture. Be sure to visit Ben and Bill's, a candy store and ice-cream parlor on Main Street, where every kind of candy imaginable is for sale.

Top: *Situated on the east side of Mount Desert Island and surrounded by Acadia National Park, Bar Harbor has long been a popular tourist spot.* Right: *A stroll through Bar Harbor will take you past some fine examples of classic Victorian architecture. The town is a visitor's delight, with many quaint shops and restaurants.*

White Mountain National Forest

Located in central New Hampshire, White Mountain National Forest (also known as "the Whites") attracts more visitors than Yellowstone and Yosemite national parks combined. Roughly 770,000 acres, it includes the Presidential Range, so named because its peaks are each named for an early U.S. president. Its showpiece is Mount Washington. Among the park's scenic deep mountain passes, called *notches,* are Pinkham, Franconia, and Crawford.

The Whites have seemingly endless trails with picturesque vistas for you to explore during all seasons. The region offers hiking, cycling, canoeing, climbing, and fishing in summer; and snowshoeing, snowmobiling, and cross-country and downhill skiing in winter.

The Appalachian Mountain Club is quite helpful for hikers. It operates a system of hikers' huts (dormitory lodges) in the Whites, chief of which is their Pinkham Notch Visitor Center.

The towns and villages in the area contain plenty of other attractions for families, including the Conway Scenic Railroad, the New England Ski Museum, Story Land, Santa's Village, and a number of water parks.

The splendor of Mount Washington overlooks the White Mountain National Forest in New Hampshire.

Lake Winnipesaukee

Longing for that relaxing, barefoot-all-day lakeside vacation? Located in central New Hampshire, Lake Winnipesaukee may be just the place for you.

Summers at Lake Winnipesaukee are all about cottages by the shore, leisurely boat rides to the store for groceries, moonlit swims on warm nights, and a rod and reel on the dock. Winnipesaukee is New Hampshire's largest lake, dotted with 253 islands and edged with coves, deep inlets, and bays. All sorts of craft share the water—ski boats, sailboats, kayaks, and elegant wooden boats dating back decades.

Each of the area's villages has something different to offer. Weirs Beach is a perennial family favorite, where you'll find arcades, bumper cars, an old-fashioned drive-in movie theater, waterslides, and tour boats. Its 1950s wooden boardwalk flanks the beach, and on certain nights in the summer, fireworks explode high in the sky above hundreds of boats. Wolfeboro is a classic New England town with white-steepled churches and gracious old houses.

During the winter months you'll find ice fishing and ice sailing on the lake, and cross-country and downhill skiing nearby. Snowmobiling is another popular pastime.

Keene Pumpkin Festival

After dark, when volunteers have lit the thousands of pumpkins in downtown Keene, New Hampshire, a switch is flipped and four immense towers of carved, light-filled pumpkins blaze in the night.

During this annual festival, held in late October, there are pumpkins aplenty—side-by-side along the streets and sidewalks and all around the gazebo in Central Square. The carved gourds take all forms—classic peg-toothed grinners, artfully chiseled ghouls, leering witches, pop-culture celebrities, and even advertising slogans.

The record for number of pumpkins lit was set in 2003, when 28,952 pumpkins were all glowing at once.

There is plenty of fun to occupy your time while you're waiting for the great pumpkin lights. The festival features trick-or-treating on Main Street, a pumpkin pie eating contest, a pumpkin seed spitting contest, a craft fair, food vendors, a climbing wall, and a kids' activity tent called Jack's House. Volunteers at a pumpkin carving station will help you create your own jack-o'-lantern. The Museum of Pumpkin Oddities exhibits the strangest pumpkins grown that year. A kid favorite, the enchanting children's costume parade is the biggest in New England, with thousands of participants.

Later, as the tea lights in the glowing orange heads begin to burn down, fireworks of all colors explode overhead.

Scary scowls and goofy grimaces adorn the collection of pumpkins at the Keene Pumpkin Festival. What began as a small-town festival now attracts thousands, with many attending the highlight of the event: the lighting of the pumpkin towers.

Odiorne Point State Park

Visit Odiorne's Seacoast Science Center before going to the beach to give your family a leg up on identifying the many creatures you're likely to spot in the tide pools. All kinds of sea urchins, starfish, mollusks, and crabs inhabit the shoreline's intertidal zone, and when the tide is low, there are many opportunities to see them. The Center's aquariums and animal exhibits showcase coastal habitats from tide pools to the seafloor. Other exhibits detail the natural and human history of Odiorne and the seacoast area.

The state park includes Odiorne Point, the largest undeveloped stretch of shore on New Hampshire's 18-mile coast. Its spectacular ocean-front is backed by marshes, sand dunes, and dense vegetation. An extensive network of trails, including a paved bike path, winds through the park. There are picnic areas, a boat launch, and a new playground. Fishing is also a popular pastime.

The land that makes up Odiorne Point State Park was purchased by the federal government during World War II and built up as a coastal defense base. Today the old bunkers are camouflaged in the hills and greenery of the park; a few are open for tours on holidays.

Kids can get up close and personal with the mysteries of the ocean at the Seacoast Science Center, located within Odiorne Point State Park. The Center's touch tank invites visitors to do some hands-on exploring.

Sand Bar State Park

Sand Bar State Park in Vermont is named for a natural sandbar between South Hero Island in Grand Isle County and the town of Milton. Its smooth, sandy lake bottom remains shallow well out from shore, making this a perfect swimming spot for young children. The park's 2,000-foot stretch of sand is considered one of the best beaches on Lake Champlain, and one where the water tends to stay a bit warmer than other parts of the lake in midsummer. Families headquarter on the sand and can take a break to picnic in the tree-shaded spots near the beach.

Next to the park is the Sand Bar Wildlife Refuge, a 1,000-acre safe haven for a variety of wildlife, such as beavers, muskrats, turtles, and waterfowl. It's also a seasonal stopover for a great variety of migratory waterfowl and other birds popular with bird-watchers.

There is a concession stand on the beach and canoe and kayak rentals in the summer. Sand Bar is also high on the list for windsurfers and kite surfers, who can be seen whipping around the lake when the wind is up.

Take a peaceful lake, add 2,000 feet of sandy beaches, and you have an instant vacation at Sand Bar State Park on Lake Champlain. Its shallow water and numerous picnic spots make it a family favorite.

Ben & Jerry's Ice Cream Factory Tour

Vermont's number-one tourist attraction is the Ben & Jerry's Ice Cream Factory in Waterbury, in the heart of the Green Mountains. Ben and Jerry began making their ice cream in the neighborhood in 1978; today they sell their products all over the world.

Kids won't get bored waiting in line (if there is one) to get in, because there are often fun activities to occupy them, including a bubbles kiosk, spin art, and temporary tattoos. The grounds of the brightly painted factory include a number of unusual items for children to climb on, as well as a small playground and picnic tables.

The tour consists of a short video presentation followed by a walk through the factory to see the ice cream–making process. Everyone's favorite part of the tour comes at the end, when two rich and creamy samples are offered. The Scoop Shop outside features 30 of Ben & Jerry's ice cream, frozen yogurt, and sorbet flavors.

Be sure to take the Stairway to Heaven to the Flavor Graveyard, where colorful tombstones honor dearly departed flavors such as Fred and Ginger and Holy Cannoli.

Gone, but not forgotten. The many ice cream flavors retired by Ben & Jerry's have been given a final resting place.

Shelburne Museum

Plan your day carefully at the Shelburne, nicknamed Vermont's Smithsonian, so you have plenty of time to enjoy its extensive collection of American folk art. You could get lost exploring its exhibition halls, restored barns, jail, and vehicle sheds with hundreds of horse-drawn stagecoaches, sleighs, and fire engines. The activities and sights aimed to delight children can alone occupy an entire day.

Start with a ride on the vintage carousel near the entrance, and stop in at the adjacent circus museum with its 35,000-piece carved miniature three-ring circus. Then head over to the grounded steamboat *Ticonderoga,* a fully restored side-wheel steamship, where children can visit the pilothouse, talk into the ship's speaking tube, and explore the engine room, galley, and cruise quarters to their hearts' content.

The Owl Cottage Family Activity Center contains historic

Top: *This 1920s carousel takes you back in time as it welcomes visitors to the Shelburne Museum.* Right: *The Shelburne Museum is known for its one-of-a-kind exhibits. The* Ticonderoga, *a 220-foot steamboat, is the last walking-beam, side-wheel passenger steamer in the world.*

Ready for a bit of nostalgia? The 1950 House features authentic details, right down to the hula hoops and Life *magazines on the coffee table.*

Apothecary Shop children can pretend to mix compounds. In the Hat and Fragrance Textile Gallery they can make a quilt with magnetic patterns and feel the textures of different types of quilts. In the doll exhibit there is a dollhouse they can play in.

Many children enjoy the museum's most popular stops for adults, such as the Stagecoach Inn, a 1783 inn relocated to the museum grounds. It is the premier gallery for weather vanes, trade signs, and painted furniture. Quilts are very popular, too, and there's always a special exhibition or highlights in the Hat and Fragrance Textile Gallery from the museum's collection of more than 400 18th- and 19th-century quilts.

There are various events for families throughout the season. Even the family dog becomes part of the fun at the museum in contests that determine the "best kisser" and "best lapdog over 50 pounds." Halloween features trick-or-treating around the museum, a pumpkin catapult contest, and pumpkin bowling.

costumes, games, a puppet stage, and a reading area where children can get comfortable. The museum staff offers free art projects and craft activities daily during July and August: Children might build a birdhouse, make a doll, or paint.

Another fun stop for kids is a 19th-century-style playground called Alyssia's Garden. The playground is surrounded by beautiful perennials and features a slide, swings, and 19th-century games such as hoops and graces. Next door, an 1840s one-room schoolhouse allows children to play old-fashioned school.

The 1950 House is something the entire family will like. This interactive 1,000-square-foot ranch house exhibit encour-

ages you to explore whatever's inside. You can open kitchen cupboards and a refrigerator to check what food is available, or sit in the living room and read *Life* magazine. The garage contains an activity center for children, where they can play 1950s board games, go on a short scavenger hunt based on 1950s pop culture, and enjoy hula hoops and other toys.

The museum's toy shop has a collection of vintage toys such as cast-iron banks, fire trucks, and boats. But the highlight is the vintage toy train. Children can operate the train and a few of the accessories in the layout.

Most of the exhibits have touch-and-learn components designed for kids. In the

Freedom Trail

A walk along Boston's Freedom Trail is like a trip back in time to Colonial America. The 16 sites along the trail describe Boston's early patriots, their notion of liberty, and the journey to independence. Exploring the 2.5-mile-long Freedom Trail is a fascinating way to experience Boston's rich history as well as the sights and sounds of the modern city.

A painted red line or red brick path connects the sites and buildings on the trail and serves as a guide on your journey. It begins in Boston Common, one of the nation's oldest public parks, which has a long-standing tradition as a place where demonstrators can exercise their right to freedom of speech without needing a permit. The trail finishes at the Bunker Hill Monument, the site of the Revolutionary War's first major battle.

Children will enjoy the variety of shops and activities at Faneuil Hall, which was built in 1742. It's a good spot for refreshments and people-watching. The house of Paul Revere, who made history with his famous ride warning of the Redcoats' arrival, is the oldest structure in Boston. It was built in approximately 1680 and was purchased by Revere in 1770. Much of the heated debate that led to the Boston Tea Party took place in the Old South Meeting House, another famous point of interest along the Freedom Trail.

Paul Revere's house is the oldest building in downtown Boston. It opened in 1908 to the general public and is one of the first museums in the United States to be situated in a historic home.

Left: *A member of the Wampanoag tribe at the Plimoth Plantation shows visitors how to use fire to fortify a dugout canoe. This practice was an important part of the Wampanoag's culture, as they depended on the ocean for transportation and food.* Bottom: *This replica of the* Mayflower *was built in England in 1957 and remains anchored in Plymouth. The* Mayflower II *gives visitors to Plimoth Plantation a chance to view the living conditions on the original boat.*

Plimoth Plantation

As you stroll the lanes of Plimoth Plantation, it's easy to envision yourself living in this settlement just seven years after the *Mayflower* landed. Costumed interpreters go about their daily lives as they would have during the early years of Colonial America—women plant medicinal herbs and cook meals over a hearth fire, servants milk cows, and children tend to baby animals in the spring. Each person has a story to tell, and it's clear that they enjoy talking. But if you ask them any questions that have to do with modern life, or for that matter, anything after 1627, you'll receive a blank stare.

The living-history museum has two main components: the reconstructed English village occupied by the colonists and a reconstructed Wampanoag Native American settlement, Hobbamock's Homesite. The homesite explores the life of one 17th-century Wampanoag person, Hobbamock, as well as traditional Wampanoag culture and history. Unlike in the 1627 English Village, the interpreters dressed in traditional deerskin clothing in the Native

American settlement are actually Wampanoag.

Another part of the museum, a reproduction of the *Mayflower* on the Plymouth waterfront near Plymouth Rock, is located a few miles away. Children's activities are scheduled throughout the year, with a concentration of fun in the summer.

Boston Children's Museum

A 40-foot-high red and white wooden milk bottle marks the entry to the Boston Children's Museum, where hands-on discovery and uninhibited experimentation are found on four floors of fun. The museum's centerpiece is the New Balance Climb, an elaborate three-story sculptural maze of brightly painted towers, colorful tubes, and wobbly walkways that seem to be suspended in the middle of the building.

The Science Playground contains several popular attractions, such as the Raceways, where kids get a lesson in physics by pushing golf balls down an intricate set of wooden tracks. Nearby, kids make gigantic soap bubbles and climb underneath oversize aquariums to observe turtles from a fresh perspective.

There is a Latin-American Supermercado, a life-size

lobster boat children can board, and a Construction Zone where youngsters can dig, tunnel, build, and tear down.

The Kid Power exhibit will inspire families to develop healthier habits. Kids can learn about good breakfasts and super foods. Kids also get all kinds of exercise

here, from climbing the walls to showing off moves on the interactive dance floor.

Many activities for preschoolers and toddlers are found in PlaySpace. There's a tree house with bridges and a slide, an interactive toy train landscape, and a see-through painting wall.

The famous 40-foot-high Hood milk bottle greets visitors at the entrance of the Boston Children's Museum. The structure actually houses a snack stand.

Boston's Public Garden

The biggest celebrities in Boston's Public Garden are characters from children's literature. In Robert McCloskey's beloved *Make Way for Ducklings,* a family of ducks travels from Boston's Charles River, with the help of local police officers, to the Public Garden, where they decide to live. The charming scene of Mrs. Mallard and her eight little ducklings all in a row waddling across the street is immortalized in one of the garden's most popular statues.

The Public Garden pond is famous for its swan boats, which have been making leisurely pedal-powered cruises around the water in warmer months since 1877. E. B. White featured the swan boats in *The Trumpet of the Swan:* Louis the mute swan made a name for himself by playing his trumpet as he swam alongside the swan boats.

Children can feed the many ducks, geese, and swans that congregate on the banks of the pond in the oldest botanical garden in the United States. Established in 1837, it has more than 600 varieties of trees and ever-changing flower displays.

A 24-acre garden within a city, Boston's Public Garden has been a favorite among tourists for years. The beautifully landscaped area gives sightseers the chance to rest their tired feet. The famous swan boats are especially popular during the spring and summer months.

Fenway Park

Baseball fans consider this storied ballpark a slice of sports history. Built in 1912, Fenway Park is situated right in the middle of Boston. Many of baseball's greatest players have played here, including Cy Young, Babe Ruth, Tris Speaker, Ted Williams, Jimmie Foxx, Carlton Fisk, and Carl Yastrzemski, just to name a few.

Of course, the best way to see the park is to attend one of the games, but if you want to step into the hallowed ground of Fenway's dugout and enjoy a behind-the-scenes peek at the parts of the park usually off-limits to spectators, take a tour. You can walk around the warning track and get up close to the hand-operated scoreboard. The numerals are printed on steel, and those used to indicate runs and hits measure

16 square inches and weigh three pounds each. Kids will come face-to-face with the legendary Green Monster, and visit the press box and the lone red seat in the right-field bleachers where the longest measurable home run, hit, of course, by Ted Williams, landed.

A tour of this classic ballpark is a must for any fan of America's favorite pastime.

Martha's Vineyard

Martha's Vineyard provides an old-fashioned beach vacation with miles of pristine beaches, clean salty air, lavish beachfront homes, and rolling farmlands. A favorite summer resort for more than a century, its picturesque towns are filled with ice-cream shops, stately sea captain's houses, art galleries, and winding lanes edged with plum trees and blackberry bushes. Bicycles are the best way to get around.

New England's largest island attracts the rich and famous, including movie stars and presidents who travel by private plane, as well as hordes of day-trippers arriving by ferry. Many rental homes and cottages have their own private beaches. One of the best public beaches for families with young children is State Beach, known for its gentle surf and wide expanse of sandy beach. Older kids enjoy the high waves at the public Katama Beach on the island's south shore, where surfboards, kayaks, sailboards, and sailboats can be rented for fun in the sun. In Oak Bluffs, don't neglect to stop by the Flying Horses Carousel, the oldest operating carousel in the country.

As they take the ferry to Martha's Vineyard, passengers can take in the view of the many Cape Cod–style houses that dot the scenic shores.

Old Sturbridge Village

Families who want to experience life in times past will be enthralled by Old Sturbridge Village, just an hour's drive outside of Boston. The largest outdoor living-history museum in the northeast, Old Sturbridge Village brings to life an 1830s New England rural community, down to the smallest details.

Its 200 acres contain 40 exhibits, including authentically restored homes, gardens, and meetinghouses; a working farm; a district school; blacksmith, pottery, and tin shops; a bank; and law and printing offices. Costumed artisans go about their work as they would have in 1830: Shoemakers stitch shoes, tinsmiths decorate lanterns, blacksmiths forge farm equipment, and families bake bread. Children can play historic games on the commons, such as hoops and graces or cup and ball, or they can practice writing on slates in the old-time schoolhouse. Music programs, storytelling, and crafts are regularly featured.

There are special activities depending on the season. Spring has budding flow-ers, as well as newborn lambs, piglets, and calves. In summer, families can take a boat ride along the Quinebaug River or an after-hours horse-drawn carriage ride.

Costumed artisans hand-stitch a quilt at Old Sturbridge Village, where visitors can step into the past and visit the early 1800s.

Salem

Salem calls itself "Witch City," so named for that harrowing seven-month period in 1692 when the townspeople put 19 innocent people to death. Today, the town commemorates its history with a number of ghoulish attractions.

There are numerous places devoted to witches and their kind—witch museums, palm readers, cemetery tours, ghost tours, shops selling magical curios, and more. The high school sports teams are named the Witches, and the *Salem Evening News* logo is a silhouette of a sorceress. The caricature of a pointy-hatted witch on a broomstick is everywhere, even on police cars.

The Salem Witch Museum, housed in a 19th-century Romanesque-style stone building, has the look of a haunted castle. It brings visitors back to early Salem through a dramatic presentation using stage sets with life-size figures, lighting, and narration. It also gives visitors an excellent overview of the Salem Witch Trials. Other witchy attractions include the Salem Wax Museum with characters from the witch trials, the Witch Dungeon Museum, and the New England Pirate Museum. Some of these may be a bit scary for children under age seven.

Witches are now welcome in Salem, where each October the Salem Witch Museum is visited by an assortment of scary folk during the town's Haunted Happenings festival.

Opened in 2002 and founded in part by author and illustrator Eric Carle, this 40,000-square-foot museum is the first U.S. museum devoted to picture book art. Children will find many of their favorite characters there, including (who else?) The Very Hungry Caterpillar.

Eric Carle Museum of Picture Book Art

Most children have seen the vibrant collage illustrations in Eric Carle's *The Very Hungry Caterpillar,* a book that has sold 25 million copies and has been translated into 35 languages. This museum, located in Amherst and founded by Carle and his wife, houses hundreds of his collages, sketches, and manuscripts. It's also home to a collection of original illustrations by other children's book artists such as

Dr. Seuss, Maurice Sendak, Chris Van Allsburg, and Leo Lionni. Art is hung a bit lower than standard museum height to accommodate young viewers, and each gallery contains copies of the books that correspond to the illustrations on the wall.

But for kids, viewing is one thing and doing is another. One of the centerpieces of the museum is Art Studio, a bright space with worktables, nonslip floors, a cleanup station, and shelves holding everything

from watercolor paints and puzzle pieces to numerous trays of colored tissue paper. A 130-seat auditorium hosts puppet shows, films, and lectures by visiting artists.

The museum's cozy "living room" contains comfortable couches and armchairs along with more than 3,000 books for visitors to enjoy. The popular Meet the Artist series includes a presentation by a featured illustrator and concludes with a book signing.

Block Island

Block Island's 17 miles of beaches, windswept dunes, gently rolling hillsides dotted with wildflowers and blackberry vines, and hundreds of freshwater ponds have lured families for decades. It offers the experience of an old-fashioned family beach vacation.

Even getting to Block Island is fun. Hop aboard a ferry for the journey from Point Judith or the two-hour jaunt from Fort Adams. Onboard, children flock to the railings to watch the seagulls dip and soar. The ferries arrive at Old Harbor, a quaint town filled with seafood restaurants, old-fashioned candy stores and ice-cream shops, and all kinds of accommodations.

If your family likes busy beaches with concession stands, lifeguards, bathrooms, and plenty of crowds, stop at Town Beach on a sunny day. Crescent Beach is a bit quieter, stretching for more than two miles along the eastern shore. Mansion Beach is wonderful for exploring tide pools, where you'll find crabs, starfish, and sand dollars. Sachem Pond is a great stop for a freshwater swim, especially for toddlers. Many visitors enjoy biking, and rentals are plentiful. Kayaking, snorkeling, and horseback riding are popular, too.

Sailboats dot the horizon as they round the rugged coastline of Block Island. Children will love exploring the island's beaches, tide pools, and dunes.

Newport

Newport has much more than magnificent mansions to recommend it as a family destination. This historic Rhode Island seaport has beautiful beaches and a bustling wharf where lobster boats unload their catch. Be sure to amble along the town's famous Cliff Walk. You can pick up the trail along Newport's eastern shore, and you'll eventually end up at Easton's Beach, where you'll find a carousel, a skateboard park, and free weekly concerts in summer.

The extravagant homes where America's wealthiest families spent leisurely summers are great to explore. The Vanderbilts, Astors, and Dukes were among the families that vacationed here. The family tour of The Breakers focuses on the more personal stories of the Vanderbilts and their children who lived in this palatial home. Older children especially enjoy Belcourt Castle's intriguing Ghost Tour.

GREEN ANIMALS TOPIARY GARDEN, PORTSMOUTH

Some of the animals in this lush garden menagerie are nearly 100 years old. Tallest of them is a giraffe, which presides over the also venerable camel, elephant, and lion. Other creatively sculpted shrubs that are family favorites include the dancing teddy bears, a unicorn, and an ostrich.

Lions, tigers, and bears—and just about every other animal imaginable—are on display at the Green Animals Topiary Garden. Eighty topiary displays are available for public viewing.

So named for the sound of the waves crashing against the shoreline beneath it, The Breakers is one of the most exquisite mansions in Newport.

Mystic Seaport

It's easy for children to fantasize about the life of an old-time sailor in this 19-acre living-history museum. They can poke around in a ship's galley and climb into actual sailors' bunks to see what it was like to have lived in such cramped quarters for months at a time. They can learn about sailors' knots and crafts, listen to old salts spin their yarns, and learn old-time sea chanties. They can even take a trip on the Mystic River in the *Sabino*, a coal-fired steamboat built in 1908.

The museum is set up as a re-created 19th-century seafaring village. It comprises historic buildings that have been transported from locations around New England. Families can stroll about the typical seacoast village and watch craftspeople at work, or they can explore its shipyard and port.

Wooden ships are still built in the museum's shipyard, and visitors can see them under construction. The town's port is filled with antique ships and boats,

The Charles W. Morgan *was built in 1841. It is the last remaining wooden whaling ship in the United States. The ship is among the collection of antique vessels anchored at Mystic Seaport.*

including the *Charles W. Morgan,* which at more than 150 years old is the only surviving wooden whaling ship. A re-creation of the historic slaving ship *Amistad* is frequently docked here as well.

Barker Character, Comic & Cartoon Museum

This nostalgic museum located in Cheshire tips its cap to beloved childhood icons such as Mickey and Minnie, the Flintstones, Charlie McCarthy, Li'l Abner, and, more recently, SpongeBob. The Connecticut museum houses the toys that founders Herb and Gloria Barker have accumulated over the years. They now have more than 80,000 items in their collection.

You'll see hundreds of Pez dispensers, 1,000 themed lunch boxes, 600 Disney and Ty Beanie Babies, several pieces of Pokémon memorabilia, and Lone Ranger and Roy Rogers toys of all types. It's a place meant for reminiscing—Dennis the Menace's "Mischief Kit"? It's here. Popeye collectibles? Sure! More than 3,000 Barbies? Present and accounted for. Rare tin toys? A whole case! Each exhibit displays the current market value of a collectible, but the toys are not for sale.

A theater shows short animated films from the 1930s and '40s featuring some of the beloved characters found in the museum. Large cartoon character cutouts are popular backdrops for photographs. An animation and sculpture gallery is located next door.

The Barker Character, Comic & Cartoon Museum features a number of collectibles to stir up a sense of nostalgia. Its exhibits include many current favorites, as well as plenty that grown-ups will remember from their own childhoods.

Yale Peabody Museum of Natural History

Towering dinosaurs and a spine-tingling mummy are just a couple of the exhibits that have made this museum a big hit with families for years. In the Great Hall of Dinosaurs you can see complete skeletons of a *Stegosaurus* and an *Archelon*, an extinct turtle species about the size of a minivan. The famous mural "The Age of Reptiles" is located here. The tomb of a 2,000-year-old Egyptian mummy has been re-created in the museum.

But the museum goes even further to lure children into the fascinating realm of natural science. Its special Discovery Room is designed just for families. Here, "please touch" is the rule, and you can examine a 100-million-year-old fossil, walk in the tracks of a dinosaur, compare your height to that of a mature black bear, and connect the bones of a rabbit. The Discovery Room also features a large collection of live animals, including an air-breathing African lungfish and brightly colored poison dart frogs from South America.

The Yale Peabody Museum boasts an impresssive display of dinosaurs among its exhibits.

THE MID-ATLANTIC

Recreation and outdoor beauty meet history and culture in this part of the country, where families can experience the excitement of a big city, observe the simple lifestyle of the Pennsylvania Dutch, or explore a harbor area that's a treat for families of all ages. The nation's capital is packed with fantastic museums and tours tailored for children, and they're all free. Enjoy the activity of a boardwalk amusement park, visit a Civil War battlefield, or experience the rocketing thrill of an Olympic bobsled track—it's all part of the fun when you visit this area of the country.

Washington, D.C.'s cherry blossoms and the Washington Monument

STATUE OF LIBERTY AND ELLIS ISLAND

For more than 100 years, the Lady with the Torch has stood watch as the country's most illustrious symbol of freedom. She is as impressive and grand a sight today as she was when she first served as the welcoming beacon for the millions of immigrants who sailed into New York Harbor.

To avoid the afternoon crowds, wake up early to board the first boat out. Tours inside the statue have been discontinued since September 11, 2001. However, you can still visit the multilevel pedestal.

Many of the boats that take you to the Statue of Liberty also stop at Ellis Island, the first American soil touched by hopeful immigrants upon their arrival in the United States. Twelve million people passed

Right: *The original torch is on display in the Statue of Liberty museum. Far right: A globally recognized icon of the United States, the Statue of Liberty is the tallest metal statue in the world. She has greeted millions of newcomers as they arrived on U.S. shores.*

through the site between 1892 and 1954, beginning with 15-year-old Annie Moore and her two brothers from Ireland. Today there is a statue on Ellis Island that pays tribute to Moore.

Many famous immigrants have contributed to the melting pot that is the United States. Among those who passed through Ellis Island were Irving Berlin, Bob Hope, Knute Rockne, and the von Trapp family, whose story was told in *The Sound of Music.* Some 40 percent of today's Americans can trace at least one ancestor back to Ellis Island.

An excellent short film describes why millions of people left their homes to come to America, and what the experience was like for them.

Top: *The Great Hall marked the beginning of a new life for millions of arrivals.*
Right: *Kids enjoy the Treasures from Home exhibit at the Ellis Island National Museum of Immigration, featuring actual items brought over by the immigrants, including clothing, musical instruments, and books.*

CENTRAL PARK

This 843-acre wooded and land-scaped oasis in the heart of New York City is studded with 21 playgrounds and many one-of-a-kind attractions. One of the park's most beautifully landscaped attractions is the Billy Johnson Playground near Tisch Children's Zoo. Its

The Alice in Wonderland Statue, sure to appeal to every child's sense of fantasy and adventure, is located at 75th Street just north of Conservatory Water. The bronze statue was dedicated in 1959 and is a favorite climbing spot for kids.

many features include a stone bridge, a 45-foot-long spiral granite slide, a seating area situated in an amphitheater, spraying water fountains, and picnic tables.

Tisch Children's Zoo and the Central Park Wildlife Center are separated by the famous Delacorte Musical Clock, which is decorated with six enchanting rotating bronze animals. The children's zoo lets

young visitors mingle with potbellied pigs, goats, and more. In the zoo's center is the Enchanted Forest, which features oversize animals, the remains of a make-believe primeval forest, and a giant spiderweb for climbing. Turtles and frogs share the central aviary with the park's expansive bird collection. A children's theater is also located here. Be sure to take a spin on the historic carousel located nearby.

It's also fun to rent rowboats at the Loeb Boathouse for a leisurely ride across the Lake, a 22-acre body of water located in the heart of Central Park. If you're looking for a boating excursion on a smaller scale, stop at Conservatory Water, where you can watch experts sail their own beautifully crafted miniature remote-controlled boats. You can even rent your own miniature sailboat at Kerbs Boathouse and join in the boat racing fun.

At the western end of Conservatory Water sit several of Central Park's most beloved sculptures. Children adore climbing on the statue that honors Hans

Christian Andersen. Balloon-animal makers and caricature artists often gather at this spot to entertain and amuse the children. On the northern end of Conservatory Water is a statue that pays tribute to Lewis Carroll's 1865 classic *Alice's Adventures in Wonderland*. Central Park hosts a storyteller each week during the summer at this location. Another beloved statue is of Balto, the canine hero of the Iditarod.

Plan to catch a show at the Swedish Cottage Marionette Theatre—its shows are based on classic fairy tales and are perfect for younger children. Older children may enjoy the summer performances at Delacorte Theatre, home of Shakespeare in the Park, but you'll have to arrive early

on the day of the performance to get free tickets for the 8:00 P.M. show.

The Dana Discovery Center at the edge of the Harlem Meer, the park's largest and northernmost pond, hosts family education programs, catch-and-release fishing, and seasonal activities such as the Halloween Pumpkin Sail of candlelit jack-o'-lanterns across the water.

You can rent bicycles or take a horse-drawn buggy through the park, which is especially fun on the weekends when it is closed to motor traffic.

Winter fun includes two ice-skating rinks in Central Park; Lasker Rink, located mid-park, and the Wollman Rink, which is one of the most picturesque in the world, set among trees and rolling hills against the backdrop of Manhattan's skyscrapers.

Right: *Skaters at the Wollman Rink in Central Park can enjoy a superb view of the city's skyline. At 33,000 square feet, the ice-skating rink can accommodate more than 1,500 skaters at one time!* Below: *A haven in the midst of the concrete and the crowds of metropolitan New York City, Central Park is visited by 25 million people annually. It contains 21 playgrounds, 125 drinking fountains, and more than 9,000 benches.*

AMERICAN MUSEUM OF NATURAL HISTORY

A colossal collection of dinosaur skeletons is a huge attraction at this museum, where more than 30 million fossils and artifacts are spread throughout 40 exhibition halls. A 50-foot-tall *Barosaurus* greets visitors in the entry rotunda, while other spectacular dinosaurs take up the entire fourth floor of the museum. Popular stops for children include the Hall of Reptiles and Amphibians, the Hall of Ocean Life, and the incredibly detailed habitat dioramas scattered throughout the halls.

Children ages 5 through 12 should visit the hands-on Discovery Room, where they can reassemble a cast skeleton of a *Prestosuchus,* a 14-foot-long reptile from the late Triassic Period. Fledgling paleontologists will enjoy examining real fossils or unearthing an *Oviraptor* nest in a re-creation of a dig site. Whether it's hunting for hidden creatures in a two-story replica of an African baobab tree or tracking earthquakes all over the world on a seismograph, young visitors are sure to find something fascinating here.

After all those earthbound adventures, it's time to head into the galaxies. What better place to explore outer space than in the museum's Rose Center for Earth and Space? Step into the Hayden Planetarium for an exploration of the 13-billion-year history of the universe. The planetarium houses both the Space Theater and the Big Bang Theater.

The skeletal displays in the American Museum of Natural History soar to the heights of the dinosaur exhibit. The museum boasts one of the largest collections of dinosaur fossils in the world.

METROPOLITAN MUSEUM OF ART

Widely considered one of the world's greatest museums, the vast Metropolitan Museum of Art houses one of the largest art collections in the western hemisphere. The highlights of the permanent collection are numerous, but certain exhibits are particularly appealing to children.

The Arms and Armor exhibit is filled with medieval mail armor, gem-encrusted knives, curved swords, and fancy firearms. There is armor of all types, including some old Japanese armor with a distinct sci-fi look. The Costume Institute displays 500 years' worth of wearables. Children will enjoy the Egyptian Temple of Dendur, with its airy, well-lit interior and collection of artifacts.

The museum has developed a number of family programs, such as scavenger hunts, kid-focused gallery talks, sketching, and storytelling to provide inspiration for budding art lovers. On Saturday nights, the museum hosts Art Evenings for Families. *Hello, Met!* greets these future artists (ages 5 through 12) with a discussion about the museum's collections and a chance to sketch a masterpiece.

The Temple of Dendur was relocated from the Middle East, where it was threatened by the construction of the Aswan High Dam, and rebuilt stone-by-stone at the Met. It arrived at the museum in 1967 and was placed on display in 1978 as part of the Egyptian Art exhibit.

TIMES SQUARE

Times Square outpaces Las Vegas when it comes to neon and electric razzle-dazzle. Formerly known for its adult-oriented entertainment, Times Square has been completely transformed and it is now filled with family attractions of all kinds, day and night.

Toy giants have added entertainment attractions to their megastores headquartered here. Toys "R" Us has a 60-foot-high indoor Ferris wheel and a 34-foot-long animatronic T-Rex. The flagship Disney store is now in Times Square, and the ESPN Zone restaurant has sports activities

such as basketball (free throws), bowling, virtual golf, and virtual boxing. Madame Tussaud's Wax Museum is another family

A celebration of neon lights and vivid colors, Times Square was once home to adults-only entertainment. Today it's a starting point for tour groups and a stop for many visitors.

favorite, as is Mars 2112, a theme restaurant that takes you to your seat in a spaceship. Even if you don't plan to eat there, it's worth a look.

Several television studios tape shows right in the heart of the action. MTV films *TRL (Total Request Live)* here, and hordes of kids line up to get into the studio. The studio is located just above the MTV store, and many shows are filmed on its balcony. Times Square visitors can also look into the studios of ABC's *Good Morning America* to see the show as it airs, and occasionally the cast comes out to visit with the crowd.

Some of New York's most unique street entertainers hang out in Times Square around the ticket booths or in Times Square station. And, if that's not enough, there are arcades filled with laser tag and virtual reality games.

Popcorn shops offering dozens of toppings, ice-cream stores doing much the same, restaurants of every ethnicity, and the ubiquitous hot dog stands and pizza vendors line the lively streets. Other attractions, such as the Children's Museum of Manhattan, American Girl Place, and the Build-a-Bear Workshop, are nearby.

There are plenty of family-oriented Broadway and off-Broadway shows playing at all times of the year, but the Disney-sponsored New Amsterdam Theater is a Broadway house completely dedicated to children's entertainment. After the *Beauty and the Beast* musical had a successful Broadway run, Disney decided to take on the renovation of the New Amsterdam. The restored theater has been home to productions such as *The Lion King* and *Mary Poppins.*

Just north of Times Square, on 6th Avenue between 50th and 51st, is Radio City Music Hall, home of the Rockettes. Radio City offers flashy Rockette shows during holiday periods, and behind-the-scenes tours of this restored Art Deco theater all year long. If you walk along Broadway to get there, look back at Times Square for a great view of all of the billboards and the building where the crystal ball is dropped on New Year's Eve.

You'll get a kick out of the Rockettes. The legendary dance group still performs in Radio City Music Hall. Many visitors to the city during the winter season attend the Christmas Spectacular, which debuted in 1933.

THE EMPIRE STATE BUILDING

Completed in 1931 and soaring approximately a quarter of a mile into the sky, the Empire State Building, with its famous Art Deco spire, is one of the most recognized of all American landmarks.

Erected as an office building, it remained the tallest building in the world for almost 40 years. More than 3.5 million visitors from all 50 states and almost every country in the world visit each year. Millions of people including heads of state, film stars, and a steady stream of tourists have enjoyed its breathtaking views, where on a clear day visitors can see up to 80 miles. The Empire State Building has been immortalized in nearly 100 movies, including *King Kong, Sleepless in Seattle,* and *Superman II.*

The building has two observation decks: an 86th floor observatory offering an open-air view; and an enclosed deck on the 102nd floor. Both offer high-powered binoculars on their promenades. The New York Skyride, a virtual-tour ride, is located on the second floor. Be sure to look up at the Empire State Building at night, when its spire is bathed in colorful lights that change to honor various holidays and charities.

A study conducted by the National Park Service found that the Empire State Building is one of the top ten travel destinations for visitors to the United States. The building's observation platforms offer breathtaking views.

MACY'S THANKSGIVING DAY PARADE

Nearly everyone in North America has heard of Macy's Thanksgiving Day Parade, with its fabulous and elaborate floats, dancing clowns, and brassy marching bands.

But what it's really known for are the signature giant helium balloons featuring favorite

characters such as Angelina Ballerina, the Statue of Liberty, Scooby-Doo, and Dora the Explorer. The parade heralds the start of the holiday season—Santa Claus rides along in his sleigh as a special guest.

Macy's employees excitedly helped organize the first parade in 1924, which featured horse-drawn floats and animals from the Central Park Zoo. In 1927 live animals were replaced by giant balloon characters. Now more than 40 million people watch the parade on television, but nothing beats being there in person.

IT TAKES THE VILLAGE

You can't have too many parades—New York City is also home to the zany Village Halloween Parade, a city institution since 1973. Nearly 50,000 creatively costumed participants—along with marching bands, giant pageant-size puppets, and stilt-walkers—march along a mile of streets in Manhattan. Anyone with a costume can join in, and there are prizes for the best costumes.

The first Macy's Thanksgiving Day Parade was held in 1924, and it has since become an annual holiday tradition. Millions of people line the streets to get a view of their favorite characters.

BRONX ZOO

The signature exhibit at this world-famous urban zoo is its breathtaking 6.5-acre Congo Gorilla Forest, a re-created rainforest complete with mist and vibrant green landscaping. As you meander along its path, you pass black-and-white colobus monkeys and walk through a fallen tree to see okapis, red river hogs, and mandrills. Then you head into a huge tree trunk for a short film about gorillas. When the movie ends and the screen goes up, you find yourself in a glass-enclosed observation room in the middle of the gorilla habitat.

The Children's Zoo lets children experience life from an animal's perspective. They can crawl through a prairie dog tunnel, listen for sounds through a fox's ear, climb a spiderweb, and shimmy up a tree to be eye to eye with the lemurs right next door.

A Bug Carousel, where children can take a spin on a shiny green mantis, a bumblebee, a ladybug, or a black beetle, sits next to the popular Butterfly Garden.

The lowland gorillas at the Congo Gorilla Forest are a favorite among the visitors to the Bronx Zoo. The 6.5-acre African rainforest habitat includes more than 300 animals.

Three times a day in the tiger area zookeepers bring behind-the-scenes activities front and center to show visitors how they keep animals stimulated and entertained. In winter, indoor exhibits such as the World of Reptiles, housed in an original 19th-century building, allow guests to stay toasty while they tour.

CIRCLE LINE TOURS

When New York's concrete jungle and nonstop hustle and bustle begin to wear your children down, plan an exhilarating Circle Line Tour. You'll get a well-deserved break from the action and relax in the fresh air while you view Manhattan's famous skyline from the water.

There are several tours available: Children with short attention spans will prefer the 75-minute tour, which takes you around the lower half of Manhattan Island and offers excellent views of the Statue of Liberty. A narrator provides plenty of historical information about Manhattan and identifies the buildings you pass.

The three-hour sightseeing cruise takes you around the entire 35 miles of the island. It passes many famous New York City landmarks, including the Statue of Liberty, the Brooklyn Bridge, Yankee Stadium, and the George Washington Bridge. Additional cruises of varying lengths cover other attractions in the city, and the sunset tour offers a nighttime perspective of New York City's skyline. Older kids will want to ride the Beast, a giant speedboat that takes passengers on an exciting 30-minute ride through New York Harbor.

One of the best ways to take in all the sights New York City has to offer is by boat. The Circle Line Tour offers rides of various lengths and speeds.

ADIRONDACK PARK

Leave the fast pace of New York City far behind when you head upstate. The six-million-acre Adirondack Park, filled with mountains, lakes, and rivers, was the first great American wilderness area to be preserved. In summer, nature lovers can escape the heat of the city (Boston, New York City, and Montreal are within a half-day's drive). They flock here to enjoy canoeing, fishing, boating, horseback riding, hiking, mountain climbing, and swimming—and that's just in warm weather. When the snow falls, downhill and cross-country skiing, snowshoeing, ice-skating, iceboating, and snowmobiling take over as recreational favorites.

There are pastoral meadows, picturesque villages, around 3,000 lakes and ponds, and dozens of towering peaks to explore. You can go on a casual hike or take a more serious backcountry pack trip. Other attractions include ski resorts; century-old country estates; scenic railroad trips; and Fort Ticonderoga, which showcases numerous muskets, bayonets, pistols, and swords from the 18th century.

AUSABLE CHASM

Ride a raft, kayak, or inner tube through the Ausable Chasm, a deeply cut gorge sculpted by the Ausable River. The ride takes you through the gorge, past towering cliffs and breathtaking rock formations cut deep into sandstone bedrock. Opened in 1870, it is one of the oldest natural attractions in the United States.

Mount Marcy, located in the Adirondacks, is the highest point in New York. It is situated near Lake Placid, twice the host of the Winter Olympics.

Left: *The Toboggan Chute at Lake Placid was formerly a 30-foot-high ski jump trestle. The chute empties onto the ice of Mirror Lake.* Below: *The bobsled track at Lake Placid will appeal to your child's need for speed.*

LAKE PLACID

Lake Placid hosted the 1932 and 1980 Olympic Games, and families who visit during the winter can sample many of the same sports and venues enjoyed by Olympic athletes. Whiteface Mountain, site of the downhill ski races, lures skiers and snowboarders of all abilities, and ice-skaters can practice their tricks at the Olympic speed-skating oval. But for sheer thrills, nothing beats the luge and bobsled rides.

Climb into a fiberglass Luge Rocket, and after you've had a brief lesson, you can hurtle down a track with 17 turns at speeds approaching 80 miles per hour. The bob-sled races down a half-mile track with a guide and a person at the brakes. Both rides are for children 48 inches and taller.

Slightly tamer is the Toboggan Chute for all ages on Mirror Lake. Participants climb a 30-foot-high platform to race down one of the side-by-side 166-foot-long wooden chutes and out onto the ice. Very young children can ride with their parents.

From December through March, watch ski jumpers as they soar off ramps at the Mackenzie–Intervale Ski Jumping Complex. From June to October you can watch them practice their landings in a 750,000-gallon pool. Take the elevator up 26 stories to the top to get the jumpers' terrifying perspective. Intermediate skiers and above can learn to ski jump at the complex.

COOPERSTOWN

Cooperstown, baseball's holy shrine, is also a walkable, picturesque lakeside village at the southern tip of Lake Otsego, surrounded by miles of rolling farmland. You won't find a Starbucks, a McDonald's, or any chain stores here. Instead, streets are lined with old-fashioned ice-cream parlors, baseball memorabilia shops, quaint bed-and-breakfasts, and historic buildings. You can enjoy the sights while riding an old-fashioned trolley around town.

Three standout museums have earned Cooperstown the nickname, "The Village of Museums." Each museum is a fine example of its genre: American art; the rural life of times past; and America's favorite pastime, baseball.

The Fenimore Art Museum boasts an enviable collection of American folk art, photography, fine art, and Native American arts and crafts. Housed in a spacious mansion built on what was once the estate of writer James Fenimore Cooper, the museum features workrooms where children can sit and draw while parents relax and enjoy the art.

Across the street, The Farmers' Museum celebrates the rural life of the area. The highlight of the museum is its collection of heritage livestock, which are farm animal breeds that were common

Cooperstown, at the foothills of the Catskill Mountains, is home to Doubleday Field, once rumored to be the birthplace of baseball.

It's everything baseball at the National Baseball Hall of Fame and Museum. Right down to the locker room that was re-created with fans in mind, the museum gives a hearty salute to America's favorite pastime.

Just down the street is Doubleday Field, where baseball was rumored to have first been played in 1839. Although this has been disproved, it's still where the Hall of Fame Game takes place each spring. Other baseball attractions abound. There's the American Baseball Experience and Heroes of Baseball Wax Museum. Several baseball bat companies that produce collectible and professional wooden bats are found on Main Street, as well as shops containing baseball cards and various other sports memorabilia.

Many families will recognize the town's Glimmerglass Lake from James Fenimore Cooper's *The Leatherstocking Tales.* In season, you can tour the lake on *The Glimmerglass Queen,* a 50-foot tour boat. You can also explore the lake by canoe. Overlooking the lake is The Otesaga Resort's Leatherstocking Golf Course, which has been enjoyed by golfers since 1909. Glimmerglass State Park features a beach, a boat launch, nature trails, a playground, and tent or trailer sites for overnight camping.

several hundred years ago but are rare today. Other family favorites include a carousel, old-fashioned games, wagon rides, and a small petting zoo. The museum is set up like a farm village, with houses, barns, and fields, as well as buildings you'd find in town, such as a church, schoolhouse, country store, and doctor's office. On a hill behind the museum is a Native American log house.

The National Baseball Hall of Fame and Museum pays tribute to the heroes of America's most beloved sport. This three-floor museum of baseball memorabilia is packed with nostalgic exhibits from the game's beginnings to the most current

Hall of Fame inductees. Rare old photographs, displays, and timelines trace the history of the game and showcase its most important players, stadiums, and leagues. You'll see Babe Ruth's record-making bat, Willie Mays's glove, Lou Gehrig's locker, and the first known baseball, found in an old trunk outside Cooperstown. The Sandlot Kids' Clubhouse, a popular hands-on discovery area designed for young visitors, has interactive features such as discovery drawers filled with museum artifacts. Very young rookies will enjoy special screenings of the short animated film *Curious George Plays Baseball.*

SEASIDE HEIGHTS

Combine sandy white beaches and perfect ocean waves with a long boardwalk promenade and amusement park fun, and you have an enjoyable family beach town. Seaside Heights, just north of Long Beach Island, New Jersey, has all of that and more.

Amusement parks are located at both ends of the mile-long boardwalk, which extends from the north end of Seaside Heights to the southern border of Island Beach State Park. Along the boardwalk are shops, arcades, seafood restaurants, and snack stands selling summertime classics such as cotton candy and saltwater taffy. The boardwalk bustles with families, teens, and fun-seekers all day and well into the evening.

The beach itself is always filled with visitors who come to catch the best surfing waves in New Jersey or to swim, sunbathe, and play in the sand. All of the town's beaches are public and have lifeguards and concession stands that rent beach umbrellas, lounge chairs, and inflatable rafts. Visitors can rent a cottage, book an oceanfront hotel, or stay at a bed-and-breakfast.

What do you get when you combine the excitement of a carnival with the activity of a beach? Seaside Heights—a family favorite that appeals to children of all ages.

SIX FLAGS GREAT ADVENTURE

Six Flags Great Adventure in Jackson is all about the biggest, the fastest, and the most. It is considered the largest regional amusement park in the country, and covers 2,200 acres and has more than 200 amusement rides, including some of the fastest thrill rides anywhere in the world. It encompasses two other parks: Wild Safari, the largest drive-through safari park outside of Africa, and Hurricane Harbor, one of the largest water parks in the world.

Wild Safari's 4.5-mile drive-through park takes you past zebras, baboons, giraffes, lions, and more, all seen from the safety and comfort of your car. Hurricane Harbor has all the water park classics: raft rides, steep and fast slides, wave pools, and lazy river rides.

The theme park's comprehensive roller-coaster collection includes some of the steepest, tallest, and fastest heart-pounding rides around. All the special terminology used by roller-coaster enthusiasts—inversions, zero-gravity rolls, high g-force speed, corkscrews, spirals, and hammerheads—is at work here. The park caters to younger children, too, at Looney Tunes Seaport and Wiggles World. Plus, there are concerts and performances all season.

Above: *The new El Toro breaks the world record for steepest wooden roller coaster drops.* Right: *There's no telling who you'll meet at Wild Safari in Six Flags.*

CRAYOLA FACTORY

Fascinated visitors watch spell-bound as swinging vats of heated wax spin around and dump their colorful contents into molds. Just minutes later, 1,200 perfect crayons pop out and move along the line toward sorting, boxing, and packaging machines. Using real equipment, these live demonstrations simulate the crayon-making process that takes place at the Crayola Factory in Easton, Pennsylvania. To date, the factory has made more than 110 billion crayons. But this place is much more than a factory tour—it's a hands-on discovery center with a number of creative activities your kids can enjoy.

Kids can play with magic modeling clay, draw on the walls, illustrate on screens that project their work, and try out the latest Crayola products from the ever-growing line of creatively designed markers, finger paints, clay, crayons, pencils, and other items. The factory features a

different theme each month, and projects are geared toward the themes. A room of Crayola history tells about the retired crayon colors, such as magic mint, blizzard blue, and maize.

Kids can take their projects home, and at the end of the tour they receive a marker and a four-pack of crayons. The Crayola Store outside carries the most complete line of Crayola products anywhere.

Children lead such colorful lives! Did you know that the average child between the ages of 2 and 8 will spend 28 minutes each day coloring? At the Crayola Factory, families are encouraged to engage in some hands-on creativity.

GETTYSBURG NATIONAL MILITARY PARK

Gettysburg is the site of the most pivotal battle of the Civil War. For three days in July 1863, 165,000 Union and Confederate soldiers fought here to determine the future of the United States. More than 51,000 soldiers were killed, wounded, or captured.

The battlefield has been preserved so visitors can tread the same varied terrain as the soldiers. The first stop on your visit should be the visitor center, where you can begin one of the many battlefield tours, including a guided bus tour, private tours with guides who will accompany you in your car, an audio tape timed to the marked plaques, a guided bicycle trip, and a horseback riding tour. Stop and see the huge boulders at Devil's Den as well as nearby Little Round Top, which holds a view of most of the battlefield.

A new visitor center is scheduled to open in April 2008. The new structure is in a more convenient location and will allow for better presentation and storage of artifacts. It will certainly only enhance the visitor experience.

Serving as a lonely guard, this cannon is a reminder of one of history's most terrible battles. It sits on Little Round Top at Gettysburg National Military Park.

HERSHEYPARK

Be sure to roll down your windows as you approach Hershey, Pennsylvania, to let the aroma of chocolate float into your car. Initially opened in 1907 by candy maker Milton Hershey as a picnic spot for his employees, Hersheypark is now a 110-acre theme park with more than 60 rides. Its attractions include an assortment of water rides, ten roller coasters, and play areas for very young children. Keep an eye out for seven-foot-tall costumed characters dressed as Hershey bars, Hershey's Kisses, and Reese's Peanut Butter Cups wandering about the park.

When the amusement park and adjacent zoo and gardens are closed during the winter months, you can still visit other chocolatey attractions such as the Hershey's Chocolate World Visitor's Center, which offers a factory tour. Visitors can climb into mechanized cars to tour the chocolate-making process, from cocoa bean to molded bar. Your family will enjoy the tour's end, when all visitors receive a free chocolate sample. The history of the chocolate empire is featured in the park's Hershey Museum.

Above: *The rides range from mild to wild at Hersheypark. The Sooperdooperlooper offers a high-speed experience. Of the park's 60 rides, 20 are designated for young children.* Left: *A Kiss (chocolate!) gets a hug at Hersheypark.*

KENNYWOOD AMUSEMENT PARK

Founded in 1898, Kennywood is the quintessential American amusement park. It represents a piece of American history as well, and is a National Historic Landmark. Located in West Mifflin along Pennsylvania's Monongahela River, Kennywood Amusement Park revisits the best of an old-style park while featuring the thrills of the new. Its classic wooden roller coasters are considered to be among the best in the world. The Racer is a particular favorite for kids. It is a single-track racing coaster, the only one of its kind in the United States, and the ride's racing aspect appeals to anyone's competitive spirit. The park's Kiddieland was built in 1927, and a few of its original rides are still there.

Winding paths edged with colorful flowers and luxuriant bushes lead visitors to the various rides. Towering trees, many there since the park opened, provide plenty of shade from the summer heat. Kennywood is also famous for its homemade fudge, funnel cakes, dip cones, and "Potato Patch French fries" that are cut fresh and served in a basket with up to eight toppings.

Make way for the Thunderbolt! Named "King of the Coasters" 40 years ago, the wooden roller coaster remains a Kennywood favorite.

MUMMERS PARADE

Take the extravagant costumes of a New Orleans Mardi Gras parade and add even more sequins, feathers, and fabric. After all, this parade takes place on New Year's Day, when the weather in Philadelphia can be frosty, if not downright freezing. Then add string-band music, dancing clowns, elaborate floats, brass bands, and an extra dose of humor, and you have the Mummers Parade, a Philadelphia institution that dates back to the late 1700s. Swedish immigrants began the tradition as part of their Christmas celebration.

The parade consists of three divisions: the Comics, a collection of costumed dancing clowns, jesters, and satirical performers; the Fancy Costume Brigade, outrageously dressed in satins and plumes; and the String Bands, with marching musicians in eye-catching costumes performing precision drills while they serenade the crowds. They move through the streets with a distinctive gait called a cakewalk, or strut. Many of Philadelphia's Mummers spend the entire year practicing dance and band routines and constructing their elaborate costumes.

All groups are judged at the parade's finishing point, City Hall, for overall originality, best theme, and best costume. The celebrations culminate with the Fancy Costume Brigade groups performing in the Philadelphia Convention Center, an extravaganza of flamboyant costumes and intricate dance routines. If you miss the parade, visit the Mummers Museum to see some of the paraphernalia and flashy outfits worn by the paraders.

Left: *Dozens of Mummers clubs work year-round to prepare the colorful costumes you'll see at the annual New Year's Day parade, a holiday favorite.* Above: *The Mummers Museum houses elaborate costumes and memorabilia from past parades. Volunteers are on hand to help your kids learn the Mummers' fancy strut.*

INDEPENDENCE HALL

The seeds of liberty were sown in Philadelphia's Independence Hall. It was here that the Declaration of Independence was signed in 1776, the Articles of Confederation uniting the 13 colonies was ratified in 1781, and the Constitution of the United States was adopted in 1787.

Kids will relate to the history of the Assembly Room, where the Second Continental Congress met to debate whether to remain a colony or fight for independence from British rule. It was here that George Washington was chosen as Commander in Chief of the Continental Army. Your kids will see the table where the Declaration of Independence was signed and the chair in which Washington sat. The Declaration was first read in public in Independence Square a few days after its signing. The famous Liberty Bell, which is now on display in a pavilion across from the hall, was rung to announce the public reading.

A number of other buildings make up Independence National Historic Park. This includes the National Constitution Center, which kids will really enjoy. It's worth a visit to experience its hands-on, high-tech exhibits.

Below: *Hands-on history awaits your children when they tour Independence Hall. The bell tower atop the hall was the former home of the Liberty Bell.* Right: *The Liberty Bell weighs more than 2,000 pounds. Its inscription reads: "Proclaim Liberty Throughout all the Land Unto All the Inhabitants Thereof."*

PLEASE TOUCH MUSEUM

This museum is petite by big-city children's museum standards, but wonderful things come in small packages. The Please Touch Museum features thoughtfully designed exhibits geared toward kids ages seven and under. This engaging Philadelphia attraction is meant to inspire a lifelong appreciation for museums.

Several enchanting exhibits are based on the classics of children's literature: A scene from *Alice's Adventures in Wonderland* lures visitors through the base of a tree and into the rabbit hole. In the hall of mirrors, your reflection becomes smaller or larger at the twist of a knob. The inter-active Maurice Sendak exhibit includes oversize settings and characters from his books *Where the Wild Thing Are* and *In the Night Kitchen*.

In the popular Supermarket, children can zoom around the aisles tossing all kinds of food into their pint-size shopping carts. Announcements such as "Attention all shoppers, it's time to put your items away," keep order in the place. Humorous theater shows and themed creative activities are offered daily.

Kids are welcome to explore the aisles and ponder the produce section at the Supermarket in the Please Touch Museum. The museum provides child-size grocery carts for the inquisitive shoppers.

FRANKLIN INSTITUTE SCIENCE MUSEUM

This Philadelphia museum's star attraction is a two-story human heart. Big enough to place inside the Statue of Liberty, the heart has been the centerpiece of this museum for the past 50 years. Visitors walk through it, following the same route that blood would take, passing through chambers and veins to the ever-present sound of the beating organ. An eight-foot-long Crawl Through Arteries feature allows children to pretend they are blood cells navigating through clear and clogged arteries. All kinds of educational information about the heart lines the walls of the walkway and nearby exhibition space.

The museum's most popular interactive exhibits geared for children include Sports Challenge, where kids can throw a variety of balls—baseballs, volleyballs, water polo balls—down a 60-foot cage to test their speed in relationship to their size, shape, and weight. Life-size photos and foot-prints of different athletes decorate the exhibit, and kids adore comparing themselves with sports greats such as Shaquille O'Neal.

Another favorite is KidScience, featuring a cave, sailboat, two-story lighthouse, and lots of water. Here younger children learn about the principles of sound, movement, and geology.

Philadelphia's Franklin Institute Science Museum is the city's most visited museum. Its most famous exhibit is a giant replica of a human heart. Children enjoy walking through the display, which was built in 1953.

SESAME PLACE

Join Big Bird, Bert, Ernie, and other fuzzy favorites from the award-winning PBS show *Sesame Street* at Sesame Place, a theme park based on the popular television program. This Langhorne, Pennsylvania, amusement park features rides, 12 water attractions, exciting stage shows, parades, and plenty of opportunities to shake hands with Muppets, Elmo, Snuffleupagus, and other life-size characters. You can also reserve dinner with the characters so your children are guaranteed to rub shoulders with their favorite cast members.

At Big Bird's Rambling River ride, parents and children share tubes as they float along a 1,000-foot-long waterway. A gigantic Ernie presides over Twiddlebug Land, where everything is larger than life, including a soupspoon big enough to slide down. Kids love Ernie's Waterworks, which has fountains, mazes, splash pools, and various waterslides for younger children.

Stage shows, such as "Big Bird's Beach Party," feature the Sesame Street cast and offer a restful break from the theme park activities. Be sure to stroll through the Sesame Neighborhood, a full-size outdoor re-creation of the classic *Sesame Street* television show set. You'll have a chance to meet Oscar the Grouch, the Count, and other friends, as well as visit Bert and Ernie's house and the fire station.

Above: *There's nothing like a lazy river ride on a hot day.*
Left: *E is for enjoy! Your kids will dance for joy when they meet their* Sesame Street *buddies up close at Sesame Place.*

First stop... Fun! The Miniature Railroad & Village has been a popular attraction of the Carnegie Science Center for the past 50 years. Look closely at the amazing detail that goes into each display.

CARNEGIE SCIENCE CENTER

There is so much for children to do at this imaginative science museum in Pittsburgh that they may never get to Exploration Station, the enormous fourth floor filled with interactive exhibits designed just for kids.

Many children become sidetracked in SportsWorks, an entire building that emphasizes the physics of sports with virtual reality rides that rival any amusement park for fun. Kids can run a race against a life-size virtual image of Jackie Joyner-Kersee on a real track with lanes or play a game of optical illusion mini golf. Or they can design their own roller-coaster ride on a special computer, then head into a simulator, get strapped down, and experience the ride they've just created.

At the Miniature Railroad & Village display, adults will marvel at the minute historical accuracy of familiar Pittsburgh neighborhoods, while kids are spellbound by its special animated features. There is a working amusement park, and if you look closely, you'll see PBS's Mister Rogers sitting on his front porch swing.

One of the museum's signature exhibits, the World War II–era USS *Requin* submarine, shows in exacting detail how the submarine would have looked onboard during its time of service. The exhibit is brought to life by dynamic sound effects.

The center has three theaters that run science shows all day long, and a planetarium has daytime star shows and evening laser light shows.

PENNSYLVANIA DUTCH COUNTRY

A common sight in Pennsylvania Dutch Country, an Amish farmer plows his field with his team of horses. The area draws many visitors, curious to see a way of life that doesn't include modern conveniences.

As you drive through this peaceful realm, you'll pass classic barns and silos, horse-drawn buggies, wooden covered bridges, and a pretty patchwork of farm fields and villages. You might even see girls in bonnets and boys in hats, but you won't see them riding bicycles to get to their one-room schoolhouses. Some children aren't allowed to have bicycles because their elders fear they might venture too far from home. That's just one of the many things that set apart the Pennsylvania Dutch Country, which hearkens back in time to a simpler era.

Plan to stop at one of the region's pretzel bakeries, such as the Sturgis Pretzel House in Lititz, which has been baking the snack since 1861. Here you can roll, twist, and fold your own pretzels, and eat them right out of the stone oven. At Central Market in Lancaster City, you can sample or purchase regional produce, flowers, meats, candies, jams, baked goods, and Amish crafts at the oldest publicly owned, continuously operating farmers' market, dating back to the 1730s.

Strasburg is a train lover's paradise. Ride the Strasburg Rail Road pulled by an old-fashioned locomotive, or visit the Railroad Museum of Pennsylvania with its vintage locomotives and cabooses. Nearby, The Choo Choo Barn, Traintown USA, showcases 22 operating model trains that chug along through elaborate miniature worlds and landscapes.

WINTERTHUR GARDENS AND ENCHANTED WOODS

Many people visit Winterthur, the lavish former home of Henry Francis du Pont, to see its collection of art and antiques and its elaborate formal gardens. Most popular with families is its Enchanted Woods, a three-acre fairy-tale garden. Children delight in the legend that fairies brought broken stones, old columns, crumbling millstones, and cast-off balustrades to this hilltop area to create a magical place of wonder for children.

The Tulip Tree House is located in a hollow tree that leads to the Faerie Cottage. With its stone walls and thatched roof, the cottage is right out of a storybook. It features running water, and kids can operate a hand pump to force water into a trough that, when filled, cascades into two lovely ponds. Nearby, a giant egg-filled bird's nest large enough for children to climb into is woven out of sticks. A magical mushroom ring sports a sign that reads, "never step into a fairy ring," and according to fairy lore, if you do you're transported to fairyland. For many children, the temptation is too great, and when they step inside, they are enveloped in a mist of fog. Kids also enjoy the estate's Touch-It Room, an imaginative play area with a child-size parlor, a small general store, and an area featuring old-fashioned toys.

The 60-acre Winterthur Gardens offer a number of beautiful formal gardens to meander through.

LEWES

A seafaring hub since Dutch settlers arrived in 1631, this Delaware seaport is situated where Delaware Bay meets the Atlantic Ocean. It is filled with both bay and ocean beaches where you can swim, surf, or comb the sand for old Spanish pieces-of-eight coins, which some say still wash up on shore from an old shipwreck.

The village of Lewes is a charmer, lined with historic homes and quaint antique stores. Several key family stops can be found here, such as Notting Hill Coffee Roastery/Lewes Bake Shoppe, home of the famous Lewes sticky bun, and the award-winning King's Homemade Ice Cream Shop. At Fisherman's Wharf, families can drop a line to fish for flounder or sea bass, or board a boat to go whale and dolphin watching.

Families with small children enjoy sheltered Lewes Beach with its gentle waters. Older children often enjoy visiting Cape Henlopen State Park, just east of Lewes,

Known as "the first town in the first state," historic Lewes is a family vacation favorite that offers miles of beautiful beaches.

which has five miles of shoreline and larger waves. Kids love exploring an abandoned military bunker that's located near one of the park's hiking trails. They can also climb to the top of a World War II observation tower and search for imaginary invaders.

ANNAPOLIS

Think Annapolis, and all things nautical come to mind. First settled in 1649, the city soon became an important colonial port. But after the Revolutionary War, shipping moved to the Port of Baltimore and Annapolis's business shifted to small-boat harvesting of oysters, crabs, and fish from the shallow waters of Chesapeake Bay.

Today, the town is known as the sailing capital of America and home to the U.S. Naval Academy. Sailing is definitely a favorite pastime for Annapolis residents, and many major national and international sailing events, as well as weekly racing events for the locals, take place in the bay.

There are plenty of opportunities to get out on the water—schooners, sailing sloops, and cruise boats offer a variety of trips, narrated tours, and even Sunday brunch. Take a guided kayak tour of downtown Annapolis or paddle along one of the many creeks that feed the bay. Sailing schools with family programs abound. A particular favorite with kids is the *Sea Gypsy,* a re-created pirate ship that offers an action-packed cruise. Kids can pretend to be pirates and defend their ship from fierce attackers by using its water cannons.

The Naval Academy is well worth a visit, and its visitor center features interactive exhibits and displays, as well as a theater showing the award-winning film *To Lead and to Serve.*

Annapolis Harbor is a fascinating place for children to explore and is sure to spark the imagination of fledgling sailors.

Baltimore's Inner Harbor

While Baltimore's Inner Harbor still operates as a working port, most of the big freighter shipping activity is in its Outer Harbor. Water taxis are now the most common boat you'll see in the Inner Harbor, as they zip tourists and locals from one terrific attraction to the next. The Inner Harbor has become Baltimore's top tourist destination, and you'll need at least a day to enjoy the museums, entertainment, and eateries at this lively, family-friendly seaport.

Several attractions are related to Baltimore's 300-year history as a maritime powerhouse. The USS *Constellation*, a restored 1854 wooden naval warship, is docked in the harbor and is open for tours. Children ages 6 and older can participate in a special program to learn about the lives of the youngest sailors—some were only 11 at the time—who spent months at sea working on the ship. Nearby at the Baltimore Maritime Museum, three docked historic ships and a restored lighthouse can be explored.

The National Aquarium features marine life from Maryland's tidal marshes, as well as creatures of the deep from all over the planet. A steamy tropical rainforest has

The last Civil War vessel remaining afloat, the USS Constellation *is on display for visitors to tour in Baltimore's Inner Harbor. More than 200,000 people have toured the historic ship since 1999.*

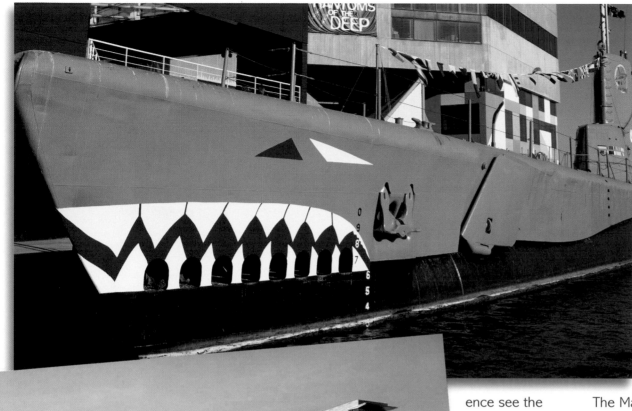

For visitors who don't mind close quarters, the Maritime Museum offers overnight stays aboard the submarine USS Torsk.

The Maryland Academy of Sciences houses the museums in the Inner Harbor, including the venerable Maryland Science Center, the state's oldest scientific institution. Children will enjoy its Kids Room and many other hands-on activities.

poisonous dart frogs, piranhas, and sloths contained in an enormous greenhouse enclosure on the top level. Underwater cameras at the dolphin show let the audi-ence see the trained mammals dive and accelerate as they prepare to leap out of the water. More than 10,000 creatures call the aquarium home.

Baltimore has a fantastic children's museum, Port Discovery, which is located one block northeast of the Inner Harbor. Disney's Imagineers designed most of the museum's exhibits. Its three floors of fun include a three-story urban tree house that has rope ladders, bridges, slides, tunnels, and even zip lines. Everything in the museum is hands-on, and kids can pro-duce movies, create all kinds of art, and make crafts with real tools. Miss Perception's Mystery House is a particularly popular stop, where young-sters help a detective solve the mystery of the disappearing Baffeld family by sifting through clues and bits of evidence—they even get to crawl through a kitchen sink as they search.

The Maryland Science Center has hun-dreds of hands-on activities that engage both children and adults. Its Kids Room is full of fun: There's a water play area and a Baltimore streetscape with doorknobs to turn, doorbells to ring, and steps to climb. There's even an area where babies can crawl on waterbeds and play with soft blocks. In other parts of the museum kids compare their footprint to that of a dinosaur, race bubbles, and touch a cloud. The planetarium and IMAX theater also offer regular programs for kids.

For a great view of Baltimore, the Top of the World is located on the 27th floor of the city's World Trade Center near the Maritime Museum. The attraction has large windows and photos that are labeled to help identify the sites below.

THE B&O RAILROAD MUSEUM

Anyone who has ever played Monopoly knows the B&O Railroad. But they may not know that "B&O" stands for "Baltimore & Ohio," a railroad company that at one time ran trains from the Ohio River to Baltimore and was one of the most important freight and passenger lines in the country. The B&O Railroad Museum is listed on the National Register of Historic Landmarks. It's situated in Baltimore, the final destination of the B&O, and it is the largest railroad museum in the western hemisphere.

Train rides are offered Tuesday–Sunday, April–December. The museum features a large collection of railroad cars. Trains are displayed in a brick roundhouse and on outdoor platforms. Kids can climb in a caboose and a World War II troop sleeper car, and watch large toy trains make their way through an outdoor garden.

Two smaller toy trains are set up in an old passenger car, and yet another railcar has been made into a theater that shows short films about trains. Other displays include the stationmaster's quarters, a waiting room, a ticket office, and a freight house. During warmer months, kids can play on an outdoor wooden train set.

The B&O Railroad Museum is an affiliate of the Smithsonian Museum. Its campus includes the original roundhouse, which features a huge collection of actual railroad cars and engines, as well as a wealth of railroad memorabilia.

FOURTH OF JULY FESTIVITIES

For America's finest Fourth of July birthday party, the place to be is in its capital city. The day begins with a rousing dramatic reading of the Declaration of Independence, followed by a parade complete with Marine Corps, Army, Navy, and Air Force bands; drill teams and marching groups representing all parts of the United States; VIPs; floats; and giant balloons. The parade winds down ten blocks of Constitution Avenue beside the National Mall, the capital's hub of activity.

After the parade, head into the Mall to check out the Smithsonian's National Folklife Festival, a dazzling display of music, song, dance, crafts, foods, and storytelling that celebrates the nation's traditions. Visitors are encouraged to join in with singing and dancing. Several events geared toward children are always a part of the festival.

At 8:00 P.M. the National Symphony Orchestra and other top-rate guest performers get the crowd in a patriotic mood with favorites such as John Philip Sousa's "Stars and Stripes Forever" and the "1812 Overture" in front of the U.S. Capitol. The grand finale is an amazing fireworks display against the picturesque backdrops of the U.S. Capitol and the Washington Monument.

The first celebration involved cowbells and bonfires, but it's come a long way since then. Don't miss the state-of-the-art fireworks display that concludes Washington, D.C.'s annual Fourth of July festivities.

THE NATIONAL MALL

The National Mall is a tree-lined stretch of parkland that runs for 2.5 miles from the banks of the Potomac River to the U.S. Capitol. It is the center of every visitor's trip to Washington, D.C. Families love visiting its grand monuments, memorials that stir the emotions, and world-class museums. Best of all: It's free.

The Mall is an easy place to take kids for museum touring because when they get bored, you can take them outside to run around or head to yet another museum with a completely different focus.

The National Museum of American History is one of the best places to start. (Note, though, that this museum closed in September 2006 for renovations; it is scheduled to reopen by summer 2008. While it is closed some of its objects are on display at the National Air and Space Museum.) There's so much to see here

The beauty of Washington, D.C.'s National Mall is just one of the reasons the city attracts visitors from all over the world. Its assortment of museums and monuments offers something to appeal to everyone.

that you can easily tailor your wanderings to your kids' interests. There are inaugural gowns of the first ladies, the original Kermit the Frog puppet said to be cut from Jim Henson's mother's coat, full-size American trains, and the ruby slippers worn by Judy Garland in *The Wizard of Oz*. When you tire of touring, stop in the Victorian–era ice cream parlor for a snack.

The National Museum of Natural History, another blue-ribbon museum for children, features a collection of dinosaur fossils; African mammals dioramas; and an insect zoo with live black widow spiders, ant colonies, and tarantulas. Its Discovery Room has hands-on activities and touch tables for young children.

Most children's favorite exhibits at the National Gallery of Art are the paintings with children in them and the colossal Alexander Calder mobiles that seem to defy gravity as they hang suspended in space in perfect balance. The outdoor sculpture garden nearby is a favorite place for kids to burn off steam.

You can view a diverse collection of art at the galleries located in the Mall. The Freer Gallery of Art and the Arthur M. Sackler Gallery are noted for their collections of fine Asian art. The National Museum of African Art features vivid exhibits of finely crafted masks, intricate wood carvings, and more.

Children of all ages enjoy climbing to the top of the Washington Monument. Inside are an elevator and an 897-step stairway, as well as an observation deck at 500 feet that offers a 360-degree view. Other monuments and memorials are worth a visit as well.

The most rousing night out on the town is free. Pack a picnic dinner and arrive before the start of the 8:00 P.M. military band concert to claim your square of turf. The kids can run around in

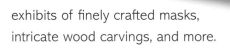

The Capitol, rich with history, is a must-see attraction. It has been the scene of many historical events, including presidential inaugurations.

between bites while you enjoy the fine sounds of the Army, Navy, Air Force, and Marine bands. The concerts are offered near the Capitol most summer weeknights, weather permitting. You're guaranteed to leave in high spirits.

It looks like Orville Wright is bringing it in for a landing. A section of the 1903 Wright Flyer, the world's first airplane, is on display at the Smithsonian's National Air and Space Museum. The exhibit also features a letter that Wilbur Wright wrote to the Smithsonian Institution requesting publications on aviation.

National Air and Space Museum

Showcasing the icons of space and aviation—*Apollo* modules, a *Mercury* space capsule, lunar landing probes, the Wright Brothers' 1903 Flyer, and full-size missiles—the most-visited museum in the world exhibits the real deal instead of models. At this Washington, D.C., museum children can touch a piece of real moon rock, activate a supersonic wind tunnel, and see John Glenn's flight suit.

There's a space station you can actually walk through (where wax astronauts sleep upright strapped to cots), and many multimedia areas that ratchet up the experience for kids.

One sure favorite is the At the Controls: Flight Simulator Zone, where visitors can flip over, twist, and turn as they pilot a full-motion flight simulator. Other such simulation programs allow visitors to fly combat missions, experience a space walk, or pilot aircraft such as an *F/A-18 Hornet*, Lindbergh's *Spirit of St. Louis*, WWII's infamous *P-51 Mustang*, and the Japanese Mitsubishi *Zero*. You can even see if you have what it takes to land a jet fighter on an aircraft carrier.

When the crowds start to drain your energy, direct yourselves to the museum's Einstein Planetarium or the IMAX theater, where films rotate continually, for a restful, educational break.

BUREAU OF ENGRAVING AND PRINTING

The buck starts here, and you can watch as bills evolve from large blank sheets of paper into complexly printed wallet-size notes. A fortune rolls off the presses every few minutes. Around $635 million is printed each day ($232 billion per year), mostly for the purpose of replacing worn bills already in circulation, since currency's average shelf life is around two years.

The presses roll 24 hours a day year-round. Tours follow the various steps involved in currency production, from the printing on 23 giant presses to the slicing of the paper into individual bills and the machines that stack and bundle them. You'll learn about the latest steps the Bureau has put in place to thwart counterfeiting and what type of durable paper is used that can withstand thousands of wallets, hands, and

ATMs. At the end of the tour, you can measure your height against imaginary stacks of money and buy uncut sheets of bills in different denominations, as well as packages of shredded cash.

While everyone wonders where their money goes, the Bureau of Engraving and Printing can tell you where it comes from. Tours of the facility offer a fascinating look at the country's production of currency.

INTERNATIONAL SPY MUSEUM

Learn firsthand how a spy operates at the only museum in the United States dedicated to the world of espionage. Upon your arrival at Washington, D.C.'s International Spy Museum, you'll adopt a "cover" and receive a new identity. You'll need to remember this information to see how well you perform as a spy, particularly when border guards throughout the museum interrogate you.

You'll learn how spies disguise themselves with fake hair and face-altering makeup and how Hollywood and the CIA worked together to come up with some amazing disguises. Some of the family programs include workshops on disguise-making, as well as on making and breaking secret codes and inventing concealment devices. On display are classic hidden spy craft tools such as buttonhole cameras, lapel knives, lipstick pistols, and hollowed-out coins concealing microdots.

Historical exhibits discuss espionage techniques used in the past, when spies shot secret messages into forts using bows and arrows and hundreds of thousands of pigeons flew secret messages across enemy lines. Other exhibits include a re-created tunnel beneath the divided city of Berlin during the Cold War and an exhibit on escape and evasion techniques in wartime.

Were you born to be a spy? Find out as you tour the International Spy Museum. You'll enjoy your journey into the world of disguises and mystery.

THE NATIONAL CHERRY BLOSSOM FESTIVAL

What better way to greet spring than with a trip to the National Cherry Blossom Festival? This two-week celebration features a kite festival, a parade, daily traditional music and dance performances, martial arts demonstrations, bike tours of the pink and white blossoms, origami lessons, a Japanese street fair, fireworks, and other special events. The festival celebrates not only the arrival of spring, it also commemorates the gift of 3,000 cherry trees to the city of Washington, D.C., from the people of Tokyo in 1912, as a symbol of friendship between the two nations.

The parade is the festival's biggest event and features spectacular floats, marching bands, taiko drum corps, costumed dance groups, and giant helium balloons. Sakura Matsuri, a Japanese street festival held after the parade, exhibits the traditions, arts, and food of Japan. You'll also see performances by children's musical ensembles. Kids will enjoy playing Japanese games and learning all about Japanese paper- and doll-making.

At the kite festival, hundreds of colorful handmade creations ride the wind as kite fliers compete for prizes. The popular trick kite showdown dazzles the crowd with fantastic aerial acrobatics. For sheer thrills, nothing beats the traditional Japanese Rokakku kite battle, where warring kites bank and dive as fliers try to force their opponent's kite to the ground.

The capital celebrates the blooming of its cherry trees with the annual Cherry Blossom Festival. The trees have become synonymous with Washington, D.C.

NATIONAL MUSEUM OF THE AMERICAN INDIAN

The newest star in a constellation of world-class Smithsonian museums, this showplace of Native American cultures, from the Arctic Circle to Tierra del Fuego, is a must-see in Washington, D.C. As visitors first step inside the museum, they are greeted by the sight of the word *welcome,* translated into multiple Indian languages and projected onto a 23-foot-wide screen. Many visitors head right to Lelawi Theater, which continually screens a short film that is projected on four Native American blankets and an adjacent dome. The film shows the lives of residents in Native American communities today.

Kids enjoy the journey through the museum's exhibits, which include steamy wetlands and lush green woodlands. They can participate in a Native American celebration of song and dance and listen to storytelling.

Exhibits at the museum include painted hides from the Plains Indians, woodcarvings from North America's northwest coast, basketry from the southwestern United States, carved jade from the Maya, and gold from the Andean cultures. Performances regularly feature storytellers, dancers, musicians, and informative talks by Native Americans. At the museum café, you can sample native specialties such as buffalo chili on fry bread, Peruvian mashed potato cakes, and smoked Northwest salmon.

The National Museum of the American Indian celebrates the history and heritage of Native Americans. It's a multimedia experience that is sure to educate and enlighten visitors.

Scientists believe that fewer than 1,000 giant pandas remain in the wild. This panda is a popular resident of the National Zoo.

NATIONAL ZOO

Start the day bright and early with a visit to the National Zoo. It opens at 6:00 A.M. so visitors can see the animals out and about when they are particularly lively. Get there early and it's easy to see the zoo's most popular guests: the adorable giant pandas from China, Mei Xiang, Tian Tian, and their offspring. Almost one-quarter of the zoo's animals are endangered species, including the pandas, Asian elephants, and western lowland gorillas.

Among the zoo's many highlights are the rare Sumatran tigers, the Bald Eagle Refuge, the Reptile Discovery Center, and Amazonia, a re-creation of an Amazon rainforest. Think Tank is a special exhibit offering visitors the chance to observe the cognitive abilities of the zoo's orangutan population. They can also observe these active apes as they climb and swing overhead and travel from the Great Ape House on the "O Line," a series of towers and cables.

Daily programs include animal training, feeding demonstrations, and animal-keeper talks. During the summer months, visitors can enjoy a popular free concert series, Sunset Serenades, performed on Lion and Tiger Hill.

THE SOUTH

The South is a natural choice for a family vacation, with its famous southern hospitality and sunny disposition. Where else can you see alligators cruising alongside your airboat, hunt shells on one of the best shelling beaches in the world, or listen to Dixieland jazz while your kids munch pralines and peach pie? It's the center of theme-park thrills and home to countless amusements such as Walt Disney World and Universal Studios Islands of Adventure. Visit the Gulf Coast beaches year-round, and stay a while—the weather's just fine.

Georgia Aquarium, Atlanta

SHENANDOAH NATIONAL PARK

Scenic Shenandoah National Park stretches along a particularly glorious section of the Blue Ridge Mountains in northeastern Virginia. It's an excellent park for families who like to hike—even young children can manage some of the easy, self-guided trails that wind past waterfalls, hemlocks, pines, and wildflowers, where white-tailed deer graze and chipmunks frolic. A couple of favorites include the Story of the Forest Nature Trail, a 1.8-mile interpretive route that provides background on the animals and plant life found in the forest. Fox Hollow Nature Trail is about a one-mile round-trip and meanders past ruins of old farm fences and a cemetery, reminders of the mountaineers who settled here long ago. More than 500 miles of hiking trails cut through the park, including 100 miles of the Appalachian Trail. The famous Skyline Drive runs 105 miles along the mountain crest of the entire park, and it offers stunning panoramas and opportunities to stretch your legs at each of the 75 viewpoints.

The park features a well-equipped Junior Ranger program: You can rent backpacks containing field guides and binoculars, and purchase a Junior Ranger Explorer Notebook that teaches children about

Some of the day hikes through Shenandoah National Park are perfectly suited for families. As you journey through this particularly beautiful part of the country, you'll come across lush forests and cooling waterfalls.

trails, streams, plants, and the woodland creatures they'll see.

MOUNT VERNON

George Washington's plantation on the banks of the Potomac River offers a fascinating glimpse of how America's first president lived toward the end of the 18th century. The home has been so lovingly restored to its early authenticity that it looks as if George and Martha might step out at any moment to say hello. An effort to locate and return the estate's original contents has been ongoing for more than 100 years; the home features an expansive collection of memorabilia.

Visit the mansion to see Martha's tea service laid out in one of the parlors; the study, containing its original globe and desk; and the bedroom where George spent his final days. Be sure to allow enough time to explore the rest of the plantation grounds, such as the stables, the overseer and slaves' quarters, the Washingtons' graves, and the slave burial ground. There are four different gardens to stroll through. Along the banks of the Potomac you can visit a four-acre working farm with a re-created 16-sided barn that showcases many of Washington's farming innovations. In spring and summer, you can journey from Washington, D.C., to Mount Vernon by boat along the scenic Potomac River.

Mount Vernon was George Washington's home for 40 years. Records show that 80 million visitors have toured the estate since it was first opened to the public in 1860.

COLONIAL WILLIAMSBURG

This former capital of colonial Virginia is the world's largest living-history museum. The town appears much as it did during the Revolutionary War. You can explore many of its more than 500 restored and reconstructed buildings: Walk through dank jails, visit elegant government buildings, and tour simple homes and neighborhood taverns.

Many of the quaint shops offer fascinating hands-on demonstrations of trades such as boot-, barrel-, and wig-making. In the homes and taverns, you're likely to see colonials cooking the day's meal over an open hearth. Horse-drawn carriages travel along the immaculate, hard-packed dirt streets, where drum corps march and fifers play.

Interpreters of all ages wander the streets in period costumes, bringing to life the stories of the working people, families, slaves, and revolutionary firebrands who

Step into the past at Colonial Williamsburg with a visit to an Early American apothecary shop. Here, medicines and healing herbs are prepared by hand.

Fifers and drummers played an important role during the Revolutionary War. Boys between the ages of 10 and 18 were trained to accompany soldiers into battle. In Colonial Williamsburg, performers include boys and girls.

blindman's bluff, make soap, dip candles, and draw water from a well. Local children working as costumed junior interpreters help visiting kids get into the Colonial spirit. The family fun continues during summer months and over school holidays with a variety of fascinating programs. You might see reenactments of famous trials, colonial and slave uprisings, and contentious town meetings. In the fall there is a popular storytelling festival and timely programs such as ghost tours and staged witch trials. Winter programs commonly involve 18th-century music, dance, and theater.

Williamsburg has more than 100 gardens that offer a shady respite from touring. The Governor's Palace Gardens is one of the prettiest and is conveniently situated near an old-fashioned hedgerow maze with plenty of confusing twists and turns that children love to navigate.

lived here 300 years ago. A staff of 3,500 people, including archaeologists and historians, are helped by more than 800 volunteers who make the 18th century come alive.

You can sample some of the Early American cuisine that is featured in many of the authentic 18th-century taverns, often to the accompaniment of lively period music. You might find mince pies, Yorkshire beef pasties, spoon bread, and apple tansey accompanied by cider and ale on the menu. Many of the restaurants also feature children's menus. After dark, enjoy the candlelit world of early America and stroll along Colonial Williamsburg's streets. Attend a concert or an 18th-century play, or enjoy games and gambols, an old form of entertainment.

Activities for children abound all year: They can help with seasonal farm chores, play colonial games such as ninepins and

The Powhatan native people were the first residents of what was later called Jamestown. One of their huts has been re-created and is on display at Jamestown Settlement.

HISTORIC JAMESTOWNE AND JAMESTOWN SETTLEMENT

Historic Jamestowne is where the settlers formed the first permanent English colony. Visitors can tour its excavations and the few structures that remain. Archaeologists working at various locations have unearthed a wealth of artifacts. Jamestowne's glassblowing industry is also depicted, with costumed workers applying their skills in the same manner as the early craftspeople.

Nearby is Jamestown Settlement. It features artifacts from the settlement, including a 17th-century child's hornbook, a wooden doll, clay marbles, and a small stoneware jug, dated 1590, which reportedly was given to Pocahontas. The settlement is best known for its re-created fort, the Powhatan Indian Village, and three ships that are open for exploration. In the fort, kids can try on armor and play old-fashioned games such as quoits and ninepins. They can pound corn and play a Native American game called cob darts in the Powhatan Indian Village. At the Riverfront Discovery Area children are welcome to climb aboard the ships and into the tiny bunks where the sailors used to sleep. They can also try the steering device that was used before wheels came into fashion and learn about early methods of fishing.

BUSCH GARDENS, WILLIAMSBURG

This Williamsburg attraction is believed by many to be the world's most beautiful theme park. Even though most young visitors care more about Busch Gardens' other features, their parents will appreciate the park's European-themed "lands." Each of the lands features its own music and dance shows, rides, exhibits, and foods, as well as classic theme-park thrills.

In the Italian Renaissance hillside village, riders on Escape from Pompeii flee the volcanic eruption of Mt. Vesuvius on a boat—amid constant rumbling, crashing beams, a ceiling engulfed in flames, and a five-story plunge. Over in the Bavarian village, the Curse of DarKastle ride goes through dizzying drops, dense fog, shattering ice, and dazzling pyrotechnics as it journeys through a grand Bavarian castle frozen in time. Costumed actors add extra fun to the theme areas.

Situated on 100 action-packed acres, Busch Gardens has more than 50 rides and attractions, with something special for all ages. It also has a small walk-through nature area that features gray wolves and other endangered animals.

You're in for a splash landing on Escape from Pompeii, a popular ride at Busch Gardens. A visit to this beautiful amusement park will take you to many different lands and an assortment of exciting rides.

Assateague Island National Seashore

Assateague Island National Seashore lies on a long, narrow barrier island that straddles the coasts of Virginia and Maryland. The island is a peaceful, windswept sanctuary to many species of wildlife, none more famous than the wild pony population. According to legend, these shaggy, sturdy animals survived the shipwreck of a Spanish galleon in the 1600s and then swam ashore to Assateague. Other stories relate that colonial farmers turned their livestock out to graze on the island to avoid livestock tariffs.

The ponies now share Assateague with an assortment of wildlife, including the unusual sika deer that makes its home in the island's pine forests. The island is also known for its lovely beaches and hiking trails that allow for plenty of exploring.

These ponies are part of the herd on Assateague Island National Seashore. They are actually horses whose growth has been stunted by their steady diet of sea grass and saltwater.

Chincoteague Pony Swim

The ponies on Assateague are separated into Maryland and Virginia herds. The Virginia herd is under the care of the Chincoteague Volunteer Fire Department, which conducts the Chincoteague Pony Swim each year. Anyone who has ever read *Misty of Chincoteague* is familiar with the event, which has taken place every July since 1925. The ponies are rounded up on Assateague Island and then herded across the narrow channel by a group of "saltwater cowboys." With crowds of onlookers cheering along the shoreline, the ponies swim ashore and are later auctioned off to carefully screened bidders. Unsold horses are returned to the island.

The swim has become a popular family event and now features a carnival. Children are thrilled by the sight of the ponies making the short swim across the channel to the mainland. It's good, muddy fun when the ponies are herded into the bidding area.

VIRGINIA BEACH

Virginia Beach is a timeless beach town, full of classic summer fun and miles of smooth, white sandy beaches. Its 3-mile-long boardwalk is perfect for inline skating, bike riding, or ambling with a stroller. If you cover its entire length, you'll come across a variety of diversions that include an amusement park, the world's busiest Dairy Queen, a Beatles museum, taffy shops, and a 1903 Coast Guard Station with a rooftop "tower cam" that kids can use to get a closer look at the ships along the horizon.

Even the most die-hard beach lovers need a break from the sand and sun. Touring the Virginia Aquarium & Marine Science Center is a wonderful way to spend the day. This contemporary science museum offers visitors the chance to explore the plant and animal life found near the Virginia coast. Its river otters habitat is a family favorite, as is its shark exhibit, which is housed in a 300,000-gallon tank. The aquarium also boasts a 70,000-gallon sea turtle habitat and an IMAX theater. Whale-watching tours are available during the winter months, and dolphin watching is a favorite activity in the summer.

In addition to the usual beach activities, Virginia Beach's Back Bay Refuge and First Landing State Park provide opportunities to view acres of beach, marshland, and woods from footpaths and bicycle trails.

Far right: You'll make some new friends when you visit the Virginia Aquarium & Marine Science Center. Right: The boardwalk in Virginia Beach is also known as "Beach Street USA."

STEVEN F. UDVAR-HAZY CENTER

The Steven F. Udvar-Hazy Center, an extension of the Smithsonian National Air and Space Museum, was built to display the thousands of aviation and space travel artifacts that could not possibly fit into the popular Washington, D.C., museum. Opened in December 2003 in Chantilly, Virginia, it showcases famous aircraft, spacecraft, rockets, and satellites, and a wide assortment of other space exploration memorabilia.

The centerpiece of the museum is a cavernous hangar that is more than three football fields in length and ten stories high. It houses the *Enola Gay,* the plane that dropped the atom bomb on Hiroshima; a Concorde that once traveled in and out of adjacent Dulles Airport; the world's fastest jet; and dozens of other aircraft displayed on three levels. The top levels can best be viewed from the elevated skywalks placed around the hangar. The space shuttle *Enterprise,* the *Gemini VII* space capsule, and the Mobile Quarantine Unit used when the *Apollo 11* crew returned are also on display in the museum. Interactive exhibits include a simulation of a shuttle flight. Special activities for families are offered throughout the year.

The comprehensive list of exhibits at the Steven F. Udvar-Hazy Center covers everything from early flight to the space shuttle Enterprise. *The huge facility took 15 years to plan and construct.*

HARPERS FERRY NATIONAL HISTORICAL PARK

Harpers Ferry was a key staging area for pioneers heading into the western frontier in colonial days—Lewis and Clark actually began their cross-continental trek here. George Washington established a federal armory at Harpers Ferry during his presidency. The armory later attracted industrial development. A canal and railroad line made the area a transportation hub. The town came to national attention in 1859, when the federal armory was raided by abolitionist firebrand John Brown in his effort to end slavery by arming slaves.

Today the town is a National Historical Park, and it still looks as it did during the Civil War. Its mixture of historic events and recreational activites draws about one million visitors annually. A number of older homes in Harpers Ferry have been converted to quaint shops, restaurants, and art galleries. Many of its historic buildings have exhibits and interpretive displays that bring the town's history to life. Walking

Rich with history and surrounded by scenic wonders, Harpers Ferry in West Virginia offers plenty of hiking trails and wildlife viewing in the surrounding Blue Ridge Mountains. Tours related to the town's history are offered during the summer months.

and hiking trails wind throughout the area, and the Shenandoah River is a preferred spot for tubing and kayaking. The town is surrounded by the Blue Ridge Mountains, where rock climbing and rappelling are popular activities.

WINTER FESTIVAL OF LIGHTS

The Oglebay Park Winter Festival of Lights in West Virginia has grown into one of the nation's largest holiday light shows. It attracts more than one million visitors per year during its two-month run, which starts in November and continues into January. Featuring more than one million lights and 50 displays, the festival covers 300 acres.

Guests take in the display of lights via car. An animated Snowflake Tunnel glows with thousands of lights as visitors drive through the exhibit of twinkling snow-flakes. Other displays lit up in holiday finery include a poinsettia wreath with candles that stands almost 60 feet high, making it the festival's tallest display. Illuminated Snoopys help guide visitors through the show.

Also on display are a nativity scene, decorated live Christmas trees, a miniature holiday village, entries from a gingerbread

The colorful extravaganza of holiday lights in Oglebay Park is one of the most widely attended displays in the country. It's been a West Virginia tradition since 1985.

contest, and a model train exhibit set in an enchanting winter wonderland. Elementary schoolchildren from the area are invited to send in their ideas for lighting displays. The Benedum Planetarium at the Good Zoo features a laser light show all festival long.

River Rafting on the Upper New River

West Virginia's Upper New River white-water rafting adventures are perfect for families. While some of the state's other rivers, such as the Gauley, are a bit too challenging for youngsters, the Upper New River is great for beginners and is safe for children. You'll raft through a magnificent 1,400-foot-deep canyon, splash in gentle rapids, and play in gorgeous emerald-green pools. You can choose from numerous licensed river rafting outfitters that guide special family trips.

In river rafting language, rapids are separated into six categories. A class one river is the easiest, and a class six river is virtually unrunnable. The Upper New River is filled with long and tranquil class one and two rapids, with an occasional class-three stretch of white water thrown in for excitement. Outfitters take families on two- and three-day trips that are appropriate for families with children ages six and older.

Trips offer inflatable rafts piloted by guides as well as individual easy-to-paddle inflatable kayaks called "duckies." Most outfitters have special small-size duckies for children who wish to paddle by themselves. The river guides cook delicious family-friendly meals and help set up camp each night along particularly scenic sections of the river.

The Upper New River offers a white-water rafting experience that kids will enjoy. The government named 53 miles of the New as a Wild and Scenic River under the protection of the National Park Service.

KENTUCKY DERBY FESTIVAL

The Kentucky Derby Festival that precedes the famous horse race is a two- to three-week extravaganza of fireworks, parades, races, and more, and it's tailor-made for families. It begins in mid-April and sets the pace for the excitement leading up to the race. The festival's trademark daylong Thunder Over Louisville Air Show dazzles viewers with more than 100 planes, as well as aerial acrobatic teams and daring skydiving teams performing breath-taking stunts.

The Army, Navy, Air Force, and Marines often get into the act, and there is a special moment when helicopters pull the largest American flag ever flown across the sky. At night, when darkness descends, the fireworks begin. Eight huge barges on the Ohio River form the stages from which the 28-minute fireworks show

ignites. It's the largest annual pyrotechnic display in the country.

The Pegasus Parade is the festival's oldest event and features a spectacle of colorful floats, marching bands, giant inflatables, equestrian teams, and celebrities parading down Broadway in downtown Louisville. Two days before the parade, at an indoor venue, you can view the lavishly decorated floats and the enormous inflatables hanging from a ceiling, including the festival's winged white mascot Absolutely Pegasus.

Friendly—and often funny—competitions are a trademark of certain festival events. The Great Balloon Race features a colorful spectrum of hot-air balloons taking flight and racing for prizes over two days.

Your kids will have a booming good time at the fireworks display that's part of the Kentucky Derby Festival. The event caps the first day of festival activities.

At night during the Great Balloon Glow, the balloons are illuminated but stay tethered and blaze against the blackness of the night sky, synchronized to a special musical score. Families arrive early to picnic on the lawn. The event offers a children's area with inflatable slides and other activities.

The Great Bed Races are a festival favorite, featuring five-person teams dressed in wild and crazy costumes pushing decorated beds on wheels around a "track," competing for the fastest times and, more important, the best decorations. They're billed as the best race you can have in your pajamas. Thousands of bed-racing enthusiasts gather to cheer their favorite beds and vote for the People's Choice award, which is bestowed upon the most popular bed.

Meanwhile, the Derby Festival Waterfront Chow Wagon features a selection of delectable goodies, such as Louisiana-style bourbon chicken, Creole shrimp, and gumbo. Concerts take place nearby at Waterfront Park on the Ohio River.

Even more activities add to the fun, including a steamboat race, a mini marathon, a spelling bee, and a children's art competition. The Kentucky Derby at Churchill Downs is the festival's grand finale. As the first jewel in the Triple Crown of thoroughbred racing, the Derby attracts more than 100,000 spectators each year.

Colorful steamboats line up in preparation for the Great Steamboat Race, a popular event at the Kentucky Derby Festival.

Louisville Slugger Museum and Factory

Ever since Bud Hillerich created the first Louisville Slugger bat in his father's workshop in 1884, baseball's biggest stars have used these finely crafted pieces of smooth white ash. A collection of famous bats lines the walls of this factory and museum; most notable is the 1927 Louisville Slugger bat Babe Ruth used to hit 21 home runs. You can still see the notches carved by Ruth himself on the top of the bat.

The world's largest bat, a 120-foot-tall replica of Babe Ruth's, leans casually against the factory near its entrance. Take the factory tour to learn about the steps used to make the bats, from the massive beginnings to the completed varnish. After the tour, all visitors receive a souvenir—their own miniature Louisville Slugger.

The museum is perfect for kids who can't sit still: They can climb all over a giant baseball glove and head out to the batting cage to swing replicas of bats used by stars such as Babe Ruth, Ted Williams, and Derek Jeter. Hitters can also try out the latest line of aluminum baseball and softball bats.

And just wait until you see the glove! There's no mistaking the Louisville Slugger Museum and Factory. Nearby you'll also find the world's largest baseball glove.

MAMMOTH CAVE NATIONAL PARK

Formed by water and time, Mammoth Cave is the longest cave system in the world: It comprises 360 miles of caverns and passages. Many of the rooms in the vast subterranean world are enormous. At 192 feet high, Mammoth Dome is as big as a palace ballroom, while the Bottomless Pit plunges 105 feet into inky blackness.

Chambers and passageways have evocative names such as Giant's Coffin, Fat Man's Misery, Fairy Ceiling, Frozen Niagara, and Drapery Room. Some are lined with sparkling white gypsum crystals, while others overflow with the twisted and dripping shapes of stalactites and stalagmites. Underground rivers with names such as Echo River and the River Styx flow through the cave's deepest sections. And surprisingly, many unusual animals live there in total darkness, including eyeless fish, near-translucent white spiders, and blind beetles.

The best way to visit the caves is to take a tour, and there are many from which to choose. A special tour just for children, called the Trog Tour, explores the connections between the cave and the sunlit world above. Wearing a hard hat and headlamp, children walk and crawl through various passageways as they learn how the cave was formed and what lives in it.

Going down? Mammoth Cave is a revelation of the beauty that can be found below the earth's surface. The national park was established in 1941 to preserve the labyrinth cave system.

THE NATIONAL CORVETTE MUSEUM AND FACTORY TOUR

The first thing you see as you drive into the parking lot of this Bowling Green, Kentucky, sports car plant are the front-row spots designated "Corvette Parking Only." That's just the beginning of the loving attention that this museum and factory shines on America's wildly popular sports car, introduced in 1953.

More than 75 Corvettes are on display at the museum, from the first cars to roll off the assembly line to the super-sci-fi, finned Stingray. Many of the cars are placed in a nostalgic tableaux, such as an old-time garage and gas station. In addition to the cars, there are videos, scale models, Schwinn Corvette bicycles, and various other rare memorabilia on display.

Visitors can tour the Corvette assembly plant across the street. Here you'll see robots welding the steel frame together and workers installing the seats, wheels, and roof. You'll witness the "marriage," which in car talk means the point at which the chassis and the engine come together, and the moment when the Corvette is driven off the end of the line. Be sure to call ahead to verify tour times; tours are sometimes canceled during pre-production of future models.

It's preferred parking all the way at the National Corvette Museum, but only if you happen to be traveling in a 'Vette.

TENNESSEE AQUARIUM

Most aquariums showcase the varied marine animals that inhabit the planet's vast oceans. But the spectacular Tennessee Aquarium in Chattanooga concentrates on creatures found in and around the earth's rivers, swamps, ponds, and lakes. It is the biggest freshwater aquarium in the world.

One section of the aquarium follows the course of the Tennessee River all the way from an Appalachian high country stream down through the steamy Mississippi Delta and out into the Gulf of Mexico, where freshwater and saltwater mix. Along the way, visitors see thousands of animals

that live above and below the water's surface, such as playful river otters, speckled salamanders, alligators, a massive 80-pound catfish, and vicious-looking moray eels. Visitors can also wander through the world's largest collection of freshwater turtles to see the unusual pancake tortoise and a nursery containing adorable baby turtles.

The Rivers of the World gallery displays creatures from warm Eurasian waters, as well as from the Amazon, St. Lawrence, Volga, and Fly rivers. Here visitors see fish of dazzling colors and creatures such as anacondas, red-bellied piranhas, massive Beluga sturgeon, and pig-nosed and four-eyed turtles.

Smile for the camera! These are just some of the creatures your family will meet at the Tennessee Aquarium. The emphasis here is on freshwater habitats and fascinating exhibits.

GRACELAND

The 24-karat-gold-plated seat belt on The King's jet airplane bed is one of the quirky highlights at Graceland, Elvis Presley's Memphis home for 20 years until his death in 1977. Most kids don't know very much about Elvis, but after touring his home and his two private jets, they definitely come to appreciate his over-the-top sense of grandeur. The Graceland Mansion is the biggest attraction in Memphis and one of the five most visited home museums in the United States.

The house tour is great fun for kids, who love to see the flashy stage costumes and the gold records. The Automobile Museum includes a 1955 pink Cadillac and a 1956 purple Cadillac convertible, as well as motorcycles and other vehicles.

Accompanying this collection are Elvis's home movies and a compilation of car-scene clips from his films, all shown in a mock drive-in-theater setting. A visit to the ice-cream parlor on the grounds is a great way to break up the tour.

Top: Elvis was larger-than-life, so don't expect anything less when you tour his home. Graceland is one of the top tourist destinations in the country. Bottom: Stained-glass peacocks and a grand piano—Elvis had an over-the-top style all his own.

NATIONAL CIVIL RIGHTS MUSEUM

This Memphis museum pays tribute to the many people involved in the struggle for civil rights in the United States. Built around the Lorraine Motel, where Dr. Martin Luther King, Jr., was assassinated in 1968, the museum chronicles the history of civil rights activities from the beginnings of slavery through the end of the 20th century.

Exhibits focus on such events as the Civil War, the Supreme Court decision to desegregate schools, the lunch counter sit-ins, the Montgomery Bus Boycott, and the March on Washington. Multimedia presentations and full-scale exhibits bring the civil rights movement to life for children. They'll see a public bus similar to the one ridden by Rosa Parks when she refused to move to the back seats, the burned shell of a freedom-ride Greyhound bus, and the actual motel room where Dr. King stayed before he was slain.

At the National Civil Rights Museum your family will gain a new awareness of the people who have struggled for equality and fairness throughout the country's history. The museum opened in 1991.

PIGEON FORGE AND DOLLYWOOD

Pigeon Forge is filled with the kind of flashy family fun that kids love. From miniature golf, go-karts, and bumper boats to waterslides, laser games, and an indoor skydiving simulator, the attractions can keep the family busy for days. But the biggest draws are Dollywood and its neighboring water park, Dollywood's Splash Country.

Graceland has Elvis, and Dollywood has Dolly Parton. As a result of its affiliation with this favorite celebrity from Tennessee, Dollywood has grown into one of the nation's most popular theme parks. It is packed with more than 30 rides and attractions, including a wooden roller coaster and rides with names such as the Smoky Mountain River Rampage and the Tennessee Tornado. Master craftspeople demonstrate old-time crafts such as glass-blowing and blacksmithing around the park each day. Shows feature the best bluegrass, Southern gospel, country, and mountain music you'll find in the area. Families that visit in the summer will enjoy KidsFest, a summer-long celebration with special activities and entertainment just for children.

Dollywood's Splash Country is a 30-acre water park open in the summer. The fun includes the multilevel Bear Mountain Fire Tower, Big Bear Plunge (a white-water rafting ride), two play areas, a 25,000-square-foot wave pool, and 23 waterslides.

The accent is on fun at Dollywood, which features high kickin', foot stompin' musical shows and exciting rides, such as Daredevil Falls.

NATIONAL STORYTELLING FESTIVAL

This event, which began in 1973, is traditionally held the first weekend of October in Jonesborough, Tennessee. Anyone can tell a story, but to perform at the National Storytelling Festival, a professional storyteller might practice reciting a tale over the course of six months or more. Performance story-telling is as much an art as dancing, acting, or making music. The commitment and artistry can be seen and heard in this three-day festival devoted to the telling of traditional stories, multicultural folktales, and contemporary legends.

On Friday, the festival's kick-off day, a special tent features storytellers and stories particularly suitable for families and young people, and local schoolchildren are invited to come to listen. All ages, but especially kids, enjoy the Youthful Voices concert, where young storytellers between the ages of 5 and 18, who have been selected through a competitive process, share their finest tales.

Young people particularly enjoy the Ghost Story Concerts that are held in a large open-air park on Friday and Saturday nights. Audience members spread out on blankets and are captivated as professional storytellers relate creepy, astonishing tales.

Above: *It's never too early to sharpen those storytelling skills. The festival gives children an opportunity to weave their colorful tales before an appreciative audience.* Right: *Presentation counts at the National Storytelling Festival. A high school journalism teacher organized the first event in 1973, and the festival has sparked a revival in the classic art of storytelling.*

Great Smoky Mountains National Park

Great Smoky Mountains National Park runs northeast to southwest, stretching across the border of North Carolina and Tennessee. The mantle of white that inspired the name Great Smokies isn't smoke at all, but low-lying clouds and a misty haze. The park protects a multitude of plant, mammal, and bird species, as well as 30 species of salamander. The park's half-million acres are filled with stately old-growth forests, wildflower-packed meadows, high mountain streams, and beautiful waterfalls. This national treasure is so rich in its variety of life that the United Nations has named the park an International Biosphere Reserve and World Heritage Site.

The park hosts more visitors than any other national park in the United States. The trick to experiencing nature without rubbing shoulders with thousands of people involves getting off the interstate and exploring the more remote parts of the park. Some of the quieter campgrounds can be a good place to start. Surrounded by a forest of hemlock and white pine, Abrams Creek Campground is at the park's western edge and is great for overnight or half-day visits. The creek is a wonderful spot for fishing. Kids also enjoy swimming in its quiet pools and exploring

Opposite page: *Hiking through the Great Smoky Mountains National Park can take you on a trip through time. You'll see weathered farms and outbuildings abandoned long ago.* Left: *The many waterfalls and shallow pools are perfect for wading and exploring.*

along the banks of the creek. Cosby Campground is another popular camping area, and it's rarely filled. Waterfalls and old-growth trees are short hikes away.

Families traveling with younger children should try the hike to Laurel Falls. The 2.5-mile trail is partially paved and leads to a refreshing waterfall. The trail to Grotto Falls is an easy 3-mile round-trip hike, and children will enjoy climbing behind the falls to get a different view of the cascading water.

Horseback riding is a popular activity and an adventurous way to see the flora and fauna. The park offers 550 miles of trails, along with horse camps, pack trips, and four commercial stables. Be sure to take the kids on a hayride out of the Cades Cove stable.

Stop by the Oconaluftee Visitor Center just inside the entrance on the North Carolina side to pick up general information about the park and see some the Mountain Farm Museum. From the Tennessee side, the Sugarlands Visitor Center near Gatlinburg is a popular stop with a film and natural history exhibits.

Outer Banks

Today a particularly serene stretch of sea and sand, North Carolina's Outer Banks belie their treacherous past. It was here that the people of Roanoke Island settled and then mysteriously disappeared in the 1580s. Among the pirates and buccaneers who hid their booty around these islands in the 18th century was the infamous Blackbeard. He materialized in the area with a

price on his head and was quickly captured and executed.

The waters off the Outer Banks are so hazardous that they have earned the name "Graveyard of the Atlantic" due to the thousands of ships that ran aground on the shoals and were destroyed by storms. Historic lighthouses that

once warned sailors of danger still dot the coastline.

Today, beach lovers visit these legendary islands to enjoy the seemingly endless stretches of ocean and soft sand. Birdwatchers tour the wildlife refuges that host millions of migratory birds along the shores and inland marshes. Families who can tear themselves away from the beach should visit lively Roanoke Island Festival Park, which has a hands-on museum, free concerts and plays, and a replica of the ship that brought over the colonists who disappeared.

The Wright Brothers National Memorial marks the site of the world's first successful airplane flight.

Not only are the Outer Banks the perfect family getaway destination for a relaxing beach trip, the area is also famous as the scene of the first airplane flight. The Wright Brothers Memorial on Big Kill Devil Hill pays tribute to the event.

WRIGHTSVILLE BEACH

Wrightsville Beach is known as the premier family beach town on the popular Cape Fear coastline of North Carolina. Located about 15 minutes from historic and activity-filled Wilmington, this peaceful seaside community has a small-island feel and miles of pure white sand. Accommodations are in cottages, condominiums, a couple of resort hotels, or simple and comfortable motels.

At Johnnie Mercer's Pier, drop a fishing line for sea trout and flounder. Crabbing on the beach is also a popular pastime. Many families enjoy swimming at the beaches between this pier and Crystal Pier, which are patrolled by lifeguards all summer long.

The Wrightsville area is considered one of the best surfing spots on the east coast, and kids of all ages can take lessons at several surf camps. Boogie boarding and windsurfing are popular, too. Paddlers can take a marked 5-mile kayak trail that winds throughout the

Summer school just became a lot more fun! Wrightsville Beach, a popular surfing spot, has a number of camps that offer instruction on the finer points of catching a wave.

island's marshes. Most of the public beaches have beach volleyball courts, and Wrightsville Beach Park has a children's playground.

EDISTO ISLAND

O ne of the oldest settlements in South Carolina, this remote barrier island offers the kind of beach vacation that is perfect for nature lovers and beachcombers looking for peace and quiet.

The island welcomes exploration: Several churches and plantations from the 1800s offer tours, and families can rent bikes for a ride through Edisto Beach State Park, which includes a salt marsh and a maritime forest with a nature trail and visitor's center.

Activities are simple and laid-back and usually revolve around lounging and playing on the long stretches of sandy beach. Children delight in lazy days spent building sand castles and hunting for shells on the beach. You can also catch your own seafood by surf casting, shrimping, or deep-sea fishing. Dolphins are regularly seen feeding off the coast. Nesting sea turtles lay their eggs from May through October on the island.

Your family will love the beautiful sunsets, relaxing strolls along the beach, and laid-back fun that are a part of an Edisto Island vacation.

CHARLESTON

Charleston is one of the most beautifully preserved cities in America, full of antebellum mansions, quaint cobblestone alleys, and carefully preserved historic buildings. Founded in 1670, the town's wealth and prosperity was based on cotton, rice, and indigo, and the resulting economic boom enlarged the city. After the Civil War devastated the community, residents were so poor that they could not afford to rebuild, so the city simply adapted its old buildings, unknowingly protecting them as historical treasures for future generations to appreciate.

Magnolia Plantation is particularly well suited for families to visit. It features a home tour, and its grounds and gardens are filled with extras that keep kids entertained for hours. Take the Nature Train tour to see the plantation's many animals, including alligators. There's also a petting zoo, a garden maze, and a wildlife observation tower. Magnolia Plantation is one of the best birding areas in the country; rare waterfowl and nesting birds can be seen from this tower.

History buffs will enjoy a tour of Fort Sumter National Monument, where the first shots of the Civil War were fired. Tour boats regularly depart from Charleston. Before boarding, stop at the Fort Sumter Visitor Education Center for more insight on the fort and its role in the Civil War. Children enjoy touring the fort and seeing its many exhibits. They can climb about its ruins and peer through the cannon turrets across Charleston Harbor.

As you look through the cannon's sights over Charleston Harbor, it's easy to imagine the exchange of gunfire that took place at Fort Sumter.

HORSE-DRAWN CARRIAGE RIDES

The best way for families to tour Charleston is to take a carriage ride through its historic neighborhoods. After the ride, ask to be dropped off in open-air Old City Market, where you can wander past vendors selling food and souvenirs, including handmade sweetgrass baskets.

KIAWAH ISLAND

Though the sand is so firm you can ride bikes on the beach, there are plenty of bike trails—more than 30 miles' worth—interlacing this unspoiled island. Much of this South Carolina island is privately owned, and only visitors with a reservation at one of the homes or resorts on the island are allowed to access most of it. Beachwalker County Park is open to the public and offers 11 miles of unspoiled sandy beaches and a large swimming area.

Nearly 10,000 acres of natural woodlands, marsh, and pine forests are protected, and the islanders have worked hard to keep overdevelopment at bay. Consequently, it is one of the quieter and more peaceful places along the east coast.

As you might expect, beachcombing is a popular activity on any of the immaculate beaches. Families also enjoy golfing on Kiawah, with some courses offering family tee programs. Canoe and kayak excursions through the creeks and marshes offer sightings of island wildlife, including alligators, loggerhead turtles, snakes, lizards, and a variety of bird species.

Above: *Kayaking and canoeing are the best ways to explore Kiawah Island's creeks and marshes.*
Left: *Kids will love the wide open spaces and bike-friendly beach at Beachwalker County Park.*

SAVANNAH

Savannah is the grand old dame of the South. Founded in 1733, the city has a colorful history. Its early residents included settlers from Europe, slaves, sailors, merchants, and pirates.

Savannah's historic district is filled with elegant homes. Among these lovely mansions you'll find the home of Juliette Gordon Low, the founder of the Girl Scouts. The home has been converted into a museum and is a popular destination for Girl Scout troops across the United States. Families enjoy touring the elegant home as well.

Another highlight of the historic city is Old Fort Jackson, which was built in 1808 and helped protect the coast from British warships during the War of 1812. During the summer the fort holds daily cannon firing demonstrations.

Another good stop is the Savannah History Museum. Here visitors can see weapons and military uniforms, items from Savannah's railway history, and an exhibit of women's fashions from the 19th and 20th centuries.

You can also tour Savannah by horse-drawn carriage. Guides will treat you to details about the city's famous characters. If your kids enjoy their history with a spooky twist, they'll like the tours of the supposedly haunted areas of Savannah.

Top: *Forsyth Park is Savannah's oldest large park and home to The Fountain, which was featured in* Forrest Gump *and* Midnight in the Garden of Good and Evil. Bottom: *When the kids tire from walking, hop into an open carriage to visit the city's lush gardens, stately mansions, and 200-year-old monuments.*

THE GOLDEN ISLES

Georgia's great barrier islands shelter the Atlantic Intracoastal Waterway and guard the coastal shoreline. The beauties known as the Golden Isles—Sea Island, Jekyll Island, St. Simons Island, Little St. Simons Island, and Cumberland Island—are about 20 minutes from each other by boat or car, and each has a slightly different personality. All have stunning beaches, as well as marshes and creeks that are great fun to explore by canoe and kayak—most outfitters can tailor their outings to fit a family's ages and interests.

Dolphin-watching tours depart from several of the islands. Along the way you might see manatees and other marine life. The islands are also nesting sites of the protected loggerhead turtle, and several of the islands allow guests to patrol the beaches at night to see the giant creatures lumber ashore to lay their eggs.

Sea Island is home to The Cloister, an acclaimed resort. Situated on five miles of sandy beach, the resort is a retreat for well-heeled guests. Even if you're not staying at the resort, it's fun to visit for a meal so you can explore its old-world Southern hospitality and cruise the mansions along the shore.

Jekyll Island is protected by offshore sandbars. As a result, the surf is particularly calm, making it a very good choice for families with young children. The island has 20 miles of paved bike paths that traverse salt marshes and beaches, past Spanish moss–draped trees and palmettos, as well as the island's National Historic Landmark District. Its ten miles of beaches offer swimming, horseback riding, surf fishing, and kayaking. The island is a major site for sea turtle conservation.

St. Simons Island is the largest and most developed of the Golden Isles. The island measures 45 square miles and boasts many beautiful old homes and estates. It's a terrific place to try surf casting, pier fishing, oystering, crabbing, or shrimping. St. Simons is home

Jekyll Island was a popular destination for the country's rich and powerful, and is now a favorite among families looking for a relaxing beach getaway. Jekyll Island Beach Club is a local landmark.

Wild horses are a common sight on Cumberland Island. The island has many quiet, sandy beaches and is a perfect spot for camping.

to one of the nation's oldest continually working lighthouses open to visitors. Families can also explore the island on its numerous biking trails.

Little St. Simons Island is privately owned and is accessible only by boat or plane. It's virtually undeveloped. Its seven-mile stretch of beach is perfect for swimming, shelling, and fishing, and other activities include hiking and bicycling.

Cumberland Island is a protected National Seashore and a haven for families seeking peace and quiet on sandy beaches. Visitation is limited to 300 people per day, and you must make advance reservations. It is accessible by ferry, and most visitors camp in designated areas, although a local lodge offers accommodations as well. The island is home to a wide variety of wildlife, including wild horses, bobcats, armadillos, and an assortment of birds. It is also sanctuary to the loggerhead turtle, which lays its eggs from May to September on the sandy shores. Families will find the park's quiet forests, salt marshes, tidal creeks, and sandy beaches a paradise for hiking, beachcombing, fishing, and swimming.

The historic lighthouse on St. Simons Island still guides boats into its harbor. The island also offers great fishing and inviting beaches.

The Okefenokee National Wildlife Refuge

Cypress trees rise up out of the water, dripping Spanish moss from their branches. Water lily–filled lakes and marshlike prairies harbor alligators and turtles that bask on logs and slide into the water at the slightest noise. Wading birds such as herons, sandhill cranes, and egrets hunt for their fish dinners, while frogs croak and trill. The Okefenokee's primitive wetlands harbor hundreds of birds, mammals, reptiles, and amphibians. It is crisscrossed with more than 100 miles of canoe trails, and visitors can best see its natural wonders by touring on the water.

The refuge has three main entrances, and all offer canoe rentals and boat tours as well as wooden boardwalks and observation platforms. Day-trippers have plenty of paddling options since a number of the canoe trails are short enough to traverse in an afternoon. Families wishing to spend a night or two can reserve wooden platform tent sites along the canoe trails or book a room near the western entrance of the park.

One of the residents of the Okefenokee National Wildlife Refuge, this alligator appears to be looking for something on which to munch.

These two giants of the prehistoric world can be viewed at the family-friendly Fernbank Museum of Natural History. It is one of the only museums in the world located in an old-growth forest.

FERNBANK MUSEUM OF NATURAL HISTORY

The scene in the light-filled atrium of Fernbank Museum depicts the struggle between predator and prey. You can almost feel the ground shake as *Giganotosaurus* chases down its intended meal, the huge *Argentinosaurus.* A flock of *Pterodaustro,* a small pterosaur species, and several larger flying reptiles swoop above the scene in the exhibit Giants of the Mesozoic. The rest of the exhibit displays a scene from the ancient Mesozoic period and reveals a fossilized tree, a prehistoric turtle, dinosaur footprints, and more.

This Atlanta museum's main exhibit, A Walk Through Time in Georgia, reflects the story of Georgia's natural history and the development of our planet with a series of realistic dioramas covering roughly 1.5 billion years. The hands-on Sensing Nature exhibit playfully demonstrates the role of our senses in interpreting our environment. The exhibit is filled with lights, videos, lasers, mirrors, optical illusions, and more, and kids can create a giant soap bubble and witness a tornado forming as they learn about human perception.

GEORGIA AQUARIUM

Whale sharks are the biggest stars of the Georgia Aquarium in Atlanta. It is the only aquarium outside of Asia to feature whale sharks. At nearly 20 feet long and growing, these creatures are members of the largest fish species on Earth. They roam the waters of a six-million-gallon tank they share with thousands of other fish, including sawfish, giant grouper, stingrays, and hammerhead sharks.

The aquarium features 100,000 animals representing more than 500 species in 60 separate habitats and has several major viewing galleries, each arranged around a theme. The Cold Water Quest exhibit is home to several beluga whales. Belugas are social creatures found exclusively in arctic and subarctic waters. They are very vocal, which earned them the nickname "canaries of the sea."

The Georgia Explorer section focuses on Georgia's coast, with touch tanks full of stingrays, horseshoe crabs, sea stars, and shrimp, as well as a children's playground.

In the River Scout Gallery, visitors are treated to a video of a river that appears to be running overhead. It teems with fish found in the rivers of Africa, South America, Asia, and the state of Georgia. Several Asian small-clawed otters play in an adjacent exhibit.

Children are mesmerized by the endless blue sea and the whale sharks of the Ocean Voyager gallery at the Georgia Aquarium. The aquarium features one of the largest viewing windows in the world.

EVERGLADES NATIONAL PARK

This national treasure encompasses 1.5 million acres of saw grass marshes, tangled mangrove forests, and fresh and brackish water wetlands. Tram tours and hiking trails are available in areas of the Everglades open to the public. However, this slow-moving "River of Grass" is best explored by boat. At Flamingo Marina you can rent a kayak, a canoe, or a skiff to see an incredible collection of animals up close: Turtles, marsh rabbits, manatees, crocodiles, otters, alligators, and hundreds of species of birds inhabit the area.

Families who want to explore on foot have a number of easy boardwalk trails from which to pick: The Anhinga Trail is one of the Park's most dependable areas for wildlife viewing, and West Lake Trail is one of the best places in the park to see American alligators.

AIRBOAT TOURS

High-speed airboats, propelled by fanlike contraptions, are a fun way to tour the swampy marshes of this unique wetland. Many outfitters just outside the boundaries of the park offer airboat tours, each with a guide who will stop along the way to point out alligators, native plants, and birds.

Top: *The Everglades is home to more than 300 species of birds, including the wood stork.* Bottom: *The Everglades contains more than 2,000 species of plants. Saw grass and freshwater marsh make up an open prairie.*

St. Augustine

Its beaches are legendary stretches of talcum-soft sand bordered by calm, blue water. But St. Augustine's real claim to fame is that it is the oldest permanently inhabited city in the United States. Founded in 1565, it's filled with reminders of its early Spanish history.

At the edge of the ocean is an authentic fort, Castillo de San Marcos. Construction of the fort began in 1672, and it was completed in 1695. It boasts an impressive moat, drawbridge, and huge cannons atop which kids can sit. The walls of the fort are constructed of coquina, a limestone material composed of broken seashells and coral. Thanks to this durable substance, the fort remained impenetrable during 300 years of enemy fire and violent storms. It once helped guard St. Augustine from pirate raids. Later, supporters of the American Revolution were locked away in its dank and creepy dungeons.

Wander through the narrow, picturesque streets of the town's carefully restored Spanish Quarter for a glimpse of how this community of Spanish soldiers, settlers, craftspeople, and families lived in the 18th century. You'll see narrow cobblestone streets, the oldest wooden schoolhouse in the country, and Ponce de Leon's Fountain of Youth. There are also a number of 17th- and 18th-century buildings housing ice-cream parlors and shops staffed by costumed interpreters who

This cannon once protected St. Augustine and the outlying sea routes used by treasure ships returning to Spain.

This old wooden schoolhouse offers a view of a classroom from centuries ago. It is typical of the history-rich architecture you'll see in St. Augustine.

lets you observe birds, turtles, and alligators swimming in a natural setting. Other interesting reptiles, such as giant Galápagos tortoises, wander about. Shows feature alligator wrestling, snake wrangling, and other crowd pleasers.

The St. Augustine Ripley's Believe It or Not! Museum was the first in the nation. It is located in Castle Warden, a historic Moorish Revival–style mansion built in 1887. The curiosities in it that kids like best are the ones that make most adults squeamish—the more gruesome the better—such as shrunken heads and other human oddities.

On a rainy day, you can head to the St. Augustine Lighthouse & Museum. Children enjoy climbing the tight spiral stairway to its top, where they're rewarded with expansive views of the area. On the way up, catch your breath on each floor and peruse the exhibits on the history of the lighthouse.

reenact life in the 18th century. A carriage tour is a great way to see the historic district, and drivers are always willing to share stories of the city's past.

The town's best beach is located on Anastasia Island across the Bridge of Lions. Here, palms and sea oats grow wild along the dunes. The warm water is shallow for many yards out, making it one of the safest places for toddlers to swim since there are no drop-offs. Older children like to ride its gently rolling waves on floats and boogie boards.

The St. Augustine Alligator Farm and Zoological Park, in operation since the late 1800s, features crocodiles, caimans, and alligators of all sizes lolling around their enclosures. A boardwalk across a lagoon

Busch Gardens, Tampa Bay

What happens when you mix the adrenaline rush of an amusement park, the beauty of a tropical garden, and the excitement of wild animals? The result is Busch Gardens. It started out as a beer garden that featured a bird show. Over the years, more animal attractions were added. The first roller coasters were built in the 1970s. As more major rides were introduced, the park continued to grow into a major tourist attraction.

The animal exhibits in Busch Gardens have an African theme and are divided into eight different areas, with 2,000 exotic and endangered animals living in natural environments. All are easily viewed from the Skyride cable car that crosses above the park, or by railway, walkway, or Land Rover. The Edge of Africa exhibit has rhinos, hippos, and more. Chimpanzees and gorillas frolic in a large enclosure in the Myombe Reserve's Great Ape Domain.

Scattered throughout the park are world-class roller coasters, rides for very young children, Broadway-style live entertainment, and plenty of water rides to cool down visitors during the steamy summer months. The gardens have mature trees,

Part amusement park, part wild animal sanctuary, Busch Gardens is all nonstop fun. In addition to its thrilling action rides, the park is home to approximately 2,000 animals.

beds thick with blooming flowers and shrubs, fountains, and plenty of benches in their many shady corners.

SANIBEL ISLAND

Sanibel Island is a shell collector's paradise. Areas of the soft sandy beaches are festooned with a variety of shells, including scallops, whelks, and kitten's paws. Shell collectors easily assume the Sanibel Stoop as they comb for tiny treasures washed up by the tide. Don't become too engrossed in your collecting, or you'll miss the dolphins that frequently feed just offshore. Visit the island's Bailey–Matthews Shell Museum before you begin your beachcombing to learn the names of the shells you'll find.

The island is known as a refuge for nesting sea turtles. Residents try to keep lights at a minimum at night in order to avoid confusing the turtles into heading farther inland. As a result, there are no streetlights to illuminate the roads at night on the island.

Bicycle riding is quite popular on Sanibel, and bike trails separate from the roads interlace the island. Most resorts have their own fleet of two-wheelers, including some with child seats and others sized for children. Bike rentals are also available on-island.

Almost half of the island is a nature preserve and sanctuary; when property is put up for sale, the residents often buy it and add it to the sanctuary. Visit the J. N. "Ding" Darling National Wildlife Refuge to see abundant bird life, alligators, and other creatures. You can explore by walking its trails and boardwalks, by canoeing or kayaking its winding water-ways, or by biking. According to building code, no structure on Sanibel Island may exceed four stories, so accommodations are scaled down and casual, and the stunning beaches are rarely crowded.

Low tide on Sanibel Island brings out the shelling enthusiast in everyone. You'll love the wide variety of seashells that wash up onshore.

KENNEDY SPACE CENTER

The Kennedy Space Center in Cape Canaveral has been the launch site for all crewed U.S. space missions since 1962. It's still the busiest launch and landing facility in the country, as well as a government site where more than 10,000 men and women work to maintain the existing space program and push the boundaries of scientific knowledge in their quest for the stars.

In 1967, a small visitor's complex was built as a launch-viewing site for astro-nauts' families. Since then, visitors have been coming to central Florida to get a glimpse of the American space program. The center has been expanded into a full-fledged spacecraft museum that is fasci-nating and fun as well as educational.

At the Visitor's Complex, guests can talk to real astronauts and dine with them during Lunch with an Astronaut. Kids enjoy hearing tales of their experiences in space, and asking the astronauts ques-tions. Younger kids love climbing in the

The space shuttle Endeavor *is prepared for launch at Kennedy Space Center. The facility attracts millions of visitors each year.*

Play Dome's Space Shuttle/Space Station Gym. In the Space Shuttle Plaza visitors will find a full-size replica of the space shuttle *Explorer* on display. In the Rocket Garden, a sculpture garden filled with ten-story-high rockets from all eras of space exploration, kids can climb into replicas of *Mercury, Gemini,* and *Apollo* capsules.

The Mad Mission to Mars 2025 exhibit transforms guests into astronauts by using 3-D computer animation, stunning special effects, and wacky characters. Visitors are then taken on an interactive imaginary tour of the universe. IMAX space films displayed on gigantic five-story screens feature dramatic footage shot by NASA astronauts during actual missions. These incredible movies will make you feel like you're floating right alongside them.

To get a look at the space program in action, take the bus tour through Kennedy Space Center. At the Observation Gantry stop, visitors get a great panoramic view of the two space shuttle launchpads and the entire complex, including the gigantic Vehicle Assembly Building (the largest building by volume in the world), where the shuttles are assembled and maintained before launch. Just down the road at the Apollo/Saturn V Center, multimedia presentations, small-scale displays, and a huge 363-foot-long Saturn moon rocket that was never launched are part of an exhibit devoted to the Apollo lunar landing program. You can also view a piece of moon rock as well as a lunar rover trainer.

The final item on the tour is an impressive close-up look at the International Space Station. Here, visitors can observe the happenings of a real NASA laboratory where components of the International Space Station are assembled and prepared for orbit. The Habitation Module is designed to give visitors a sense of life in space. You will see a replica of the living and working area used by astronauts.

Six miles away, the U.S. Astronaut Hall of Fame pays tribute to the country's space heroes and is filled with personal artifacts of the astronauts who first ventured into space. Visitors can experience a sample of the training that astronauts undergo, including a ride in a space flight simulator that turns you upside down and lets you experience zero gravity and g-forces firsthand. You can see what it feels like to squeeze into a replica *Mercury* space capsule, bungee-bounce to experience a stroll on the moon, or try on a pair of astronauts' gloves that are so big and bulky it's hard even to wiggle a finger.

The U.S. space program comes alive during the fascinating tour of the space center. Kids love the sheer size of the exhibits and the immense space vehicles.

DESTIN

Destin is renowned for its deep-sea fishing, but kids also love its white-sand beaches that are a shell-collector's paradise. In fact, Destin is considered by many to be one of the top five shell-collecting areas in the world. Many visitors believe it's the best beach in the South. Families come to Destin to enjoy its soft sand and clear emerald waters, suited to a range of recreational activities. The clarity of its warm waters makes it especially inviting for snorkeling and scuba diving enthusiasts.

Home to the largest and best-equipped fleet of deep-sea fishing charter boats in Florida, Destin is the spot if you're fishing for cobia, grouper, blue marlin, or sailfish. Kids enjoy fishing off Destin's pier and beaches, and there are plenty of fish for them to catch: Pompano, whiting, and mackerel are favorites. The area is home to excellent year-round golf courses that cater to all skill levels. Condos, beach houses, and resort hotels with children's programs abound.

Top: *A peaceful pier and a sunny afternoon add up to a perfectly relaxing day in Destin.* Bottom: *Known by deep-sea fishing enthusiasts as the "World's Luckiest Fishing Village," Destin also features some of the best beaches Florida has to offer.*

VENETIAN POOL

This unusual and enormous swimming pool in Coral Gables is reminiscent of a Venetian grotto and looks like a movie set from an old-fashioned Hollywood musical. Honored with a listing on the National Register of Historic Places, the pool dates from the 1920s and was constructed out of an old limestone quarry.

The free-form coral rock lagoon is bordered by lavish displays of blooming bougainvilleas, birds of paradise, palms, and vine-covered loggias, as well as three-story Spanish porticos with viewing areas at their top. The Venetian Pool features lovely cascading waterfalls, a cobblestone bridge, and even a sandy beach.

Children love to swim and play under the falls and around a palm-fringed island and explore a rocky cave grotto at the far end of the pool, all while lifeguards keep a watchful eye. A deeper section of the pool is roped off for older children and good

Venetian Pool has been a popular attraction for decades. During its heyday, movie stars and prominent politicians lounged poolside while gondolas glided across its waters.

swimmers. During summer, the pool's 800,000 gallons of water are drained and refilled nightly from an aquifer that flows beneath it.

WALT DISNEY WORLD

Most families plan at least one trip during their lifetime to the biggest Disney complex in the world: Disney World in Orlando. Four major theme parks make up Disney World, and more than a dozen other attractions and two evening entertainment districts are also deserving of a visit.

The Magic Kingdom, with its Cinderella Castle centerpiece and costumed characters including Mickey, Minnie, Donald, and other Disney favorites, is the best known and possibly best loved of all the Disney World parks. Parents can take their children on the rides they enjoyed as children, such as the Mad Tea Party, Space Mountain, and the Jungle Cruise, as well as The Haunted Mansion and the recently added Magic Carpets of Aladdin.

At Disney's MGM Studios, guests can tour the MGM back lot and see sets from favorite TV shows or visit the animation studios to observe the artists who work on Disney's animated features. Adrenaline junkies can hop onto the Rock 'n' Roller Coaster and thrill to its high-speed loops and drops, or free-fall 13 stories on the Twilight Zone Tower of Terror ride. There are a number of excellent live stage shows featuring Disney characters, including the family favorite *Beauty and the Beast*.

Part zoo, part theme park, Disney's Animal Kingdom is a blend of nature and adventure packaged with all of the imaginative touches and attention to detail for

Above: *Epcot Center is filled with dazzling shows and amazing experiences. This family favorite celebrates the wonders of the world.* Right: *Do you dare descend in the haunted elevator? The Twilight Zone Tower of Terror at MGM Studios will send you plunging in a special effects–filled thrill ride.*

which Disney is known. Like Magic Kingdom, Animal Kingdom has different themed lands. In this park you'll find more than 1,000 creatures from all corners of the world living in re-created habitats. Guests with small children will find the safari-themed tour buses very useful for seeing as much of the park as possible. Be sure to catch the Festival of the Lion King show, one of the very best in any of the Disney parks. The park also features a number of rides.

Epcot Center showcases world culture and technology in a unique mix of attractions and educational exhibits. It consists of two areas, World Showcase and Future World. Eleven countries are celebrated in the festive World Showcase; each country offers performances, traditional food, craft shops, and exhibits that spotlight its culture. Future World has cutting-edge interactive exhibits and rides that take you to the outer limits of the human imagination.

In addition to the four theme parks, Disney's empire, which stretches 44 square miles, includes water parks (see page 126), a sports complex, five golf courses, shopping areas, and two nighttime entertainment complexes. On-site lodging includes more than 20 resort hotels and campgrounds, each featuring witty and amusing themes.

The kids won't be late for breakfast at Cinderella's castle. The princess herself hosts breakfast each day at the castle's Royal Table Restaurant.

Blizzard Beach and Typhoon Lagoon Water Parks

Legend has it that when an unexpected (and, of course, completely fictional) winter storm dumped a mountain of snow on Orlando, the folks at Disney decided to create Florida's very first winter resort, complete with chairlifts, slalom runs, and sleds. When temperatures returned to normal, the snow began to melt, turning the slalom course, bobsled, and toboggan runs into waterslides. And so the winter resort was turned into Blizzard Beach.

The park's centerpiece for thrill-seekers is Mount Gushmore, where visitors ride a chairlift to the top and choose from a number of hair-raising routes back down: The Downhill Double Dipper is a side-by-side racing slide that can hit a top speed of 25 miles per hour; Summit Plummet, at 120 feet, is the fastest, tallest free-fall flume ride in the world; Tike's Peak is meant just for toddlers and features kiddie slides and a snow castle fountain play area.

Nearby is another Disney water park, Typhoon Lagoon, which was supposedly "created" when a huge storm struck and a ship was stranded high on a mountain by a giant wave. Left in the typhoon's wake are twisting slides, roaring rapids, and a 2.5-acre wave pool, as well as tamer water fun.

You won't need your boots, and leave your winter coats at home. Blizzard Beach may sound cold, but the Florida water park offers the best in refreshing fun.

UNIVERSAL STUDIOS AND ISLANDS OF ADVENTURE

Universal Studios in Orlando has two entertaining attractions that kids in particular will love. Universal Studios Florida, which focuses on movie-based rides and behind-the-scenes displays, and Islands of Adventure, a theme park based on cartoon characters, which features thrill rides and wonderful play areas for young children.

Universal Studios theme park has more than 40 rides, shows, and attractions, including the popular Shrek 4-D and the high-tech Revenge of the Mummy that hurtles guests through Egyptian tombs on a psychological thrill ride. Younger kids particularly enjoy A Day in the Park with Barney and Fievel's Playland in Woody Woodpecker's Kidzone.

At Islands of Adventure, thrill rides are tops with kids school-age and older. Some favorites include the Amazing Adventures of Spider-Man, which combines 3-D action and dizzying special effects with a surprise drop into total darkness; and The Incredible Hulk Coaster, which goes from 0 to 40 miles per hour in two seconds flat. Younger children like to linger in Seuss Landing, which is based on the popular Dr. Seuss books. They can play in the If I Ran the Zoo water playground or enjoy a ride that transports them into the pages of *The Cat in the Hat*.

What's huge, green, and really, really fast? The Incredible Hulk, of course! It's one of the many thrill rides you'll find at Universal's Islands of Adventure.

U.S. Space and Rocket Center

The U.S. Space and Rocket Center in Huntsville, Alabama, showcases a fascinating and comprehensive collection of rockets, missiles, boosters, and space memorabilia. On display are capsules and space suits used over the years in NASA missions and a mock-up of the *Apollo II* Saturn V, the 363-foot rocket that helped launch astronauts to the moon. There's also a full-size mock-up of a space shuttle and a lunar rover vehicle that features tires made of piano wire to ensure that they would be able to withstand extreme temperatures.

At Kids Cosmos, would-be astronauts under the age of eight can crawl around a space station. Adults and kids alike will enjoy the journey to Mars to attempt the Mars Climbing Wall. Space Shot conveys the experience of a real rocket launch, and if you take a spin on the G-Force Accelerator, three times the force of gravity will lift you right out of your seat! The Center's remarkable Space Camp program for children under 18 years old offers hands-on experience in space and aviation. Kids use state-of-the-art simulators to learn about space missions, rocket building, and robotics.

Your family is sure to enjoy the U.S. Space and Rocket Center. The facility showcases the hardware used in the space program and houses a multitude of artifacts.

GULF SHORES

The fine, white sand on the beaches of Gulf Shores must have inspired the phrase "white sugar sand." There are 32 miles of white sand beaches, and the temperate water is swimmable eight months of the year. The towns of Gulf Shores and Orange Beach have plenty of accommodations lining the shore and are filled with family fun such as miniature golf, water parks, marinas, and ice-cream parlors. Gulf State Park has 2.5 miles of uncrowded dunes dotted by sea oats.

In spring and fall, this area is filled with migrating birds, especially around historic Fort Morgan, which is the first and last landfall for migrating songbirds. Every April and October, skilled bird banders arrive and stay for two weeks, gently catching and banding birds such as indigo buntings, warblers, and scarlet tanagers as they fly through. Children can watch the banders go about their work and can "adopt" a bird and watch as it is released. They learn its name and habitat. Banders show how to hold a bird gently, and then demonstrate how to release it.

The pristine beaches of Gulf Shores now shelter a wildlife refuge, and the area is a favorite among bird-watchers.

Beautiful sunsets and pristine beaches are among the pleasures you'll find at Gulf Islands National Seashore. Your family will enjoy exploring its historic sites.

Gulf Islands National Seashore

The 160-mile stretch of barrier islands and coastal shores that make up Gulf Islands National Seashore has been described as the Crown Jewel of Mississippi, and it's easy to see why. Visitors can enjoy miles of sparkling white sand beaches, warm gulf waters, idyllic barrier islands, and fertile salt marshes. Bayous thick with alligators, turtles, and frogs are waiting to be explored. These areas are accessible by kayak and canoe. Trails wind through forests of magnolias, historic sites, and cozy campgrounds. Families can relax and spend their days swimming, sunning, fishing, boating, and paddling year-round.

Pristine West Ship Island is located 12 miles south of the Mississippi coastline. Tour boats carry visitors to the island, where motorized vehicles are not allowed.

Day-trippers can mosey across the island on a wooden boardwalk and take in a tour of its historic Fort Massachusetts. The fort was never fully completed, but it did play a role in the Civil War. Tours are available March through October. You can still see the immense 300-pound cannons that were installed in 1874—these weapons were capable of firing cannonballs as far as three miles.

After a long day of hiking in the Ozarks, the bathhouses in Hot Springs offer a relaxing soak for the weary traveler.

HOT SPRINGS NATIONAL PARK

Hot Springs National Park protects 47 different hot springs and their watershed on Hot Springs Mountain, as well as the eight historic bathhouses in the town of Hot Springs. For more than 200 years, vacationers have come to the waters in Bathhouse Row in hopes of curing all kinds of ills, and tourists can still enjoy a soak in several bathhouses that have remained open.

Be sure to take a walk along the Grand Promenade, a landscaped walkway behind Bathhouse Row, to get a glimpse of the protected springs. A number of hiking trails that wind through the Hot Springs Mountain area begin here, including Dead Chief Trail, which leads to an observation tower at the top of the mountain. If the 1.4-mile uphill hike sounds too strenuous, take a trolley from town. An elevator car-ries visitors to the top of the tower, which offers breathtaking views of the surrounding park and beyond. The town of Hot Springs grew around the springs themselves, and it has a number of family attractions: an alligator farm and petting zoo, an amusement park, a water park, a riverboat tour, a wax museum, go-karts, and horseback riding. The park's visitor center offers a junior ranger program.

BLANCHARD SPRINGS CAVERNS

Blanchard Springs Caverns is a living cave that continues to grow moment by moment as drops of water thick with minerals add to its columns and walls. It is located in the Ozark St. Francis National Forest.

The cave has two paved, lighted trails, one of which is especially fun to visit with younger children. The Dripstone Trail tour begins with an elevator trip down 200 feet. At the bottom, concrete pathways with handrails wind through water-carved passages. Forest Service guides lead the tour and provide interesting facts about Blanchard. Discovery Trail is more strenuous than Dripstone and explores the middle portion of the cave.

Visitors can view the natural stone shaft where the first explorers descended by rope and discovered one of the largest flowstones in the world. Participants on the Wild Cave tour head into more undeveloped reaches of the cavern system, where they crawl up and down dirt slopes, squeeze through tight spots, and scramble over large rocks.

Above: *Watch out—low ceiling. Older children will enjoy the guided tours of the more challenging parts of the cavern.* Left: *The underground formations found in the Ghost Room of Blanchard Springs Caverns are just amazing. Various tours will take you through different regions of the cave system.*

OZARK FOLK CENTER STATE PARK

Take a step into the past with a visit to the Ozark Folk Center in Mountain View. You'll be treated to an old-fashioned way of life that was retained well into the 20th century. The center celebrates these traditions in a state park designated specifically to preserving the culture of the early pioneers in the Ozark Mountains.

Old-time music and dance performances are a staple on the grounds, where you're likely to hear an assortment of foot-stomping folk tunes played on fiddles, banjos, autoharps, dulcimers, and other instruments through-out the day. Special evening concerts are held in an indoor hall and feature the kind of traditional music and dance that have been popular for decades in this part of the United States.

Craftspeople work throughout the park in little cottages, where they make house-hold goods such as soap, quilts, brooms,

Above: *Visitors to the Ozark Folk Center will observe a way of life that is long past. This black-smith is demonstrating one of the many crafts that are re-enacted at the center.* Left: *The Ozark Folk Center features some old-time folk music that's sure to get your toes tapping. The center sponsors a number of concerts throughout the year.*

and barrels. Many of the items are for sale.

The park's Young Pioneers program introduces visiting children to the life of a child growing up in the Ozarks. They can learn a variety of pioneer skills, such as making pinch pottery and beeswax can-dles, carving an apple-head doll, and learning to make and write with a feather quill pen.

NEW ORLEANS JAZZ AND HERITAGE FESTIVAL

Food and music are a winning combination, and the New Orleans Jazz and Heritage Festival serves up heaping portions of both at its spring celebration spanning two action-packed weekends in late April and early May. Twelve big stages and five performance tents offer an eclectic selection of jazz, blues, gospel, funk, Cajun, zydeco, bluegrass, and much, much more. Decision-making is the toughest act of the day, as you may be forced to choose among artists such as B. B. King, Herbie Hancock, the Zydeco Twisters, and dozens of others, all performing at the same time in a variety of different venues.

Food choices are even more mind-boggling: Muffulettas or po' boys? Crawfish Monica or the pheasant-quail-andouille gumbo? Pecan pralines, peach cobbler, or a New Orleans sno-ball? The tantalizing entrées, snacks, and desserts are influenced by local flavor and showcase New Orleans cuisine and Southern cooking at their best.

Kids enjoy touring the festival's many marketplaces and villages. The Louisiana Marketplace is a showcase for the state's finest artists; in the

Louisiana Folklife Village you'll see crafters creating miniature Mardi Gras floats out of papier-mâché.

Families like to hang out at least part of the day at the Kids' Tent and the Cultural Village, which has crafts, projects, and a huge mural for youngsters to paint. Nonstop performances for children are offered here, too, such as storytellers, kids' drum corps, funny jazzy jug bands, singers and dancers from around the world, and costumed Mardi Gras krewes.

Colorful costumes and talented performers are part of the scene during the Jazz and Heritage Festival. Younger visitors will enjoy the daily storytelling and craft activities that take place in the Kids' Cultural Village at the Kids' Tent.

Spooky Cemeteries and Haunted House Tours

Tours with mysterious, eerie, and downright scary themes are popular in New Orleans, and many tour companies have popped up to take visitors through the city's bewitching old cemeteries and haunted buildings. These tours may be too spooky for younger kids, but older children adore the spine-chilling opportunity to explore the shadowy streets and buildings and creepy cemeteries while listening to fascinating tales of New Orleans history.

Cemetery tours usually wind through St. Louis Cemetery #1, established in 1789 and the oldest existing cemetery in the city. Voodoo queen Marie Laveau is purportedly buried here. Many tours also visit the crypts, tombs, and historic headstones of Lafayette Cemetery, depicted in many of Ann Rice's vampire novels. The cemetery was also featured in the movie *Interview with the Vampire,* based on Rice's bestseller.

Ghost tours of the French Quarter share hair-raising tales about the ghosts, spirits, and phantoms of its various residences and businesses. You'll hear chilling narratives of duels, murder, and intrigue along with stories of unexplained forces, and you will see buildings haunted by legendary characters such as the Ghost of the Quadroon Mistress.

You won't find any conventional cemeteries on your tour of spooky places. Because the high water table in New Orleans prevents digging to any great depth, the city's deceased are placed in vaults located aboveground.

MARDI GRAS WORLD

While the spectacular floats and the sequined-and-feathered costumes of Mardi Gras would appeal to just about any child, most parents find the parade and the accompanying debauchery a bit too racy for the kids. So, to get into the Mardi Gras spirit year-round, visit Mardi Gras World, where 80 percent of the floats that travel down the New Orleans streets during Carnival season are designed and built.

It's an actual working studio, where artists sketch, sculpt, and paint the colorful figures and floats for the next year's parades. You'll tour enormous warehouses filled with floats and learn about the traditions surrounding Mardi Gras parades, balls, and music. You'll also learn the inside scoop on float designing and building. There's a chest full of bejeweled costumes for children to try on, and king cake, a tasty Mardi Gras tradition, is served at the end of the tour.

Colorful feathers, fancy flowers, and beautiful beadwork—that's only a fraction of the items that go into your typical Mardi Gras parade float. At Mardi Gras World, you can see the preparation and work that is involved in these unique creations.

NATIONAL WORLD WAR II MUSEUM

The National World War II Museum in New Orleans celebrates the courage and sacrifice of the American men and women of World War II. It tells the story of the war on both the European and Pacific fronts through multimedia: interactive exhibits that include letters from soldiers, films, and photographs; planes; battle gear; and a re-creation of a German lookout post on the Normandy coast.

Highlights include nine oral history stations that feature emotionally touching videotaped interviews with D-Day veterans and others who were involved in the war effort. Artifacts accompanied by the personal stories of those who owned them give audiences a rich insight to the veterans' experiences during the war. One of the museum's main attractions is a replica of the Higgins landing craft that allowed for a mass landing of troops, tanks, and artillery at Normandy.

The museum also shows two movies several times each day: *Price for Peace* and *D-Day Remembered.* There are also reenactments and musical performances for holidays throughout the year, such as Veterans Day, Pearl Harbor Day, D-Day, and Fourth of July.

The National World War II Museum opened its doors on June 6, 2000, the 56th anniversary of the Normandy Invasion.

THE MIDWEST

The Midwest has an astonishingly diverse collection of riches. It's the breadbasket of the nation, filled with fertile farmland and prairies rich in wildlife. The thick forests and pristine lakes of the northern reaches are waiting to be explored on foot, by canoe, or even by dogsled. Vibrant cities such as Chicago and Minneapolis rival any of the world's capitals for culture and points of interest. Excellent zoos, aquariums, and festivals that focus on all-American institutions such as car racing and football are part of the fun. You'll also find destinations celebrating Christmas, the country's pioneer past, and *The Wizard of Oz*, all vying for your attention in the heartland.

The Dinosphere, Children's Museum of Indianapolis

ROCK AND ROLL HALL OF FAME AND MUSEUM

Rock and roll's most celebrated performers, producers, song-writers, and disc jockeys are honored in this chart-topping museum of memorabilia. It was in Cleveland in 1951 that disc jockey Alan Freed popu-larized the phrase "rock and roll." It's fitting that the city is home to the dra-matic glass-and-steel museum designed by I. M. Pei. The building cantilevers high above Lake Erie, and as you enter its soaring atrium to the music of its various inductees you are immediately taken with the rock-star coolness of the place.

Known as "the house that rock built," the Rock and Roll Hall of Fame and Museum offers a range of activities that will appeal to your inner rock star. You can sit for hours, listening to the museum's selection of 500 songs that shaped rock and roll. Or you can watch short film montages that focus on rock's pioneers and early innovators, featuring interviews with artists from the 1960s to the present day.

Memorabilia buffs can linger over Jimi Hendrix's handwritten lyrics, John Lennon's childhood report card, and Tina Turner's memorable concert costumes, plus a variety of other artists' concert posters, ticket stubs, and more. Kids particularly enjoy the Hall of Fame wing; at the

entrance visitors can see footage of past induction ceremonies. Once inside kids hear the stories of the artists and view artifacts from the latest honorees. At the Hall of Fame exit there are juke-boxes that play nearly every song by the inductees.

Above: *The bold, geometric form of the Rock and Roll Hall of Fame and Museum has become a landmark on Cleveland's North Coast Harbor.* Right: *Pink Floyd's* The Wall *is an eye-catching display at the Rock and Roll Hall of Fame and Museum.*

THE NATIONAL UNDERGROUND RAILROAD FREEDOM CENTER

Cincinnati was once a major hub of Underground Railroad activity due to its location on the Ohio River. In the 1800s, the city offered refuge to thousands fleeing slavery in the South. The National Underground Railroad Freedom Center showcases the importance and relevance of human struggles for freedom in the United States and around the world, in the past and present.

Local educators helped design many of the exhibits to parallel the curriculum of area schools. As a result, the exhibits are child-friendly and use storytelling, role-playing, and hands-on activities to engage young visitors. Several local companies give guided half-day, full-day, and two-day Secret Passage Tours that bring the Underground Railroad experience to life. The Center presents eight galleries of historical exhibits. Visitors can view a two-story slave pen and attend live cultural performances. A wide range of educational programs take place most weekends, including concerts, lectures, and workshops. In addition, the Center features two theaters and a café.

Above: *The National Underground Railroad Freedom Center is noted for its thought-provoking exhibits and informative tours.*
Left: *Everyday Freedom Heroes is just one of the exhibits you'll find at the Freedom Center, which opened its doors in 2004. The center has three buildings that symbolize the cornerstones of freedom: courage, cooperation, and perseverance.*

CEDAR POINT AMUSEMENT PARK

Cedar Point is a 364-acre peninsula in Sandusky, Ohio, that first became popular in 1870 as a bathing beach. Today it is home to the world's largest collection of rides and roller coasters. It is considered by many to be among the best amusement parks in the world. Critics rave about it, roller-coaster enthusiasts love it, and families enjoy its full range of theme park entertainment. Besides its menu of heart-pounding coasters and various other amusement park rides, Cedar Point boasts a water park, four resort hotels, a luxury RV campground that includes cottages

Roller-coaster enthusiasts believe it's not enough to build them—you have to build them BIG! That's what the folks at Cedar Point have been doing since 1892, when its first roller coaster was constructed.

which are some of the tallest and fastest around. The Top Thrill Dragster reaches a height of 420 feet, hits a speed of 120 miles per hour in four seconds, and plunges riders into corkscrews and a stomach-in-the-throat freefall. The Millennium Force coaster reaches a height of 310 feet and blasts riders along at 93 miles per hour through the center of the park and across a lagoon.

If rocketing through the stratosphere at breakneck speeds seems too much for your child, Camp Snoopy offers a selection of activities sure to appeal to the younger set, such as a Snoopy's Sing-A-Long. Here kids can

dance and sing with Snoopy and some of his friends. Camp Snoopy's centerpiece attraction is the 38-foot-tall Woodstock Express, an excellent introduction to roller coasters for small children. When it's time to take a quiet moment, head to Early Petting Farm, where families can visit and feed barnyard animals that roam the area.

Frontier Trail, a charming wooded hollow filled with arts, crafts, and shaded benches, offers a look at the artisanship of earlier times. Visitors are treated to demonstrations of pottery-making, weaving, and glassblowing. You can also watch a real blacksmith at work and visit woodworking shops.

Nearby, Thunder Canyon sends rafts through 1,600 feet of churning rapids. Snake River Falls, an 82-foot-tall water flume, features a gigantic tidal wave that soaks riders as well as onlookers standing on a bridge over the splash-landing zone. There are rides for all ages, as well as shows featuring extreme diving stunts, Snoopy and his gang of comic characters, and elaborately staged singing and dancing productions.

Adjacent to Cedar Point you'll find Soak City, an 18-acre water park that has more than a dozen slides; Challenge Park, where you pay as you go for thrill rides, a speedway, and mini golf; and Castaway Bay, an indoor water park and resort open year-round that features 38,000 square feet of tropical-themed fun. Families visiting Cedar Point by boat can dock at the marina during their stay.

and cabins, and two large marinas. In addition, the park has an entertainment complex, live shows, gift shops, restaurants, kids' areas, and much more.

The adrenaline junkies in your family will love Cedar Point's 17 roller coasters,

Pro Football Hall of Fame Festival

Football fans who visit the Hall of Fame in early August, just before induction time, can score extra points for fun at the Pro Football Hall of Fame Festival, a ten-day celebration of everything football. To kick it off, nearly 2,000 children line the streets of Canton, Ohio, and pass an official football along a route more than two miles long, which ends at the Pro Football Hall of Fame. The same ball is then used in the AFC–NFC Hall of Fame Game later that week.

The festival features an array of foods, including a competition among rib vendors from all over the United States. Looking to burn off some extra energy? There's an assortment of activities, including seven football inflatables and a children's entertainment area that has a rock-climbing wall, kiddie rides, and more.

A parade features spectacular floats, marching bands, helium balloons, clowns, and costumed characters, plus returning Hall of Famers and the current class of enshrinees and their presenters. Later, the nation's top drum and bugle corps perform. Plus, there's a hot-air balloon event, sky-divers, concerts, and fireworks. The highlights of the festival are the Hall of Fame Game and the induction of new Hall of Famers.

Above: *The Balloon Classic, which features more than 70 giant figures, is just part of the fun at the Pro Football Hall of Fame Festival.* Left: *The induction ceremony naming the newly enshrined in the Football Hall of Fame caps the annual Pro Football Hall of Fame Festival.*

KINGS ISLAND

Kings Island is a 364-acre amusement and water park with a number of rides based on movies, as well as seven themed areas, two of which are designed for visitors of all ages. Located near Cincinnati, Kings Island boasts 80 world-class thrill rides, live entertainment stage shows, and attractions. Boomerang Bay, a huge Australian–themed water park, has 50 water activities, including 30 slides.

Rides for younger kids include a carousel and a swinging pirate ship. There's also Nickelodeon Universe and Hanna-Barbera lands with a variety of Dora the Explorer and SpongeBob SquarePants–themed attractions, as well as the Rugrats Runaway Reptar, the world's first suspended roller coaster designed for younger children.

Older children will like The Beast, a legendary ride that's been called the best wooden roller coaster in the world by ride aficionados. On a roller-coaster ride based on *The Italian Job,* guests board their own Mini Cooper cars and peel off on a thrilling excursion.

Above: *Who cares who crosses the finish line of the Coolangatta Racer first? The 54-foot-high waterslide is fun all the way down. Located in Boomerang Bay Water Park at Kings Island, the ride features four slides that merge for a final dash.*
Left: *Driving a Mini Cooper has never been so much fun. The Italian Job: Stunt Track at Kings Island takes you on a wild joyride.*

MACKINAC ISLAND

Visitors take a step back in time when they arrive at this leisurely island escape in Michigan. Cars are prohibited on Mackinac Island—they were banned shortly after the first "horseless carriage" motored off the ferry in the early 20th century. Visitors tour the island—which measures three miles by two miles—by bicycle, on foot, or in a horse-drawn taxi. Hotels and bike shops rent fleets of two-wheelers, and many guests bring their own bikes to the island on the ferry.

More than 75 percent of the island is Mackinac Island State Park, which includes 18th-century Fort Mackinac. Inside the fort you'll see enthusiastic reenactors and 14 original buildings with interesting displays that tell about life for American soldiers and their families circa 1880. In the Kids' Quarters, children can revisit the styles of the 1800s.

Lively fife-and-drum performances take place daily during the summer months.

The island's quaint Victorian–era town is also known for its fabulous fudge. Children enjoy visiting the many candy shops to sample the creamy confection. It's an extra treat to watch as it is poured from large copper kettles onto marble cooling slabs and folded into fudge loaves.

Inset: *You'll leave the traffic jams behind on Mackinac Island, but don't let the relaxed pace of life fool you. The island is the summer home of the governor of Michigan, and over the years political figures such as presidents Kennedy and Clinton have visited here.* Bottom: *Historic Fort Mackinac was built by the British in 1781. Today it's a popular stop for island visitors.*

SLEEPING BEAR DUNES NATIONAL LAKESHORE

These steep slopes of sand rise as high as 460 feet above the blue waters of Lake Michigan. The dunes are among the largest in the world, matched only by those in Colorado, the Sahara, and Saudi Arabia. You'll huff and puff your way to the top—it's quite a climb—but it's worth it to tumble, run, or cartwheel down the soft, sandy slope.

Enjoy a picnic lunch and relax after your climb. You'll probably spot some hang gliders who like to launch from the dunes' peaks. The waters of Lake Michigan are a very short walk from the bottom of the dunes and are a great place to linger for a swim or a picnic until you muster the energy to go up…and down again.

Enough beach for everyone is just one of the attractions at Sleeping Bear Dunes National Lakeshore.

While the dunes are a popular attraction in this protected area, the entire 35-mile stretch of Lake Michigan's eastern coast-line, as well as North and South Manitou Islands, are worth a visit.

HENRY FORD MUSEUM AND GREENFIELD VILLAGE

The eclectic Henry Ford Museum in Dearborn was founded in 1929 by the Ford family primarily as a place to house inventor Henry Ford's immense personal collection of Americana. It also serves to honor America's technological ingenuity and innovative thinking. Instead of focusing on a single time period or location, the museum spans 350 years of American history.

Both the museum and neighboring Greenfield Village reflect the quirks of their eccentric founder, who collected whatever tickled his fancy. The collection is so diverse—from the bike shop where the Wright Brothers designed and built

The emphasis is on authenticity at the Henry Ford Museum. Information in a newspaper article about the 1955 arrest of Rosa Parks was matched with bus company records to verify that this is the actual bus Parks was riding when she refused to surrender her seat.

Right: Experience 300 years of American history in Greenfield Village, immersed in the sights, sounds, and sensations of America's past. With more than 90 acres of authentic historic structures; four living history farms; period-clothed presenters; and nationally renowned glass, pottery, and tin artisans, Greenfield Village is a place like no other in the world. Visitors can even take a ride in an authentic Model T or historic steam engine.

their first airplane to Thomas Edison's last breath, captured in a test tube. It's wise to study the visitor's guide and pick out some of the museum's unique treasures for a closer look.

Visitors may choose from several delightful and unusual forms of transportation to travel around the museum grounds. They can ride in a vintage Model T, a horse-drawn carriage, a 1931 Ford Model AA bus, or an historic train.

As you might imagine, automobiles are well represented in the museum, with dozens of cars of various shapes and sizes, as well as an exhibit that explains how the car influenced everyday life in the 20th century. You'll also find on display old racecars, the ill-fated Edsel that was named after Henry Ford's son, and a 1953 Stout Scarab that was billed as a living room on wheels. Children can see a car shaped like a hot dog that was used to advertise a popular brand of wieners, they can sit on the same Birmingham bus on which Rosa Parks refused to give up her seat, and they can view the presidential limousine that carried John F. Kennedy on that fateful day in Dallas. Also on display are various bicycles, baby buggies, planes, and trains.

Greenfield Village contains more than 80 historic structures. Ford's admiration of Thomas Edison is especially apparent in here, as he relocated or re-created many of the buildings in which Edison lived and worked. Visitors can also tour Ford's childhood home, the log cabin where George Washington Carver was born, a home that once belonged to Robert Frost, and the room where Noah Webster wrote the first American dictionary. Other sites in Greenfield Village include operating sawmills, a glass-making plant, and a working farm with animals.

FORD ROUGE FACTORY TOUR

Visitors can board buses at the Henry Ford Museum for a narrated drive past famous landmarks and the manufacturing complex on their way to tour the factory where Ford trucks are built. They can also view an interesting short film on the history of the factory and the city that grew up around it, followed by a virtual reality experience that takes them to the center of the car-making process. After a tour of the factory's innovative living roof, a 454,000-square-foot garden atop the assembly building, visitors move into the plant and onto an elevated walkway to watch Ford employees and robots assemble F-150 pickup trucks.

Costumed reenactors roam the grounds, and there are many guided tours for visitors of all ages.

There are programs available at the Henry Ford Museum and Greenfield Village throught the year, such as festive holiday events in the winter, somber Civil War remembrances in the spring, an historic baseball tournament in the summer, and the Old Car Festival in the fall.

FRANKENMUTH

You'll enjoy the magic of Christmas year-round at this quaint village that seems to have jumped from the pages of a German fairy tale. Downtown shops and restaurants have a Bavarian theme—right down to the old-fashioned candy shops and restaurants with lederhosen-clad servers. A 35-bell carillon housed in a glockenspiel tower rings throughout the day and reenacts the story of the Pied Piper with carved wooden figures that move about on tracks.

The town's best-known attraction is Bronner's Christmas Wonderland. It's the world's largest Christmas store, welcoming two million guests each year from all over the world. Visitors are greeted by a 17-foot-tall Santa and the country's largest year-round lighted outdoor Christmas display. The store is the size of several football fields and contains thousands of ornaments, nativity sets from miniature to life-size, and just about every other type of Christmas item you can possibly imagine. From June through December, it snows for two minutes every half hour in Bronner's west lobby.

The glockenspiel tower is just one of the quaint sights in Frankenmuth, also known as "Little Bavaria." Your kids will think they are in a fairy tale as they tour the town's shops.

Right: *It's always Christmas at Bronner's Christmas Wonderland. This family-run store began operations 50 years ago and has grown into an enterprise that imports ornaments from all over the world.* Below: *In Frankenmuth visitors can see demonstrations of various artistic techniques, such as painting and glass blowing.*

CONNER PRAIRIE

Conner Prairie in Fishers, Indiana, gives families the opportunity to travel back in time to the 1800s, where they can experience firsthand how everyday life has changed over the past two centuries. Known especially for its entertaining, yet authentic, presentation of the past, this living-history museum has several different areas replete with costumed interpreters and hands-on experiences that bring the past to life.

Prairietown is a restored and re-created 1836 Indiana frontier village. Be sure to visit Pastport, where families can dip candles, churn butter, and wash clothes on a washboard. At the 1816 Lenape Indian Camp, you can enter a Native American wigwam, learn to throw a tomahawk, help make a dugout canoe, and even chat with a fur trader at the trading post.

Step across a covered bridge to Liberty Corner, an 1886-era rural community, where visiting children can attend the local school as long as they behave accordingly. Conner Prairie offers summer camps, a pioneer program for young children, and special holiday events.

A friendly pioneer greeting awaits you at Conner Prairie, where kids can experience history firsthand.

INDIANAPOLIS 500 AND THE 500 FESTIVAL

Mom and Dad can start their engines and take the family minivan—and the kids—for a lap around the famed Indianapolis Motor Speedway four days before the superstars of the raceway hit the track. Kids can pedal tiny racecars around a section of the official track, and the entire family can watch the actual crews practice their pit stops or get autographs from current Indy car drivers and past champions. It's all part of Community Day, one of the many 500 Festival events that precede the big race.

The festival also hosts a Kids' Day of free activities in downtown Indianapolis. The event features performances by costumed characters, inflatable rides, arts and crafts, and other kid-pleasing classics such as face painting, clowns, and games. A parade with race drivers, marching bands, floats, and inflatable characters winds its way through the streets of Indianapolis the day before the race.

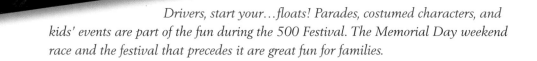

Drivers, start your…floats! Parades, costumed characters, and kids' events are part of the fun during the 500 Festival. The Memorial Day weekend race and the festival that precedes it are great fun for families.

CHILDREN'S MUSEUM OF INDIANAPOLIS

This world-class collection of hands-on fun makes up the largest children's museum in the world. Its exhibits continue to amaze and entertain local children as well as families who make the trek to the city just to visit this renowned attraction.

The astonishing *Fireworks of Glass,* a blown-glass exhibit in the five-story atrium, is the largest permanent sculpture that artist Dale Chihuly has ever created. The 43-foot-tall glass tower rises above what appears to be a floating glass ceiling. A number of innovative hands-on activities are offered to promote an appreciation of the work that went into the sculpture. Children can create their own sculptures using colorful plastic shapes or view a film that demonstrates the sights and sounds of glassblowing at the museum's planetarium.

The popular Dinosphere exhibit immerses children in the Cretaceous Period

of more than 65 million years ago and lets them examine actual fossils and fossilized bones. Kids can learn about the preparation of fossils in the Paleo Prep Lab, where they can watch real paleontologists at work.

The Playscape Preschool Gallery is designed specifically for kids up to age five. Little ones can splash around at the water table and play in the sand dome, and they can plant flowers in the

Above: *Water clocks are amazing timepieces that date back to ancient Egypt and Greece. On display at the Children's Museum of Indianapolis is the largest water clock in North America.* Left: *The largest artifact in the Children's Museum is also a fun ride. The 1900s–era carousel, found in the Carousel Wishes and Dreams Gallery, is one of the few surviving wooden carousels left in the United States. It was originally located in an Indianapolis amusement park.*

garden while a friendly scarecrow looks on. Storytelling sessions are also part of the fun.

All generations enjoy the Carousel Wishes and Dreams Gallery, where families can ride a real carousel under a starry sky, explore the inside of a giant kaleidoscope, and navigate a mirror maze.

The ScienceWorks exhibit teaches children about the natural and physical sciences. Here kids can explore a real freshwater pond, change the flow of a 30-foot-long creek, and experiment with water levels. There's also a crawl-through area that shows kids how some creatures live underground. At the simulated construction site kids can use basic engineering principles to move stuff around; there's even a child-size bulldozer they can use.

Other attractions include a 26-foot-tall water clock that contains 40 parts made of glass vials, vacuums, and colored liquid, and it somehow manages to keep perfect time. The museum houses a collection of more than 50,000 pieces of folk objects and toys, more than 500 of which are on display at any given time in the Passport to the World gallery.

The museum features holiday favorites such as a festive Winter Wonderland complete with a Yule Slide and Snow Castle, ice-fishing in the fishing shack, and a cookie café.

The amazing Fireworks of Glass, *sculptor Dale Chihuly's innovative creation, is made up of 3,200 pieces of brilliantly colored, individually blown glass.*

HOLIDAY WORLD

This holiday-themed fun spot is appropriately located in Santa Claus, Indiana. While its wooden roller coaster and traditional thrill rides are popular, the park is geared toward preschoolers. It's a favorite of parents who enjoy its low-key pleasures.

Built in 1946, the park was first known as Santa Claus Land and was billed as the nation's first amusement theme park. In 1984 the park was expanded to include three holiday motif sections: Christmas, Halloween, and Fourth of July. A water park was added nine years later, and in 2006 Thanksgiving was added.

Holiday World's child-friendly attention to detail makes parents happy: Soft drinks, lemonade, and water are free, and complimentary self-serve sunblock dispensers are found throughout the park. Kids can sit on Santa's lap year-round and enjoy a variety of rides and play areas. Family-friendly shows are a summer highlight and include musicals, professional diving, and Santa himself singing songs and reading stories.

Top: *It's a funnel of fun—and it's called Zinga. You'll find this eight-story water ride at Holiday World's Splashin' Safari.* Right: *The flying carousel called the HalloSwings is an enduring favorite at Holiday World. The ride will send you flying like a witch on a broomstick.*

SHEDD AQUARIUM

The Shedd Aquarium opened in 1930 as the first inland aquarium to have a permanent saltwater exhibit. Water was shipped by railcar from Florida. Today the Shedd Aquarium boasts a collection of 8,000 aquatic animals and an Oceanarium.

The Shedd's exhibits bring you close to exotic underwater worlds. The Shedd's original galleries make up Waters of the World. This exhibit includes hundreds of different kinds of fish— from bighead and silver carp to clown anemonefish and sea stars. Kids will also see paddlefish and giant gourami and even sea horses and sea dragons. The Shedd's oldest resident, an Australian lungfish that arrived in 1933, also lives in the Waters of the World exhibit.

Visitors to the Shedd Aquarium will be treated to a performance by the Oceanarium's dolphins that also demonstrates the care and training each one receives.

The 400,000-gallon Wild Reef habitat has one of North America's most diverse displays of sharks. Its floor-to-ceiling aquarium windows give guests a diver's-eye view of a coral reef teeming with more than 500 species of fish.

The Caribbean Coral Reef tank is filled with just about every species you'd expect to find in tropical waters. A variety of rainbow-colored fish share the space with several sharks and sea turtles. Divers hand-feed the animals at scheduled times during the day. At Amazon Rising, anacondas, piranhas, and spiders the size of dinner platters bring the diverse Amazon basin to life. The expansive Oceanarium exhibit re-creates a Pacific Northwest marine environment, with dolphins, harbor seals, sea otters, penguins, and beluga whales visible through underwater viewing windows. During scheduled shows each day in the Oceanarium, visitors will be entertained by the exciting acrobatics of the Shedd's dolphins.

Chicago International Children's Film Festival

North America's largest and longest-running festival of films for children, the Chicago International Children's Film Festival brings together some of the best animated and live action films from 40 different countries. The festival traditionally begins in October and spans an 11-day period. There is something to appeal to children of all ages, with special programs directed at four different age groups ranging between 2 and 13.

The films and videos—dramas, documentaries, comedies, social commentaries, artistic vignettes, and animated shorts—compete for recognition and prizes, and children who attend the festival vote for their favorites. One of the categories is Child-Produced Work, which features the works of aspiring filmmakers under the age of 14.

In past festivals, films such as *Lucky* from South Africa, *The Little Monsterette* from Switzerland, *Domo-Kun and the Egg* from Japan, and *Runaway Bathtub* from the United States have been presented. The films shown at the festival are carefully selected to present humanistic, nonexploitative, culturally diverse, and nonviolent work. The festival also sponsors a number of workshops for kids interested in making movies.

Kids count at the Chicago International Children's Film Festival. Young film buffs are invited to join the Young Chicago Critics Program and sit on the Children's Jury. This young man is awarding a top prize at a recent festival.

ZOOLIGHTS AT LINCOLN PARK ZOO

During the holiday season, it's hard for a meerkat to get a good night's sleep when millions of tiny lights brighten the grounds of the Lincoln Park Zoo and add a festive glow. You'll see the animals with thick winter coats lolling about in the cool night air, while their less-insulated brethren remain indoors in heated enclosures.

You can take in the sights on foot or jump aboard the Holiday Express train to view the more than 100 light displays and giant illuminated animal figures located throughout the zoo. Other highlights include ice-carving demonstrations and family crafts and activities in the Kovler Lion House. Children can pay a visit to Santa in his workshop, listen to stories and music, and ride the zoo's carousel. Carolers offer entertainment during the evening, and when little zoo-goers get hungry, there are plenty of hot treats.

It's cool to go to the zoo in the winter, especially during ZooLights. This popular holiday event features ice sculptures, fabulous light displays, and an amazing laser show.

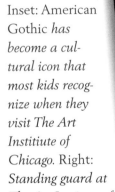

Inset: *American Gothic has become a cultural icon that most kids recognize when they visit The Art Institute of Chicago.* Right: *Standing guard at The Art Institute of Chicago are two bronze lions that flank the entrance to the building. The statues are traditionally dressed in sports finery whenever a Chicago team is in the playoffs.*

THE ART INSTITUTE OF CHICAGO

Some of the world's most famous paintings are housed in The Art Institute of Chicago. The collection includes the works of Impressionists and Post-Impressionists, as well as other notable works such as Grant Wood's *American Gothic* and Edward Hopper's *Nighthawks*. Children can traipse through the many galleries of paintings, prints, sculptures, and photographs. The collection of arms and armor, which contains shiny suits of armor, wicked swords and daggers, and ancient firearms, is a particular favorite among children.

The 68 dollhouse-size rooms in the Thorne Miniature Rooms exhibit are filled with exquisite tiny furniture, household objects, and works of art. Painstakingly constructed and handcrafted, many of the rooms are duplicates of those found in European palaces and homes throughout the United States.

Family programs are highly emphasized at the museum. Many activities are located at the Kraft Education Center, which offers exhibits, games, puzzles, interactive computer games, and a children's library. Families can explore world cultures in an exhibition called Faces, Places, & Inner Spaces. The Art Institute offers a variety of workshops, and an artist's studio is open most weekends so kids can create their own masterpieces.

MILLENNIUM PARK

What was once an eyesore of decaying railroad tracks and parking lots along Chicago's lakefront is now a stunning 24.5-acre urban jewel called Millennium Park. Among its major attractions are two extraordinary

pieces of public art that have captivated visitors. One is a highly reflective 110-ton polished steel sculpture officially named *Cloud Gate* but affectionately called "The Bean." Visitors can wander under and around it to see the park and cityscape reflected in its curves. The other, the Crown Fountain, is a reflecting pool flanked by two 50-foot towers onto which close-up images of Chicagoans are projected. The lips on the faces purse, and water sprays from them, making the ever-changing faces look like giant gargoyles. On warm days,

children splash in the shallow water between the two towers and delight in the spray from the fountains.

There are plenty of lawns for picnicking, walkways among hedges and gardens, a performing arts venue, and a bicycle rental center so visitors can tour the park on wheels. A large outdoor ice-skating rink is open throughout the winter months.

Below: Cloud Gate *is a highly polished public sculpture that has become a major attraction. The "gate" is formed by a 12-foot-high arch.*

Above: *Both a technological marvel and an impressive work of public sculpture, the Crown Fountain is made up of glass blocks erected in front of two gigantic video screens. The screens display a continuous loop of faces that smile, laugh, and squirt water, much to the delight of onlookers.*

NAVY PIER

Chicago's lakefront playground is a fabulous 50-acre complex of parks, promenades, shops, and restaurants. Much of it is quite literally a pier overhanging the blue waters of Lake Michigan. Navy Pier is a wonderful place to bike or roller blade, and rental shops offer both.

The pier is home to a wide array of family-oriented events and entertainment. Its most visible attraction is a 150-foot-high Ferris wheel that was modeled after the one built for Chicago's 1893 World Columbian Exposition. It is a great way to get a bird's-eye view of the area. Other attractions include a musical carousel, old-fashioned Viennese swings, miniature golf, a maze, an IMAX theater, and an excellent children's museum.

Two stages offer free music and theatrical performances during the summer, and many shows are geared especially to families. Tour boats depart the pier regularly—you can choose between speedboat rides that will have you zipping across Lake Michigan at 40 miles per hour or restful cruises whose guides provide background about Chicago's architecture. On select nights during the summer, Navy Pier stages a fireworks display that lights up the city's skyline. Special cruises that depart from the pier offer a perfect vantage point.

The original Navy Pier, once called Municipal Pier, dates back to 1914 and was once used as a naval training base. Today, it's alive with activity. What better way to take in all the sights and sounds of the pier than from atop its famous Ferris wheel?

MUSEUM OF SCIENCE AND INDUSTRY

This innovative Chicago museum is one of the best in the country and features a myriad of thoroughly engaging exhibits for family members of every age. You can climb through a cramped World War II German U-boat to get a feel for life undersea, descend into a coal mine like a real miner, and operate a series of 12 toy-assembling robots that can produce 300 gravitron toys per hour.

Peek into the world of miniatures at The Great Train Story, which features 34 model trains racing along an elaborate cross-country set that starts at Seattle harbor and ends in Chicago. The astonishing Fairy Castle, designed by Colleen Moore, is a wonderland of miniature treasures from around the world. In the dining room, King Arthur's table is set with real gold plates, and the stitches in the Viennese tapestries lining the wall are so small that you can barely see them, even under a magnifying glass. In Cinderella's drawing room, the chandelier is hung with real diamonds, emeralds, and pearls.

The Chick Hatchery is a favorite among children. It's a daily event where visitors witness the chicks carefully pecking their way out of their shells. Networld takes visitors on a multimedia tour into the technology that keeps our modern world connected every day.

It was once the terror of the Atlantic Ocean during World War II. This authentic U-505 German submarine was captured off the coast of Africa in 1944 and is now on exhibit at the Museum of Science and Industry.

WISCONSIN DELLS

Nearly two dozen water parks lure families to the Dells year-round: It's considered to be the water park capital of the world. Many of them are themed—pirates, King Arthur, the lost world of Atlantis—and each one tries to outdo its neighbor with more lavish rides, bigger splash-and-play pools, and longer and faster waterslides.

The Dells was a popular family vacation spot long before the first water park opened its gates. Visitors first came to take boat tours through the unusual sandstone cliffs along the Wisconsin River. In

Listening to tall tales from your guide and looking for images in the swirling patterns in the sandstone cliffs are part of the fun on a tour of the Wisconsin River.

the mid-1950s, "Ducks"—World War II water/land vehicles once used for beach invasions—were introduced to the Dells and used for tours. A flashy water-ski show also debuted. Both the Duck tours and the water show are still popular today, but the water parks are the area's biggest draw year-round.

In the summer the behemoth Noah's Ark is open to everyone. It is a Dells landmark and offers 70 acres of waterslides, endless rivers, and children's play areas. Its popular Dark Voyage ride speeds four-person rafts through 600 feet of total darkness.

While some of the water parks allow only guests of their affiliated hotel, most, including the enormous African-themed Kalahari, offer day passes for nonguests. The hotel features an indoor water park under a massive glass roof, where families can slide and splash on even the frostiest of days. One of its most popular rides, the Tanzania Twister (nicknamed the Toilet Bowl), swishes riders around a giant funnel at dizzying speeds and then "flushes" them into a pool. The resort's signature attraction is the Botswana Blast, a water coaster that shoots riders uphill using strategically placed water jets.

The Wilderness Resort is another indoor giant, with 160,000 square feet of rides and slides. Its most popular attractions include Fantastic Voyage, a fast 500-foot-long, five-person raft ride. The southwestern desert–themed Chula Vista Resort has both indoor and outdoor water parks built around its hotel.

Feeling a little waterlogged? Check out Tommy Bartlett's Ski, Sky, Stage Show and watch the incredible feats of daredevil skiers and aerial performers, as well as a laser light show. There's also an Exploratory next door filled with interactive activities.

Who's up for one more ride? Noah's Ark, the premier water park in the Dells, offers a huge selection of water rides and activities.

Ready for some sleight of hand? Head to the Rick Wilcox Theater. You can visit Ripley's Believe It or Not! Museum or the Circus World Museum in nearby Baraboo. Visitors can choose among plenty of other attractions, such as train rides, horseback riding, miniature golf, and go-karts.

Jelly Belly Warehouse Tour

The Jelly Belly tasting bar is definitely the highlight of this sweet-smelling, family-oriented factory tour, which offers visitors samples of many of the 100 candies this Pleasant Prairie, Wisconsin, company makes, including a wide variety of Jelly Bellies. Tours begin at Jelly Belly Junction, where visitors hop on the Jelly Belly Express train for a narrated tour through this large warehouse and distribution center. The train passes under colorful six-foot-long jelly beans suspended from the ceiling in Candy Alley and past a dancing chorus line of Jelly Belly characters.

As the train makes its way through the facility, it stops at various stations with large video screens showing how the company makes its famous jelly beans, candy corn, taffy, and gummies. The tour ends in the taste-testing shop, where all kinds of Jelly Bellies and other candy are sold. The shop also often sells Belly Flops, which are jelly beans that have not made the cut because they're slightly imperfect in shape.

A warehouse full of jelly beans? Sweet! Kids will love the entertaining tour of the Jelly Belly warehouse. A visit to Candy Alley offers a behind-the-scenes look at the candy's manufacturing process.

DOOR COUNTY

The long, finger-shape peninsula that separates the main body of Lake Michigan from the city of Green Bay, Wisconsin, is called Door County. It is known for its quiet beaches, picturesque towns, and scenic farms. Scandinavians settled here in the 1850s, and their influence is evident in the delicious food specialties offered throughout the region, such as Icelandic pancakes with lingonberry syrup, and skorpa, a sweetly spiced Swedish toast.

Kids will love exploring Door County's expansive shoreline and its historic lighthouses. If they grow tired of its beautiful beaches, they can travel its many bike paths or pick in-season produce at various fruit farms.

Fish boils are a tradition you won't want to miss: They date back to the time Door County was populated by settlers and lumberjacks. Today's fish boils consist of fresh whitefish steaks cooked with onions and potatoes in a huge pot over an open fire. The dramatic flare-up, or "overboil," is a sure sign that dinner is ready.

WASHINGTON ISLAND

Washington Island is accessible by ferry. Families come to bike its quiet lanes and to enjoy soft sand and smooth pebble beaches. Fishing enthusiasts enjoy angling for smallmouth bass, trout, and king salmon. Field Wood Farm is noted for its herd of rugged Icelandic horses. The farm offers guided trail rides.

Looking for authentic Wisconsin cuisine? Try a fish boil. Everybody waits for the sizzle of the overboil, which helps remove the oil from the whitefish.

Boundary Waters Canoe Area Wilderness

Some families' idea of a cruise is paddling along a peaceful waterway. If this sounds like a perfect vacation to you, head to the Boundary Waters Canoe Area Wilderness in northern Minnesota and the Quetico Provincial Park in Ontario. Together they comprise one of the largest areas of protected wilderness in North America. Glaciers have carved out a breathtaking series of more than 1,000 interconnected waterways linked by portage trails.

This labyrinth of lakes served as a travel network for Native Americans for thousands of years and was once one of the main routes to the west for European explorers and fur traders. Known as the Voyageurs' Highway, it ran through what is now the Boundary Waters and Quetico Provincial Park.

There are more than 1,200 miles of canoe routes, and motorized boats are only allowed in certain areas. There are paddle-in campsites throughout the park. The rugged terrain is populated by moose, beavers, otters, minks, and loons. Fishing is superb, and lake trout, smallmouth bass, walleye, and northern pike are plentiful.

Entry points are established to control the flow of visitors and protect the wilderness area. The town of Ely is considered the gateway to the Boundary Waters, and here you'll find outfitters of all kinds that sell supplies and specialized equipment, rent canoes, and provide guides.

During your visit, stop by the International Wolf Center to meet the center's resident wolf pack and take a wolf-howling lesson. After dark, you can practice what you've learned to exchange calls with the wild wolves.

In winter, the area is known for ice fishing, cross-country skiing, and snowshoeing. Dogsledding is also popular, and special trails have been created just for that sport. Several outfitters operate sleigh rides in the evening to take advantage of the crystal-clear view of the starry sky and the northern lights.

If your family loves a wilderness vacation that includes fishing, canoeing, and wildlife viewing, head for northern Minnesota's Boundary Waters. What was once a major travel network for explorers and trappers is now the most visited wilderness in the United States.

The Winter Carnival originated in 1886 after a visiting reporter complained that St. Paul was "unfit for human habitation" in the winter months. The city's response? An exciting, imaginative event that turns the snowy season into a festive delight!

St. Paul Winter Carnival

This gala is a much-anticipated event in St. Paul and is the country's oldest and largest winter festival. The city is filled with parades, car races on ice, and ice-carving contests.

The crowning of the festival royalty—King Boreas and the Queen of Snows and their court—heralds the beginning of two weeks of frozen fun. The coronation is followed by the Grande Day Parade, when outrageously decorated floats wind through downtown. A second procession, called the Torchlight Parade, features floats aglow with giant flames and festive lights.

The carnival offers all kinds of sporty events, including ice hockey, softball played on ice, a children's ice fishing contest, ice skating, snow volleyball, ice golf, and more. A frozen winter playground and a giant snow slide are popular stops for younger children. The intricate and elaborate sculptures of the ice-carving competition are on display throughout the entire carnival.

One of the most anticipated events of the festival is the treasure hunt for the special Winter Carnival medallion, which is worth thousands of dollars to the winner. It's a tradition that has St. Paul residents following daily clues in the local newspaper and searching high and low for the hidden prize.

MALL OF AMERICA

You can spend the whole day at Bloomington's Mall of America (MOA) and never even set foot in any of its more than 520 stores on four floors. The Park at MOA is a seven-acre playground with more than 30 rides and attractions for children. It is the nation's largest indoor theme park, complete with its own food court and restaurants.

There is a 14-screen movie theater, a NASCAR simulator, a four-story Lego play area with more than 30 full-size Lego models, a lively, interactive dinosaur museum, and much more.

The MOA's popular Underwater Adventures Aquarium is a 1.2-million-gallon tank that teems with more than 4,500 sea creatures. It is the world's largest underground aquarium. Visitors cruise by on a moving walkway inside a transparent tunnel to observe sharks, stingrays, sea turtles, and all kinds of fish. Its Creepy Crawly Corner features tarantulas and giant isopods. Visitors can even pick up the isopods, if they dare! Many people think they look like giant cockroaches.

It's the mall that has it all. The Mall of America attracts about 40 million visitors a year and boasts an indoor amusement park, an IMAX theater, and a major aquarium that is home to thousands of exotic animals. It's become one of the biggest tourist attractions in the country.

CHILDREN'S THEATRE COMPANY

North America's flagship theater for young people brings to the stage classic children's stories such as *The Magic Mrs. Piggle-Wiggle, Pippi Longstocking,* and *How the Grinch Stole Christmas.* The productions are brilliantly staged with wildly imaginative, colorful sets and vivid costumes. The shows are performed by a troupe of talented professional adult and child actors.

The Minneapolis theater company also commissions new works from significant artists, such as Pulitzer Prize–winning Nilo Cruz, who adapted for the stage the short story *A Very Old Man With Enormous Wings* by magical realist author Gabriel García Márquez. In 2003, the Children's Theatre Company was the first theater for young people to ever win a Regional Theatre Tony Award. Plus, its musical adaptation of the Arnold Lobel story, *A Year with Frog and Toad*, had a successful Broadway run.

The theater complex has two stages, where the company features an average of ten different plays and performances each year. A separate floor of classrooms and a state-of-the-art performance studio round out the educational facilities for kids.

Founded in 1965, the Children's Theatre Company presents imaginative, lively productions for children of all ages. Classic tales such as The Wizard of Oz *are family favorites.*

MINNEAPOLIS SCULPTURE GARDEN

Dozens of awe-inspiring and extraordinary sculptures by 20th-century artists such as Henry Moore, Isamu Noguchi, and Frank Gehry are situated about the grassy landscape of the Minneapolis Sculpture Garden. Its most famous work is the playful *Spoonbridge and Cherry*, a 50-foot-long teaspoon with a 15-foot-high, water-spouting, bright-red cherry perched on its rim. Created by Claes Oldenburg and Coosje van Bruggen, it sits in the middle of a lily pond.

The unique setting is the largest urban sculpture garden in the country; it's also a place where children can run around and blow off steam while enjoying some of the world's finest modern three-dimensional works of art. A map with pictures and explanations of each piece is available. Children enjoy using it as a treasure map to hunt down the various artwork depicted. The adjacent art center offers a Free First Saturday family program with various activities and entertainment.

Kids love the unexpected—just watch their reactions when they see the unusual, creative artwork in the Sculpture Garden. Spoonbridge and Cherry is just one of the imaginative sculptures on display.

Iowa State Fair

When it comes to state fairs, Iowa brings home the blue ribbon. It has more competitive events—almost 900—than any other state fair in the nation. It seamlessly blends old favorites such as pie baking, quilt making, and prettiest pig contests with some unusual competitions that are great fun to see. The ugliest cake contest is a favorite for children. It's not judged on appearance only, however; the cake must be tasty as well. Other tests of skill include a yo-yo contest, a nail driving competition, a rubber chicken throwing contest, and a hog calling competition.

Each year Duffy Lyon, an Iowa resident, crafts 550 pounds of locally produced butter into the form of a cow. This life-size sculpture has been a fair trademark for nearly 100 years.

You'll find rides and games on the fair's expansive midway, plus concerts featuring chart-topping performers, acres of farm equipment, one of the world's largest livestock shows, and agricultural displays of all types. The food ranges from fair favorites such as funnel cakes, corn dogs, and cotton candy to chocolate-covered cheesecake on a stick, sweet potato fries, and fried ice cream.

It's not destined to become an Olympic event anytime soon, but it's a crowd-pleasing favorite at the Iowa State Fair. The rubber chicken throwing competition is just one of the many wacky contests you'll find there.

BRANSON

This country music hot spot calls itself "The Live Music Show Capital of the World," and it features dozens of performances daily, as well as a variety of attractions that can keep the fun going for days.

You'll find entertainment for all ages at Branson. The Dixie Stampede is a dinner theater that features costumed stunt riders on horseback, ostrich races, and live buffalo, while the Kirby Van Burch Show offers exotic animals and magic. There are also acrobatics shows, a lively 1950s music review, and family-friendly comedy shows. Amusement parks, go-kart tracks, train rides, and festivals add to the fun.

Combine a down-home dinner, six tons of charging buffalo, and magnificent performing horses, and you get the Dixie Stampede, one of Branson's enduring dinner theaters.

SILVER DOLLAR CITY

Most families visiting Branson spend at least one day at Silver Dollar City, an 1880s, Ozark Mountains–themed amusement park, and its sister park, Celebration City. Both parks offer traditional Ozark food, music, and crafts along with water rides, thrill rides, roller coasters, and special play areas and rides for younger kids. Silver Dollar City's summer-long National Kids' Fest features activities and special performances just for kids.

THE MAGIC HOUSE

This enchanting 1901 three-story Victorian house in St. Louis is jam-packed with hands-on learning disguised as fun. Ranked by *U.S. Family Travel Guide* and *FamilyFun* magazines as one of the top family destinations in the country, it has more than 100 exhibits, and most of them encourage children to touch, poke, push, pull, or play.

Kids can glide down a three-story slide, make their hair stand on end with static electricity, record their own music, and become a news anchor on the KIDS-TV news station. Children under the age of two have their own play area, For Baby and Me, complete with a peekaboo house and a toddler-size bus.

The Magic House's interactive exhibits show kids how to lift themselves off the ground with pulley power and demonstrate the powerful force of air as they launch an air rocket and spin a wind generator. They

Very impressive! First Impressions, *now on exhibit at The Magic House, is one of the largest movable art sculptures in the United States. It stands eight feet tall and is made up of 75,000 plastic rods.*

can change their shadows into a multitude of colors, tap out messages in Morse code, and crawl through tunnel mazes. It's all fun in the name of science.

THE GATEWAY ARCH

The soaring Gateway Arch in St. Louis is the tallest monument in the nation. This graceful 630-foot-high stainless-steel arch commemorates the city and the thousands of pioneers who stopped here to rest and replenish their provisions before continuing west. Visitors can take a tram up either side of the Arch to an observation room for views of the city, the Mississippi River, and the vast plains stretching out into the distance.

The Museum of Westward Expansion is located at the base of the monument and features exhibits on the exploration of the West and noteworthy people who formed its history, including Lewis and Clark, the Plains Indians, and the Buffalo Soldiers. Two theaters beneath the Arch show movies daily, including an informative documentary on the history and construction of the Arch. Viewing the film before journeying to the top of the Arch helps visitors appreciate the work that went into this monument.

The elegant Gateway Arch, which was opened to the public in 1967, rises above the St. Louis skyline. During peak sightseeing months, the tram located inside the Arch makes about 80 trips per day to the top of the monument.

St. Louis Zoo

While the St. Louis Zoo takes its commitment to worldwide animal conservation issues seriously, visiting the zoo is all about fun. In the children's zoo, kids can pretend they're animals. They can slide through a transparent acrylic tube that takes them to an observation area in the middle of the otter pool. They'll enjoy navigating the strands of a giant spiderweb, digging in the sand like an aardvark, and measuring their height against that of a grizzly bear.

The zoo is filled with excellent exhibits that will take you right into the middle of the animals' habitats. You're hit with a blast of cold air as you enter the indoor penguin habitat in the Penguin and Puffin Coast. Here you can watch penguins swim underwater and waddle around on shore in a remarkably natural-looking habitat with high coastal cliffs. In the ten-acre River's Edge exhibit, a river path that meanders through four continents—Africa, Asia, South America, and North America—features an underwater hippo tank. You'll also see cheetahs, giant anteaters, elephants, and many creatures who live near the rivers and riverbanks.

Above: *The St. Louis Zoo has set the standard for re-creating realistic animal habitats. Its Penguin Cove was the first walk-through subarctic penguin exhibit in North America.*
Right: *Do I know you? The playful activity in the otter habitat is an entertaining sight.*

KALEIDOSCOPE

Hallmark Cards, Inc., created an art studio for children right next door to its visitor's center in Kansas City. Called Kaleidoscope, it's an 8,000-square-foot space divided into various colorful theme areas with all kinds of art supplies and creative materials.

Children need only bring their imaginations and willingness to create. Ribbons, papers, melted crayons, cutout shapes, and all kinds of other craft materials are provided. In one part of the room, children color a plain piece of cardboard that is then cut into a puzzle by a special device while they watch. Another area is deco-

rated in an outer space motif. It is lit by black light so that the ink of the fluorescent markers glows as children color. Broken fluorescent crayons are melted, and children can paint with the wax using long sticks tipped with cotton.

Every day there are different projects, and supply bins are placed throughout to hold the inviting castoffs from the Hallmark studios—curly bows, old ornaments, parts of pens,

little lockets from old journals, circles and squares stamped out of gold or silver paper, and alphabet letters. They are available for a collage or whatever masterpiece a child wishes to create.

Right: Don't bug the artist! Kaleidoscope invites children to create, create, and then create again. The Hallmark-sponsored activity center provides the materials, and the rest is up to the kids. Left: This is one art studio that never runs out of anything! Kaleidoscope is full of colorful, jazzy "junk" that will be put to good use by these young artists.

DODGE CITY

Back in Dodge City's heyday, rough-and-tumble gunslingers fought and died with their boots on. They took up permanent residence in Boot Hill Cemetery alongside paupers who couldn't afford a burial. The actual graves have been moved, but the tombstones have been re-created. They now display colorful epitaphs such as "Here lies Lester Moore. Four slugs from a 44. No Les. No more."

The cemetery is now part of Boot Hill Museum, a reconstruction of notorious Front Street in 1876, the business district of Old Dodge City, Kansas. Carefully researched through photographs and diaries, the historic buildings include an 1879 cattle driver's home, the jail from Fort Dodge, and a one-room schoolhouse.

Care to rub elbows with some of the Wild West's most colorful characters? Stop by the Gunfighter Wax Museum and say howdy to Jesse James, Buffalo Bill, Calamity Jane, and a host of others. You can wet your whistle at the re-created Long Branch Saloon, a popular watering hole during Dodge City's lawless years. For a more sedate evening during the summer months, enjoy the open air concerts of the Dodge City Cowboy Band.

Gunslingers and desperadoes used to haunt Dodge City's Front Street. The town has been re-created as a family tourist attraction, so leave the six-shooters at home.

The Oz Museum houses more than 2,000 artifacts representing all things inspired by the L. Frank Baum book of 1900.

THE OZ MUSEUM

Y ou won't need a broomstick, a tornado, or even ruby slippers to visit this museum in Wamego. Just step through the screen door of the old wooden farmhouse, where you'll be greeted by life-size figures of Dorothy and Toto. Other favorite Oz characters, such as the Scarecrow and Tin Man, are also in the museum, where thousands of Oz items

from the classic children's book series by L. Frank Baum and the famous 1939 MGM production of *The Wizard of Oz* are on display.

A Munchkin vest, an original movie script, and a rare flying monkey fashioned from rubber with a chenille-stem tail are among the memorabilia from the movie that you'll find at the museum. Original

costume sketches and first-edition books are on display, as well as Diana Ross's dress from *The Wiz* and merchandise tie-ins that coincided with the publication of each new Oz book. A well-stocked gift shop seems to have every item ever created in honor of the worldwide phenomenon that is Oz.

Henry Doorly Zoo

Workers at Omaha's award-winning zoo like to say the animals roam free and its visitors are captive. This claim is partially true. In Hubbard Gorilla Valley, a 520-foot-long window-lined tunnel allows visitors to travel into the middle of the three-acre gorilla habitat to observe these majestic creatures. The zoo's orangutans can study their visitors from two 65-foot-high banyan trees—they even have a view of downtown Omaha. In turn, visitors can view the orangutans from a 70-foot-high platform that is accessible by elevator.

As you traverse an elevated treetop walkway through the award-winning Lied Jungle exhibit, you'll pass lush vegetation and fascinating animals native to the misty jungles of three continents. The authentically re-created habitat features waterfalls, cliffs, caves, medicinal plants, and giant trees. Approximately 90 animal species from forest floor to highest canopy reside in the exhibit.

The zoo's Desert Dome has viewing areas at two levels. Kingdoms of the Night, the world's largest exhibit of nocturnal animals and their habitats, is located beneath the Desert Dome.

Housed in the Desert Dome at Henry Doorly Zoo you'll find Kingdoms of the Night. The exhibit covers 42,000 square feet and is home to 75 animals.

FORT ROBINSON STATE PARK

Rich in the history of the Great Plains, Fort Robinson offers visitors modern-day dude ranch activities and a fascinating Old West background. Its 22,000 acres of wide-open plains, forested hills, and sandstone bluffs are home to herds of buffalo and longhorn sheep. Guests can explore on horseback, by stagecoach, by jeep, by mountain bike, or on foot.

Fort Robinson was once one of the U.S. Cavalry's largest remount depots and held 17,000 horses. Established in 1874, it survived through the last tragic days of the Plains Indian wars. It's also where famed Sioux Chief Crazy Horse was fatally wounded. Visitors can stay overnight where bluecoated members of the cavalry once bunked or in campgrounds or cabins.

Summers are packed with activities for families. The breakfast trail rides and fireside buffalo stew cookouts and sing-alongs are popular events. Rodeos and melodramas are featured at the Post Playhouse. History buffs like to explore the Fort Robinson Museum and the Trailside Museum, which displays fossils that date back 200 million years. Other activities include swimming, trout fishing, and crafts. In winter, cross-country skiing is popular.

Fort Robinson was formerly the headquarters of the famed Buffalo Soldiers and housed German POWs during World War II. It is now the site of the Fort Robinson Museum.

Buffalo Bill Ranch State Historical Park

Frontier legend William Cody started out as a Pony Express rider, and he earned the nickname Buffalo Bill after he won a buffalo-hunting contest while working as a scout and ranger along the Santa Fe Trail.

Buffalo Bill lived on a ranch just north of North Platte and toured the United States and Europe with his famous Wild West Show. Today, his home is part of the Buffalo Bill Ranch State Historical Park. When you tour the house and its outlying buildings you'll find a wealth of memorabilia from the Wild West days, including original posters, costumes, and film clips from his show's tours. Families can camp in the park, and hiking trails and picnic areas are available.

Fort Cody Trading Post

The Trading Post, described as "Nebraska's Largest Souvenir and Western Gift Store," features a museum displaying authentic cow-hand gear, U.S. Calvary and Native American war relics, and a stuffed two-headed calf. Children are enthralled by the Buffalo Bill Miniature Wild West Show dioramas that display 20,000 hand-carved cowhands, Native Americans, wagons, classic Wild West scenes, and even Annie Oakley.

Fascinating in both their detail and their depictions of scenes from the Wild West, the dioramas at the Fort Cody Trading Post capture the imaginations of young visitors.

WIND CAVE NATIONAL PARK

One of the world's longest and most complex caves, Wind Cave was named for the eerie whistling noise that can be heard at its entrance. The caves were formed when limestone was deposited and consolidated on the inland seafloor about 320 million years ago. When the modern Black Hills began to rise some 60 million years ago, the limestone fractured, and water began to seep in and carve the labyrinth of dramatic caverns, tunnels, and crystalline artistry that you see today.

There are five tours of the caves. The Natural Entrance Tour is very popular among families with children. You enter through the hillside and exit by elevator. The tour provides an excellent opportunity to see boxwork, an unusual formation the cave is known for, which is composed of paper-thin calcite fins that resemble delicate honeycombs. Other tours go deeper into the caves but involve more stairs. Older kids and teens who want to experience real spelunking can don headlamps and crawl through the caves on special tours offered during certain months.

In the mid 1800s the owners of the Wind Cave mine determined that the contents of the cave were of no value. In 1890 they began to market the cave as a tourist site, and the immense cave system remains a popular stop for vacationing families.

MOUNT RUSHMORE

This presidential face-off of monumental proportions is a jaw-dropping feat of art and engineering. Blasted and chiseled out of granite, Mount Rushmore features four famous presidents: George Washington, Thomas Jefferson, Theodore Roosevelt, and Abraham Lincoln. The faces on the 5,725-foot-tall landmark tower over a majestic forest of pine, spruce, birch, and aspen trees in South Dakota's Black Hills.

The herculean effort began in 1927, with sculptor Gutzon Borglum and a team of dedicated South Dakota workers. They blasted and crafted this shrine to democracy over a 14-year period.

Before you begin walking the half-mile Presidential Trail to get a closer view of the faces, visit The Lincoln Borglum Museum to listen to interviews with the workers on Mount Rushmore, view historic footage of the carving process, and learn more about the monument's sculptor. There is even an exhibit where you can become a worker on Mount Rushmore, "detonating" dynamite charges on the mountain. You can take a ranger-guided walk along the Presidential Trail or travel at your own pace. The

President George Washington peers between the South Dakota pines with a steady gaze. The dedication to this portion of Mount Rushmore was held in 1930.

Sculptor's Studio features an interesting display of tools used to carve the mountain. The studio also offers ranger-led discussions about the sculpture's history.

The towering faces on Mount Rushmore are illuminated year-round. During the summer months, there is a nightly lighting ceremony in the park's spacious amphitheater. The 30-minute program consists of a short ranger talk and a film about the four presidents. At the conclusion of the film the audience sings the National Anthem as the lights slowly rise to illuminate Mount Rushmore.

Children's programs are also offered during the summer. The Junior Rangers program is for children ages 5 through 12, while teens 13 and older can join the Rushmore Rangers. A special walk led by a ranger is available for kids of all ages.

Another summer event is a Sculptor-in-Residence program that features an artist

Park Service records state that 2.6 million visitors tour Mount Rushmore each year. The epic project took years to complete and resulted in one of the largest sculptures in the world.

demonstrating the art of sculpture using a variety of media. The sculptor explains the processes used to create works of art today and compares them to those used by Borglum and his assistants when they carved Mount Rushmore.

CRAZY HORSE MEMORIAL

The nine-story-high face of Crazy Horse, the famous Native American leader, is just the beginning of this monumental sculpture that already dominates the vista of the Black Hills. It will be the largest sculpture in the world when it's completed. The memorial has been a work in progress since 1948, and upon completion it will show the famed Lakota warrior as he sits astride his horse with his arm outstretched and pointing forward. It is an astonishing feat of artistry and engineering that is particularly interesting because visitors can see one completed portion of the carving and compare that with the progress on other sections.

Throughout the years, the Crazy Horse Memorial has grown into a major Native American center of activity. It now features a visitor complex and an Indian Museum and Cultural Center that displays photographs, artifacts, ceremonial dress, and paintings. The museum is built out of the very rock that has been blasted from the sculpture. In the summer, many Native American artists and craftspeople create artwork and visit with guests in the Cultural Center building. The center also provides a hands-on opportunity for children to stone-grind corn and examine replicas of artifacts.

Progress on the Crazy Horse Memorial is visible in the background. The statue in the foregound depicts what the sculpture will look like upon completion. It is on display at the visitor complex.

MAMMOTH SITE

This treasure trove of fossils in Hot Springs, South Dakota, was discovered in 1974 when excavation for a housing development unearthed the remains of a woolly mammoth. Since then, budding paleontologists and their parents have visited the site to get hands-on experience in an actual dig.

To date, the fossilized skeletons of 55 mammoths have been identified, along with the remains of a giant short-faced bear, a camel, a llama, a prairie dog, a wolf, fish, and numerous invertebrates. Walkways throughout the excavation afford visitors close-up views of the skulls, ribs, tusks, femurs, and even nearly complete skeletons visible in the mass grave that resulted when these prehistoric animals fell into a sinkhole. Visitors can also see the Ice Age Exhibit Hall, which showcases some of the skeletons alongside a painting or replica of the animal as it would have looked, and they can view a working paleontology laboratory.

A simulated excavation for junior paleontologists is held daily during the summer months. Children learn excavation techniques including how to identify the fossils of different animals. They dig up replicas that are buried in a special area next to the actual sinkhole.

Left: The fossils of animals that existed 26,000 years ago are revealed at the Mammoth Site. Your family will be fascinated by the in-depth tours. Above: Kids can get pretty dirty at the supervised dig adjacent to the actual Mammoth Site, but it's fun in the name of science.

THEODORE ROOSEVELT NATIONAL PARK

Theodore Roosevelt once remarked, "I never would have been president if it had not been for my experiences in North Dakota." While visiting The Badlands on a hunting trip in 1883, he became alarmed by the extent of damage to the land and its wildlife. Overgrazing was displacing native species such as bison and bighorn sheep and ruining the grasslands as well as the habitats of small mammals and songbirds. Conservation became one of Roosevelt's prime concerns. He established numerous national parks and protected areas, and it's only fitting that this national park, where he had a home and ranch, be named for him.

In the park's South Unit, families can visit one of Roosevelt's former ranch cabins next to the Medora Visitor Center. Children will find the town of Medora a fun stop, as it offers carriage and stagecoach tours of the area. Or they can saddle up a horse and explore the paint-

brush canyons, buttes, rugged hills, and grassy prairies that are so typical of The Badlands.

Left: *The area of North Dakota occupied by Theodore Roosevelt National Park is a delight for families who revel in the unspoiled, untamed beauty of the wilderness. Herds of wild mustangs still roam freely throughout the park.*

Below: *Captivated by the rugged beauty of North Dakota, President Roosevelt dedicated himself to its preservation.*

INTERNATIONAL PEACE GARDEN

The International Peace Garden that celebrates the peace between the United States and Canada is made up of 2,339 acres of gardens along the world's longest unfortified border. Visitors can stand with one foot in each country as they straddle the border.

The International Peace Garden features a number of exhibits, including the September 11 Memorial Site. Ten steel girders salvaged from the rubble of the World Trade Center are on display; a formal memorial is in the planning stages.

There are miles of hiking trails, dozens of bike paths, and several campsites. The entire garden is a wildlife area where you're likely to see loons, grouse, moose, deer, and beavers.

International music, art, and dance performances are regular features of summer programs. Children can participate in craft-making sessions and scavenger hunts and learn about creatures such as monarch butterflies and tadpoles. The area is home to a sports camp for kids on the Canadian side and a music camp on the U.S. side. If you visit in June, you can catch the annual fiddler contest that features a category for children ages eight and younger.

Left: *The 120-foot-tall Peace Towers stand in the background at the International Peace Garden, which keeps alive the hope that peace will one day prevail throughout the world.* Below: *The enormous Floral Clock, which is made up of thousands of flowers, is a popular attraction.*

THE SOUTHWEST

Year after year the mystique of the sunny Southwest lures families to ancient cliff dwellings and Native American pueblos, as well as rodeos and pristine beaches. Nature has certainly been busy in this part of the country, creating spectacles such as the Grand Canyon, the otherworldly red rocks of Sedona, and the Painted Desert. San Antonio and Santa Fe are two vibrant, fascinating centers of Tex-Mex culture. A parade in Houston blends down-home creativity with an appreciation of the automobile, and a sand castle competition in Galveston allows architects to pull out their shovels and pails to create masterpieces along the beach.

The Grand Canyon, Arizona

SPACE CENTER HOUSTON

Where on Earth—or any other planet, for that matter—can you dock a space shuttle, touch an authentic moon rock, and watch an astronaut train for a space mission all in the same day? Space Center Houston, that's where.

Located in the Johnson Space Center complex, Space Center Houston was designed by Walt Disney Imagineering with both entertainment and education in mind. It's a perfect place for space buffs to get a close-up look at the country's space program. Younger children enjoy its expansive play areas.

Space Center Houston's interactive exhibits show what life in space is like. Did you ever wonder how astronauts perform simple daily tasks such as eating and bathing in zero gravity? The live demonstrations in the Living in Space module address those questions and many more. The hands-on exhibits demonstrate some of the daily chores that space exploration involves. Kids can attempt tricky tasks such as trying to to land a space shuttle and maneuvering a robotic arm to pick up a minute object.

In Kids Space Place, would-be astronauts can take a simulated ride across the moon in a Lunar Rover and test their skills in a re-created *Apollo* command module. Starship Gallery offers the real deal: The evolution of crewed space flight in the United States is revealed with authentic artifacts from different space missions. You'll see the actual *Faith 7* Mercury space capsule and the *Gemini 5* spacecraft, as well as *Saturn V,* which was also called the Moon Rocket. It was the largest, most powerful rocket ever built. It took astronauts into space and to the moon. Visitors will also see an assortment of memorabilia from other space missions, and the Astronaut Gallery exhibit displays the largest collection of authentic spacesuits in the world.

The Martian Matrix is a five-story play structure that provides plenty of mazes, tunnels, and passageways that are just perfect for burning off that extra astronaut energy. Families will also enjoy the virtual reality stations that transport visitors to a space station for a tour, including a simulated space walk. On the exciting Blast Off ride, visitors

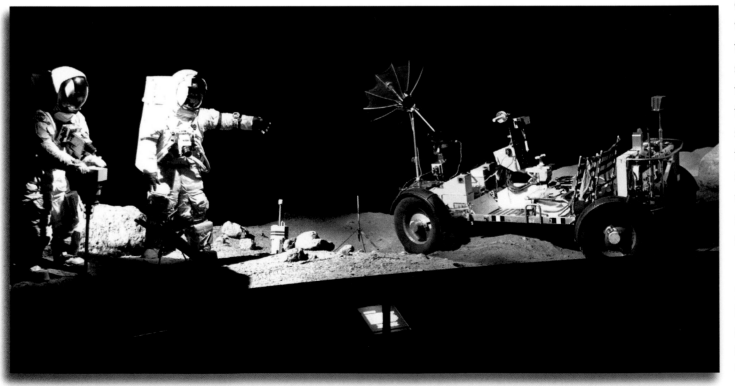

The barren lunar landscape is vividly brought to life at Space Center Houston.

will experience the thrill of launching into space like a real astronaut.

Space Center Houston boasts the largest IMAX movie theater in Texas. The five-story screen takes you right into the experience of an astronaut undergoing training. For the true space aficionado, check out the Level 9 tour of the space center. Only 12 people per day are admitted on the escorted tour, which takes you right into NASA's control center and onto the observation decks of the neutral buoyancy lab. The tours are available for those 14 and older and include lunch with astronauts who are in training.

Tram tours to Johnson Space Center depart from Space Center Houston every half hour. Some popular attractions include a tour of Rocket Park, which holds a number of the massive NASA rockets that were used in the early days of the space program, and a visit to the Mission Control Center.

Above: Kids Space Place was created for kids of all ages. It offers an out-of-this-world experience for aspiring space explorers. Right: Launching a ball, launching a space shuttle—at Space Center Houston, kids will learn it's all a matter of physics.

HOUSTON LIVESTOCK SHOW AND RODEO

The biggest and best rodeo in Texas has star-quality bull riders, barrel racers, ropers, steer wrestlers, and bucking bronco riders competing for big cash prizes. The livestock show attracts the top stars of the animal world and features some of the finest examples of cattle, pigs, chickens, horses, donkeys, sheep, goats, rabbits, and llamas.

The rodeo and parade, complete with marching bands, giant helium balloons, wagons, clowns, and horseback riders, were incorporated into the livestock show in 1938. The finest popular entertainers perform every evening after the conclusion of the arena events.

Several events are particularly popular with children. The calf scramble is exactly as it sounds: Picture 28 kids running around after 14 calves. Fledgling bronco riders can try their skills on a mechanical bull, or go on pony rides. Kids can also watch pig races

and see newborn animals as they attempt their first steps. At Rodeo University, children can meet rodeo athletes who give roping demonstrations and share their experiences.

Just hang in there! The bareback bronco riding event is just one of the many exciting competitions at the Houston Livestock Show.

HOUSTON ART CAR PARADE

Picture a car completely covered in singing fish—that's the Sashimi Tabernacle Choir car, and it's one of more than 250 outlandishly decorated automobiles, motorcycles, bicycles, and other contraptions that are featured in the Houston Art Car Parade. Approximately 200,000 people gather for this outlandish event, which features creative and outright crazy-looking vehicles parading through the city streets.

The event, held the second weekend in May, starts on Friday, when art car caravans travel to schools and hospitals. Saturday is parade day, and by 9:00 A.M. the cars are parked in ready position at a tailgater carnival. This part of the festivities allows families to view the cars while enjoying entertainment and food. In the early afternoon, the zany parade winds its way through the streets of Houston, followed by a big street party.

Some entries from previous years may give you an idea of how crazy these cars can get. You might see a car that looks like a giant dolphin, or "R U Game," a car completely covered in game boards and pieces and spouting bubbles from a bubble machine. Other jaw-dropping favorites include a car covered bumper-to-bumper in buttons, a racecar transformed into a sleek metallic lizard, and a car completely covered in grass from a recently mowed yard.

Prizes in all types of categories are awarded to the cars on Sunday. There's an award for Best Everyday Driver; Best Classic Car; Best Contraption (which can be just about anything that moves, including couches, lawnmowers, wheelchairs, scooters, and even a touring bathtub); Best Lowrider; Best Political Statement; and many others. Parade-goers get to vote for their favorite to decide the people's choice.

"Orange you glad"
you visited Houston? Where else
could you see the eccentric Fruitmobile, one of the
many imaginatively detailed and outrageously decorated automobiles
that appear in the Houston Art Car Parade?

SCHLITTERBAHN WATERPARK RESORT

Schlitterbahn is nestled on the banks of the spring-fed Comal River in New Braunfels, about 175 miles west of Houston, near San Antonio. Its natural setting amid towering trees gives it a unique character among water parks. Several of the rides make use of the river and its fresh springwater. The Raging River Tube Chute transports riders through a tube and into twisting turns, then spills them out into another ride called the Congo River. Three of the park's water coasters actually shoot riders uphill, including the six-story Master Blaster. Many water park enthusiasts believe that this ride is the best of its kind.

There are six shallow-water playgrounds for younger children, some featuring activities such as padded tube slides, pirate ships with play features, and a five-story water funhouse. Older kids have plenty of thrill rides to sample, including the surfing simulation Boogie Bahn and a tidal wave river. Visitors can stay in lodgings in the park that overlook the river and rides.

The Master Blaster, Schlitterbahn's high-tech water ride, uses a patented system of water jets to propel its riders through the looping and swooping course.

BAT WATCHING AT THE CONGRESS AVENUE BRIDGE

Bat-viewing veterans debate the best place to see the 1.5 million Mexican free-tailed bats that blast out of their daytime home beneath Austin's Congress Avenue Bridge every evening. Some think it's best to stand or even lie down on the riverbank and look up as the sky darkens with the largest urban bat colony in North America. Others like to stand on the bridge for the panoramic view. Many tourists take to the water on Town Lake and reserve a place on a bat-viewing boat tour to watch the event, which can take as long as 45 minutes.

The bats began congregating in Austin in the 1980s after the bridge underwent structural changes. The construction provided just the right kind of crevices for them to hang out in (literally) during the day. Austinites reacted with fear and loathing until they learned that the bats consume between 10 and 15 tons of insects—including mosquitoes—each night. The bats begin their migration to Austin in early March and give birth to their pups in June. They spend the summer in Austin and head south again in November.

Hundreds of people congregate at dusk to watch the Mexican free-tailed bats take flight into the Austin night sky. Many restaurants offer special seating to patrons who want to observe the nightly event.

SAN ANTONIO

This Texas city has been shaped by many cultures. Its Wild West roots are evident, but you'll find a wonderful blend of Native American, Spanish, German, African-American, Asian, French, Polish, Irish, Mexican, and Czech diversity throughout San Antonio. This mix of nationalities results in a busy calendar of ethnic festivals, a wonderful selection of restaurants, and a down-home friendliness that says "Howdy" to its visitors.

For the sake of convenience, plan to find lodgings in the downtown area, where everything is a short walk or trolley ride away. You'll be near the famous Paseo del Rio, or Riverwalk, where giant cypress trees shade 2.5 miles of meandering pathways, shops, and sidewalk cafés along the San Antonio River. Kids enjoy seeing the city from a river's view. Riverboats with narrated tours travel back and forth throughout the day and evening.

One of San Antonio's most famous landmarks is the Alamo, immortalized by the rallying cry

"Remember the Alamo!" as Texas fought for independence from Mexico. Davy Crockett and Jim Bowie were among the brave defenders of the mission who died

during the battle. Before touring the fort, stop at the IMAX theater across the street see the docudrama *Alamo...The Price of Freedom* to understand the events that unfolded there.

Kids familiar with the story of the Alamo love touring the venerable fort. The Alamo represents 250 years of Texas history and is visited by more than 2.5 million people each year.

San Antonio's lively downtown area is known for its Riverwalk, a tree-lined, flower-filled oasis of cool walkways, shops, and cafés located along the river.

There's plenty more to do in this scenic city. Billed as the largest Mexican market-place outside of Mexico, bustling Market Square is filled with mariachi bands; restaurants featuring fresh fajitas, tamales, and gorditos; and shops selling everything from pottery to piñatas. Six Flags Fiesta Texas is a theme park with thrilling rides, country-western music shows, and a water park. San Antonio's SeaWorld (see page 204) has an aquarium with animal shows, an amusement park, and a water park. The 750-foot-high Tower of the Americas at HemisFair Park, site of the 1968 World's Fair, offers rides to its top. There you'll find a wonderful view of the city and a restaurant. Another family favorite is Schlitterbahn Waterpark Resort (see page 198).

Fiesta San Antonio

This big ol' Texas house party is held every April. It's a ten-day event that celebrates San Antonio's diverse culture and recognizes the heroes of the Alamo and the Battle of San Jacinto. Numerous ethnic groups have contributed to the rich culture and history of Texas, and just about every one of them is honored during the fiesta. More than 100 events are held throughout the city, including three distinctly different parades, each one worth seeing.

The first Battle of Flowers Parade took place in the late 19th century when a group of women in decorated horse-drawn carriages paraded in front of the Alamo and pelted each other with flower blossoms. That event was the beginning of the Fiesta, which continues today. You can still see costumed ladies tossing petals during the parade, which also features flower-covered floats, horse-drawn carriages, and high school and military bands from all over the United States.

The floats in the Texas Cavaliers River Parade really do float—down the San Antonio River—in this unusual water parade. The Famous Fiesta Flambeau Night Parade is a glowing splendor that features

A Texas tradition on the grandest scale, Fiesta San Antonio has been called the state's biggest party. Opening ceremonies take place in front of the Alamo and include music, dancing, and a colorful balloon send-off.

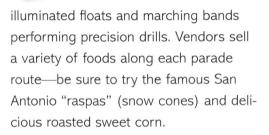

illuminated floats and marching bands performing precision drills. Vendors sell a variety of foods along each parade route—be sure to try the famous San Antonio "raspas" (snow cones) and delicious roasted sweet corn.

Music is a big part of the celebration, and mariachi, norteña, and German polka bands play throughout the festival. During four nights of the fiesta mariachi groups perform on the river as they drift along the Paseo del Rio on colorful floats.

Children's events are seamlessly woven into the fiesta: A Taste of New Orleans features food and entertainment from the Big Easy along with a children's play area. One day is devoted to a Children's Festival with live entertainment, interactive games, face painting, clowns, storytelling, miniature golf, and wildlife exhibits. Another family favorite, the Fiesta Pooch Parade,

features canines of all types decked out in fiesta garb.

Fiesta Fantasies is a staple of the festival. It takes place in Market Square and continues through all ten days of the event. People come to dine on local specialties and watch dancers and music performances of many different genres, including tejano, jazz, and country-western, on any one of the six stages. The final event of the night features nonstop live entertainment, a children's carnival, aerial acrobatics, and military pageantry. The fiesta's grand finale is a fireworks display.

Top left: *Beautiful bows and twirling taffeta add to the colorful Fiesta Flambeau Night Parade.* Top right: *That's why they're called "floats." Onlookers line the city's Riverwalk at the Texas Cavaliers River Parade, a much-anticipated event during Fiesta San Antonio.* Bottom: *The Battle of the Flowers Band Festival, staged during Fiesta week, is a high-spirited event that features many talented young musicians.*

SeaWorld

It's a four-in-one experience at the world's largest marine life adventure park. SeaWorld is 250 acres of fun in San Antonio, featuring an amusement park, a water park, animal attractions, and live entertainment.

World-famous killer whale Shamu shows off surprisingly graceful jumping skills, performing in a special stadium that has an overhead camera and plenty of splashing. In the comical sea lion show, The Cannery Row Caper, pinniped stars Clyde and Seamore reveal a great appetite for solving a disappearing fish mystery. Dolphin shows and beluga whale performances are also popular, as are the daring water-ski stunt shows. A water park keeps young visitors cool during the heat of the day, with daredevil slides and water play areas for little kids.

The fun continues with classic amusement park rides such as an inverted steel roller coaster and a Ferris wheel. Animal exhibits include a 450,000-gallon shark habitat, penguins, lorikeets, and much more.

Right: *The Steel Eel at San Antonio's SeaWorld will take you on one wild ride. Hold on to your hats during the 15-story drop.* Inset: *And who can resist that smile? Dolphin shows are just a fraction of the enjoyment you'll experience at SeaWorld. Amusement park rides and animal attractions will fill your day with fun.*

BIG BEND NATIONAL PARK

Big Bend is a land of dramatic contrasts. It covers 801,000 acres of west Texas and encompasses a vast section of the Chihuahuan Desert, approximately 69 serpentine miles of the Rio Grande Wild and Scenic River, and the Chisos Mountain range. The spectacular scenery includes deeply chiseled canyons, windblown dunes, and 60 species of cacti. It's home to more than 450 types of birds, more than any other U.S. national park.

Since the park is about the size of Rhode Island, it's important to plan ahead to maximize your visit. River rafting, kayaking, and canoeing through the canyons of the Rio Grande are activities you won't want to miss. Another great way to see the park is on horseback or by mountain bike, and numerous outfitters in the area can make arrangements. There are several easy hikes that kids of all ages enjoy, including the Window View Trail and the Chihuahuan Desert Nature Trail. A 4.8-mile round-trip hike, Lost Mine Trail provides a good challenge for older children, and it's an excellent day hike.

If you follow Big Bend National Park's Pine Canyon Trail, you'll travel through desert grasslands that are alive with an assortment of unusual cacti.

PADRE ISLAND NATIONAL SEASHORE

The pristine beaches, wind-sculpted dunes, and saltwater marshes of Padre Island National Seashore stretch for 80 miles along the Gulf of Mexico. It's the longest span of undeveloped beach in the United States and the longest undeveloped barrier island in the world. A major migratory bird flyway is found here, making this area one of the prime bird-watching regions in the world. A board-walk stretches over a section of wetlands where kids can observe some of the many bird species that occupy the seashore.

Padre Island National Seashore is a fishing enthusiast's paradise. It offers speckled trout, black drum, redfish, and flounder. The saltwater lagoon between the island and the mainland is a perfect place to learn to windsurf—it's only three to five feet deep with a soft, sandy bottom. Pack a picnic and watch one of the world-class wind-surfing competitions held throughout the year.

The spacious beaches of Padre Island National Seashore are perfect for an oceanside family camping trip. You'll find great fishing and plenty of wildlife as well.

AIA SANDCASTLE COMPETITION

Every June, the American Institute of Architects (AIA) sponsors a sand castle–building competition in Galveston that puts all others to shame. On the day of the event, about 80 teams of architects, engineers, and students of these two professions each go to work in their own 22×25-foot section of beach. They have just five hours to sculpt their creations. Past exhibits have included towers, walls, characters, monuments, and an assortment of innovative surprises.

The designs have become so complicated and detailed that some teams use large molds, scaffolding, tampers, and tiny clay sculpting tools during the creative process. The results of their painstaking efforts are elaborate, often humorous, eccentric creations, that frequently reflect current attitudes.

Many contestants bring blueprints to guide them in the construction of their work. Their creations are judged on concept, artistic execution, technical difficulty, carving technique, and utilization of the site. Additional awards, such as Most Hilarious, Most Lifelike, and Public Favorite, are also given out.

Take a group of design and building professionals, add a lot of imagination, and turn them loose on a beach, and you get a battle of the sands. The American Institute of Architects Sandcastle Competition is the largest event of its kind in the United States.

Red Earth Native American Cultural Festival

Every June, more than 100 Native American tribes from North America gather in Oklahoma City for a foot-stomping celebration of their culture, history, and artistic handiwork. A parade kicks off the festivities and features master drummers, dancers, and tribal princesses resplendent in feather headdresses, buckskins, and beads.

One of the highlights of this festival is the Red Earth Dance Competition, which features thousands of participants competing in war dances, victory dances, and more. In the jingle dance category, women compete wearing buckskin dresses decorated with hundreds of aluminum cone-shape bangles. In the men's fancy dancing competition, Native American braves don the traditional clothing of their people and demonstrate incredibly intricate footwork.

There's even a children's dance competition.

Traditional storytelling, music, and crafts are part of the festival as well. The Red Earth Art Market features about 170 Native American artists selling both traditional and contemporary art and handcrafted pieces that include paintings, woven items, and wood carvings. Art competitions honor the finest in each category, and prizes are awarded to artists ages nine and older. Food vendors prepare everything from tacos and fry bread to Okie Taters and fried bananas.

These young participants exhibit the enthusiasm you'll see at the Red Earth Native American Cultural Festival.

NATIONAL COWBOY & WESTERN HERITAGE MUSEUM

Much of this enormous complex in Oklahoma City is devoted to Western-themed artwork of the highest caliber. It also has a number of exhibits that are particularly engaging to children. At the Children's Cowboy Corral, kids can dress up in authentic chaps, boots, spurs, and vests, and hit the trail on make-believe ponies. They'll enjoy listening to a resident cowhand talk and sing about life on the range; for a taste of life on the trail, they can help build a campfire and fix some grub at an authentic chuck wagon.

After a long day of herding cattle, it's time for a trip to Prosperity Junction, the museum's turn-of-the-century cattle town. The streets are alive with music from the saloon's tinny piano, and visitors can wander in and out of the many buildings, including Prosperity's church.

The museum's exhibits span a wide range of Wild West material. Older children will enjoy the assortment of firearms in the Weitzenhoffer Fine Arms Gallery. The American Rodeo Gallery celebrates the history, people, and events of the sport that made the Wild West famous.

In the American Cowboy Gallery, you'll find a wealth of information about these icons of the West. Exhibits include an impressive collection of cowboy hats, clothing, and a display of branding tools.

Once you've toured the museum, step outside and enjoy the beautifully landscaped grounds where children can stretch their legs. Shady walkways and a plaza provide lovely places to relax while the kids check out the lily pond that has been stocked with exotic fish.

The sculpture The End of the Trail *by James Earle Fraser has become a symbol of the American West. It's on display at the National Cowboy & Western Heritage Museum.*

CHUCK WAGON GATHERING & CHILDREN'S COWBOY FESTIVAL

Each Memorial Day weekend, a Chuck Wagon Gathering & Children's Cowboy Festival is celebrated at the museum. The event features shows and authentic chuck wagon crews who prepare delicious cowboy specialties such as sourdough biscuits, stews, beans, brisket, and cobblers. Kids will enjoy pony rides, rope making, leather crafting, and blacksmith demonstrations where each child receives a ring made from a horseshoe nail as a souvenir.

TAOS PUEBLO

The Taos Pueblo in northern New Mexico is the oldest continuously occupied structure on the continent. Dating back to A.D. 1000, its adobe walls today house about 150 Taos Native Americans who maintain the ancient traditions of their ancestors. The Pueblo is not a historical artifact or a re-creation; it is an actual town that offers a fascinating introduction to Native American life.

The Pueblo's distinctive style has influenced much of the region's architecture. It consists of two long, multistory adobe structures, one on each side of a fresh-water creek. Explore on your own or take an escorted tour that recounts the Pueblo's history, which includes occupation by Spanish conquistadors in 1540 and by Franciscan friars in the 1590s.

There's more family fun to be had in the Taos area. You can choose among rafting trips on the Rio Grande, llama treks, and horseback riding. In the town of Taos, stop by the Kit Carson Home and Museum to learn more about this legendary scout and adventurer of the Southwest.

At Taos Pueblo, children will see an actual ancient Native American village, still occupied, that's interconnected with a living-history museum. The Pueblo is a World Heritage Site and a National Historic Landmark.

CARLSBAD CAVERNS

Nature's artistic streak takes a fanciful turn in this famous and enormous cave system created by water dripping through an ancient reef made of porous limestone. More than 30 miles of the main cavern have been explored, and the three miles of caves that are open to visitors are among the largest and most magnificent underground formations in the world.

A variety of self-guided and ranger-led tours are available year-round, and high-speed elevators make the caves accessible to everyone. Visitors can independently tour parts of the biggest room in the cave complex, aptly named the Big Room, by using a state-of-the-art portable audio guide, and they can explore several other caves on guided tours.

The vast Big Room has a ceiling that arches 255 feet above the floor, and it contains a six-story stalagmite and the so-called Bottomless Pit, which is more than 700 feet deep. In the summer months

Spooky, awesome, eerie—kids will run out of adjectives to describe their experiences at Carlsbad Caverns. The cave tours range in difficulty from an easy walk-through to the crawling, climbing, and sliding variety.

bats that inhabit parts of the caverns are an additional attraction. Each evening at sunset the winged creatures swarm out of the cave's entrance to feed on insects in the surrounding area. The event is best observed at the Bat Flight Amphitheater at the cavern entrance.

Santa Fe

Santa Fe is the second oldest city in the United States. It's a place where the merging of three cultures—Anglo, Hispanic, and Native American—can be seen in its vibrant art, architecture, and food.

The center of the town is the Plaza, which once marked the official end of the Old Santa Fe Trail. It is now lined with shade trees, famous landmarks, and museums, including the Palace of the Governors. Native American artisans display their wares on beautiful blankets in front of the Palace: You'll see silver-and-turquoise jewelry, pottery, leatherwork, and handwoven blankets for sale.

The town is filled with numerous galleries that exhibit exquisite

southwestern art, shops that offer the best in fashion, and sophisticated restaurants. For a decidedly unsophisticated culinary treat your kids will adore, stop at the Five and Dime General Store on the Plaza and order a Frito Pie: A bag of corn chips opened and piled high with chili and cheese. You can top it off with chopped onions and jalapeños if you wish; stick a fork in it, and you're ready to enjoy this delicious Santa Fe specialty.

The town is rich with excellent museums. The Museum of International Folk Art has proved to be a children's favorite. Among its collections are toys from all over the world, including folk dolls and figurines creatively placed in dioramas that show scenes of festivals, funerals, parties, and simple activities of daily life. There are puppets, costumes, masks, and more. Be sure to visit the innovative Lloyd's Treasure Chest, located in the lower level of the

Santa Fe has the second largest art market in the nation. Pictured is one of the many galleries you'll find in the city's Canyon Road art gallery district.

museum. Visitors are encouraged to peek into its storage drawers and get a behind-the-scenes look at museum collections. The museum's lounge features books about different cultures as well as a wide assortment of toys.

On the outskirts of Santa Fe, El Rancho de las Golondrinas is a living-history museum that demonstrates life in early Spanish colonial New Mexico. Self-guided tours are an option throughout the summer, and special docent-led tours focus on the life of the American Girl character Maria Josefina Montoya, a Hispanic girl growing up on her family's ranch in New Mexico. Also just outside the city, you'll find jackalope, a zany seven-acre bazaar filled with knick-knacks, pottery, and furniture, along with a petting zoo of barnyard animals and a prairie dog village.

Above: *The craftsmanship of Southwestern architecture is evident in downtown Santa Fe's adobe buildings.* Right: *Palace of the Governors has a thriving market-place where kids love to explore and shop for handcrafted items.*

ALBUQUERQUE INTERNATIONAL BALLOON FIESTA

Hot air balloons of all shapes, sizes, and colors fill the fall sky during Albuquerque's balloon festival, the largest of its kind in the world. You'll see a string of chili peppers, a reclining chair, Chinese pagodas, and Russian dolls as they ascend into the sky.

For the best viewing, choose early morning when the majestic balloons are beginning their ascents. The sonorous hiss of hot air filling the balloons as they are prepared for their skyward journey adds to the excitement. Certain mornings have mass ascensions—a simultaneous launch of all the festival balloons. Later in the day, book your own balloon flight and take your family up into the clear New Mexico sky.

Come back in the evening for the Balloon Glow, when more than 100 balloons are lit in unison and the night sky blazes in a panorama of luminous colored globes. For two nights only, shaped balloons are featured in an event called the Glowdeo.

Your family will enjoy the dawn-to-dusk activities of the Albuquerque International Balloon Fiesta. The daytime sky is dotted with a rainbow of colors, and evening events include fireworks displays. On certain nights, there are dramatic presentations of illuminated balloons.

SEDONA

The eerie red rock formations around Sedona resemble the desert landscape of an alien planet. Children will be fascinated as they take in the striking red spires and sculpted burgundy buttes that have been given unusual names such as Devil's Bridge and Coffee Pot Rock. The formations soar dramatically above the dry gulches and exotic saguaro cacti of the rugged terrain.

Hiking trails lead to Native American ruins and overlooks; jeep tours whisk visitors over hard-packed dirt, through arid gullies, and past odd configurations of crimson rocks and walls covered with ancient petroglyphs. Nearby is the historic mining town of Jerome and a towering cliff dwelling that was once inhabited by the Sinagua Indians.

Mogollon Rim dominates the landscape of Sedona. You can hike through the area or get the big picture with an aerial tour—it's one of the most beautiful locations in the country.

THE GRAND CANYON

Millions of years of erosion caused by wind and water have carved and sculpted the Grand Canyon, truly one of the world's most dramatic natural wonders. At 227 miles long and 18 miles across at its widest point, this breathtaking abyss plunges more than a mile from rim to river bottom at its deepest point.

The Colorado River flows along the bottom of the canyon, but because of the canyon's depth, the river is visible only from certain viewpoints above. Families can book a rafting trip on the Colorado for one or more days, and it's an unforgettable way to explore the canyon.

The North and South rims are 215 miles apart by car, so if your time is limited, it's best to visit just one. The South Rim area attracts roughly 90 percent of the park's visitors, largely because the views are thought to be better and it has the majority of the park's

Explorer John Wesley Powell launched the first major exploration of the Grand Canyon in 1869 and traveled through it via the mighty Colorado River. Today families enjoy rafting on the river, which alternates between placid waters and ferocious rapids.

accommodations and restaurants. Not far from the South Rim Visitor Center is Hopi Point, the gathering spot for a famous view of the sunset. Early birds who awake before dawn can catch an awe-inspiring view of a Southwest sunrise over the canyon. You'll have the place practically to yourselves.

Stroll along the paved South Rim Trail (an easy walk, even with a stroller) or exercise your legs on the steep switchbacks of Bright Angel Trail to get a real view of the landscape. Kids love the donkey and mule rides down into the Canyon, but children must meet a minimum height requirement to be permitted to ride. Many families take aerial tours for the ultimate bird's-eye view of the canyon.

Numerous horse rentals are available, and there are dozens of shops and small arcades in Grand Canyon Village on the South Rim. You'll also find several small museums highlighting Native American culture and local flora and fauna. An IMAX theater offers a virtual tour of the Grand Canyon and is packed with information about the park.

Visitors seeking tranquility should head to the less-visited North Rim. It has lodge accommodations, hiking trails, camping, and somewhat limited services. The rim is usually buried in snow during winter, but in summer, it's the first choice of serious hikers and outdoorsy people hoping to get away from the crowds. Mule rides are also available at the North Rim, and families with kids over the age of seven should look into the half-day tours down the rim to Uncle Jim's Point or the easy-going five-mile Widforss Trail.

Above: *Native Americans termed it "mountain lying down," and early explorers said it was "a grand canyon." The awesome beauty of this natural wonder and the many activities associated with it are what make the Grand Canyon a top family travel destination.* Right: *The majestic wonder of the Grand Canyon draws tourists from all over the world. The canyon was first mapped in 1871, and shortly afterward visitors began journeying to the awe-inspiring landmark via train.*

THE PETRIFIED FOREST NATIONAL PARK AND PAINTED DESERT

This Arizona park encompasses portions of the Painted Desert and is one of the largest tracts of petrified wood in the world. The ancient log fragments are littered about the park, and visitors can see them as they hike or drive through the desolate dreamscape of layered, multicolor badlands formed during the late Triassic period. The entire area is a treasure trove of 225-million-year-old fossils, and new finds are excavated frequently in the remote sections of the park.

Visitors can travel through the park on a ten-mile paved road that runs through the Painted Desert. Signs that explain features of the park are located at various stops, and there's a visitor center and the Rainbow Forest Museum. Kids particularly enjoy the museum's variety of ancient animal fossils and the huge, petrified logs found along the Giant Logs Trail.

SLIDE ROCK STATE PARK

For most kids, the best part of Slide Rock State Park is a natural sandstone waterslide created by Oak Creek as it meanders through a small canyon. Children of all ages enjoy climbing along the creek to the top of the chute. There, they slide into the water and the current does the rest, propelling them through the slick rock grooves and mild white-water rapids into a gentle pool. Large slabs of red rock line the creek—stretch out and enjoy them in the warm Arizona sun.

Top: *A surprising splash of colors decorates the rugged terrain of the Painted Desert. Colorful layers of sediment create patterns throughout the rock formations.* Bottom: *Archeological artifacts show that people first visited the area that is now the Petrified Forest National Park 10,000 years ago.*

WHITEWATER PARK AND KAYAK SLALOM RACING COURSE

Cutting right through the middle of downtown Reno, this white-water rafting course was created out of the Truckee River. It is open year-round for kayaking, rafting, canoeing, and tubing. The mile-long course features 11 drop pools and a slalom racing course, and there are 7,000 tons of smooth flat rocks along the riverbanks that are perfect for picnicking or watching the paddlers pass by. At one point the course splits into two channels that later reconnect; one channel offers the drops, bumps, and pitches of an aquatic rodeo course, while the other is better suited for beginning kayakers.

During the summer months the course is popular with kids who enjoy floating down the river in inner tubes. Concessionaires rent all types of watercraft, including tubes and river-boards, and kayaking lessons are available for all ages. A river festival in May brings out some of the world's best professional and Olympic kayakers for white-water competitions, clinics, and demonstrations. On Friday nights in the summer you can enjoy music from the Rolling on the River concert series as you float down the river.

Reno's Whitewater Park offers a great kayaking experience. It's become a popular downtown attraction as well.

LAS VEGAS

Las Vegas is a city divided when it comes to family vacations. Long known for its glittering casinos and adult entertainment, the city has reinvented itself in recent years as a family vacation destination. As a result, Las Vegas now offers an array of family-oriented shows and themed hotels that kids are sure to love.

Family-friendly resorts include the Excalibur Hotel, inspired by castles in Europe. Its Tournament of Kings is a must-see extravaganza, and its Court Jester's Stage features magicians, jugglers, and puppeteers. Outside the Sherwood Forest Café, kids can climb on giant dragons.

If your family's tastes include pirate adventure, try out Treasure Island Resort, based on the tales of Robert Louis Stevenson. There's a lagoon facing The Strip and plenty of talking skeletons and treasure chests inside the resort. It's also home to *Mystère,* the fantastic Cirque du Soleil performance many consider to be the best show in town. Circus Circus shows are daily from 11:00 A.M. to midnight in its mezzanine, along with dozens of carnival games and an arcade with more than 300 video and pinball games. Behind the hotel is an amusement park.

Las Vegas's selection of shows is legendary, and many of them are suitable for families. In addition to *Mystère,* the inventive Cirque du Soleil theater group offers two other breathtaking performances—one of which is completely underwater. Star Trek: The Experience is a huge hit with kids over the age of seven. Part museum, part movie, and part ride, this exciting attraction combines live theater, a motion-simulation ride, and dazzling special effects.

Lance Burton's magic show features some of the best sleight-of-hand in the business, and children are often called out of the audience to assist onstage. The

From his turret, Merlin welcomes you to Excalibur Hotel. You'll cross into a land of jousting knights and amusing court jesters.

The dramatic display of music, water, and lights at the Bellagio's dancing fountains provides a free show that will captivate the entire family. The show features 1,000 fountains timed to different musical pieces, with water shooting up to 240 feet into the air.

HOOVER DAM

A visit to the Hoover Dam is a must, especially since it's less than an hour's drive from Las Vegas. Witness this marvel of engineering built between 1931 and 1936 to harness the flow of the Colorado River. It's often referred to as the eighth wonder of the world, and even the most jaded teen will be rendered speechless by its size and power.

spectacular Fountains of Bellagio are a family favorite. They are located in front of the opulent Bellagio resort. The fountains are synchronized to music and enhanced by dramatic lighting. The show is free.

Other Las Vegas attractions include Stratosphere Tower, reaching some 1,150 feet above The Strip. It offers thrilling rides, freefall jumps, and roller coasters. While younger children will enjoy the view, the rides are better suited for older kids.

The Secret Garden of Siegfried and Roy and the Dolphin Habitat are greats stop for animal lovers, as is the Wildlife Walk at the Tropicana. M&Ms World, with 26,000 square feet of chocolate, is a mouthwatering shop for kids to visit. Dozens of other kid-pleasing attractions include Madame Tussaud's Wax Museum, the Guinness World of Records Museum, the Lion Habitat at MGM Grand, racecar driving experiences, the Manhattan Express roller coaster, and much more.

THE ROCKIES

The legendary wilds of the Rocky Mountain region make for exciting outdoor adventures. This area contains some of the continent's most majestic national parks, including Glacier and Grand Teton, where families can fish, explore on horseback, and raft on some of the wildest rivers in the country. Cowhands are a common sight, and you can visit Cody, Wyoming, to watch a rodeo every night of the summer. This is the part of the country you'll want to visit to introduce your children to the simple pleasures of hiking through alpine meadows filled with wildflowers, scouting for wildlife, and camping under a star-filled sky.

Arches National Park, Utah

MESA VERDE NATIONAL PARK

Mesa Verde National Park in Colorado offers visitors a spectacular opportunity to learn about the lives of the Pueblo people who lived in cliff dwellings they chiseled out of the solid mountainside. Visitors can hike to three of the dwellings with a ranger guide and crawl through tunnels and climb ladders to get a closer look at the ancient caves. Children can imagine the lives of the Anasazi people who lived in these primitive dwellings for thousands of years before they mysteriously disappeared about 700 years ago.

Touring the cliff dwellings can be a rigorous trip that is more appropriate for older children. To explore the ruins of Cliff Palace, visitors descend about 100 feet into the canyon on a steep trail with 120 uneven stone steps and ultimately climb five wooden ladders to get into the dwelling. A tour of Balcony House is a bit more challenging. The trip begins with a climb down a 100-foot-long staircase and then up a series of ladders. After crawling through a tunnel and climbing another 60 feet on ladders and stone steps, visitors will find themselves perched a precipitous 700 feet above the ground. Early residents of Balcony House built a wall around it to keep anything and anyone from falling off.

Above: *The scope and mystery of Mesa Verde National Park's ancient dwellings will fascinate your family. The tour of Cliff Palace provides a wealth of information about the civilization that once lived here, then curiously disappeared.* Right: *Wear your climbing shoes, because touring the cliff dwellings can be tricky. Ascending to Balcony House involves navigating some ladders, but the view from the top is remarkable.*

GREAT SAND DUNES NATIONAL PARK

The ever-changing landscape of Great Sand Dunes National Park contains 39 square miles of dunes, and some are more than 750 feet high. The park is set against a rugged backdrop of the Sangre de Cristo Mountains, the southernmost range of the Rockies. The dunes are a result of the wind and rain eroding the Sangre de Cristo and San Juan mountains.

Left: *A national park since 1932, Great Sand Dunes National Park seems to have been created by nature with kids in mind—they love the thrill of a downhill trip on the slopes of North America's tallest dunes.* Below: *The serpentine shapes in the sand are created by winds blowing in opposite directions.*

Sledding is a popular pastime in this part of the country; it's merely done without snow. Carrying their sleds, kids climb to the tops of the dunes and then slide down the steep sides. Many bring skis or snowboards to slalom down the sandy slopes. Forgot your sled? No problem, simply roll your way down, and ignore the sand in your pockets—it's part of the fun.

In spring and early summer, kids love to play on the beach and splash around in the cool water of Medano Creek, which flows at the base of the dunes. By the middle of the summer this creek dries up, however.

ROCKY MOUNTAIN NATIONAL PARK

The rugged grandeur of Colorado's Rocky Mountain National Park is only a 90-minute drive from the bustling mile-high city of Denver. These mountains range in elevation from 8,000 feet in the grassy valleys to 14,259 feet at the top of Longs Peak. Sixty of its peaks rise above 12,000 feet. Visitors to the park have countless opportunities for hiking, mountain climbing, camping, horseback riding, and wildlife viewing in the summer; cross-country skiing and snowshoeing are popular in winter.

Estes Park, just east of the national park, features an abundance of family activities. A number of horseback riding stables offer trail rides, and a small lake comes complete with boating and fishing. Other activities include bicycling and cultural events. Be sure to head as deep into the park as time allows in order to hike its more remote trails and take in all of its majestic mountain beauty. Estes Park offers a number of family-friendly accommodations for those who don't care to camp out.

Longs Peak stands tallest in Rocky Mountain National Park. Hikers can take the Keyhole Route to ascend almost 5,000 feet.

Getting to the top of Pikes Peak is half the fun. You'll ride in style on the world's highest cog railway and travel through a variety of ecosystems. Kids will enjoy trying to spot wildlife along the route.

THE MANITOU AND PIKES PEAK COG RAILWAY

Pikes Peak in Colorado Springs is second only to Mount Fuji in Japan for having the most travelers to its summit. Although you can get there on foot or by car, the best way to get to the top is to take a ride on the delightful old-fashioned cog railway. The railway began service in 1891, and it hasn't changed much since then. During the ride, which lasts just over three hours round-trip, visitors often catch glimpses of the state's largest herd of bighorn sheep, as well as marmots, deer, and elk.

The view from the 14,110-foot summit is astonishing and offers a panorama of Denver from 60 miles away, as well as the Sangre de Cristo Mountains, the historic Cripple Creek Gold Camp, and the majestic mountains that form the Continental Divide. It so inspired Katherine Lee Bates, a Massachusetts author and teacher who visited the summit in1893, that she composed the lyrics to *America the Beautiful*.

At the top of Pikes Peak, be sure to sample the world-famous high-altitude donuts. These tasty treats have been made with the same recipe since the early 1900s.

GLENWOOD HOT SPRINGS POOL

Open all year, no matter what the weather, this king-size swimming pool in Glenwood Springs, Colorado, is more than three city blocks long. Located about 40 miles northwest of Aspen, it's the world's largest hot mineral pool and is naturally heated to a comfortable 90 to 93 degrees year-round.

Kids love cascading down the pool's two giant waterslides and playing in the warm, relaxing water. There are lanes for lap swimmers, diving boards, a special shallow pool for younger kids, and plenty of splashing room for everyone. Tired from a day of hiking and sightseeing? You can relax in the smaller therapy pool heated to 104 degrees. Pop a quarter into the "bubble chairs" for a special massage.

During the winter months, steam rises from the pool in thick, misty clouds, and snowflakes melt the second they hit the water. It's not uncommon to see swimmers hop out of the pool and do a polar bear roll in the snow on the deck. During summer, families pack up the picnic baskets and stake out their turf in the lawn area or on the patio next to the pool. It's a relaxing way to spend the day.

Surrounded by the beautiful Rocky Mountains, mile-high Glenwood Hot Springs Pool is located along the banks of the Colorado River. President Theodore Roosevelt often spent summers here enjoying the soothing spring-fed waters.

BUFFALO BILL HISTORICAL CENTER

The five museums at the Buffalo Bill Historical Center in Cody contain an internationally acclaimed collection of Western Americana. Featured within its walls are masterworks of Western art, a rich collection of Native American artifacts, exhibits on the natural history of the greater Yellowstone area, and an enormous Winchester gun collection.

The museum staff has developed special materials, events, and exhibits just for the younger set. At the Whitney Gallery of Western Art kids can pick up a family guidebook. After completing its questions, they can trade it in for a souvenir. In the Draper Museum of Natural History, kids receive a passport that gets stamped at various stations.

CODY NITE RODEO

Cody hosts a full-out rodeo every night of the summer. You'll see wild broncos try to buck their riders, an assortment of mystifying rope tricks, fearless bull riders, tough barrel racers, and daredevil rodeo clowns. Children can join in stick horse races and calf scrambles, take a spin on a real clown barrel, and get their picture taken on a live bull.

Inset: *Buffalo Bill Cody once called his Wild West Show an "educational exposition." The same applies to the Historical Center, which displays a wealth of artifacts from the early West.* Left: *These authentic wagons show the wear and tear of their frontier travels.*

YELLOWSTONE NATIONAL PARK

The National Park Service doesn't hand out gold medals, but if it did, Yellowstone would win, hands down, for special effects. Its geothermal attractions, from one corner of the park to the other, dramatically spout, steam, and bubble. Fueled by a giant underground volcano that is still active, 10,000 geo-thermal show-offs lend an otherworldly appearance to the Wyoming park's terrain.

Old Faithful is the biggest star, but a supporting cast includes some 300 spouting geysers, plus boiling mud pots, hissing steam vents, steaming fumaroles, and billowing vapors. At the Old Faithful Visitor Center, pick up a schedule of eruptions to see the famous geyser in all its glory, and don't forget to walk the mile or so of boardwalk that winds around the bizarre field of other geysers and hot pools.

Old Faithful Inn, a magnificent national park lodge that looks like a gigantic, elegant log cabin, is just a short walk from Old Faithful. Its striking six-story lobby has rough-hewn pine walls and a 40-foot-high lava rock fireplace.

Visitors can see a large part of the park by driving on one or more of its looping roads, which enter from each of its four sides. Exploring the surreal landscape is best done on foot. One favorite stop is Boiling River, a 50-yard-long band of soaking pools near the north entrance. The river is a half-mile walk upstream from the parking area. It's hard to miss the swimming spot, which is marked by large clouds of steam, especially in cold weather.

The park contains the largest concentration of free-roaming wildlife in the lower 48 states. Bison gather along the side of the road, and moose graze in lakeside meadows. Elk, bighorn sheep, coyote, and an occasional wolf can also be seen. Haden Valley and Lamar Valley attract bison, deer, antelope, and elk to their grasslands and are particularly good for open viewing. The park's most famous and rarely seen inhabitants are the grizzly bears. Grizzlies are occasionally spotted in the meadow to the east of Dunraven Pass, along the road between Yellowstone's Canyon and Tower Junction. The best chances to spot bears are at dusk and dawn.

Opposite page: *It took an earthquake to knock Old Faithful off its schedule. The geyser erupted every 76 minutes until a 1998 earthquake rocked the area. Eruptions now occur every 80 minutes.* Top: *Bear sightings, although infrequent in Yellowstone, are thrilling all the same. Your family will remember these magnificent animals for their power and grace.* Bottom: *Old Faithful isn't the only show in town. As you walk along the boardwalk path in Yellowstone you'll have plenty of opportunities to observe similar steamy spectacles.*

GRAND TETON NATIONAL PARK

The spectacular, craggy, cloud-high peaks of the Tetons seem to rise out of nowhere into the endless Wyoming sky. These mountains offer a vacation experience of unspoiled nature, with ample opportunities to hike through untouched forests, fish for five kinds of trout, and splash in pure mountain streams and lakes. An abundance of wildlife thrives in the park's Jackson Hole Valley: Moose, elk, bison, and deer frequently graze in the area.

Ranger-led activities abound and are an excellent way to learn more about the park for free. There are wildlife walks and talks, daytime and twilight hikes, campfire programs, and special activities for children. The park's rivers and lakes also offer a wealth of activities, such as half-day float trips on the Snake River and canoe excursions on Jenny Lake.

In the gateway town of Jackson, an arch made entirely of elk antlers welcomes people to the town center. In summer, families can take a stagecoach ride throughout the town or watch cowhands and outlaws reenact a shoot-out in the town square.

The craggy peaks of the distant Grand Tetons are reflected in Snake River. Outdoor activities abound here, and if your family enjoys camping, fishing, and hiking, this is a great vacation spot for you.

DEVILS TOWER NATIONAL MONUMENT

The sheer drama and spectacle of this vertical rock monolith has been a beacon to visitors for hundreds of years. Hiking through the adjacent meadows and exploring nearby forests and boulder fields are fun activities, but climbing stands out as the most alluring activity. When people see a rock that tall, they just naturally want to climb it.

A number of climbing schools are licensed to operate at Devils Tower. Each offers play days where visitors learn the basics of rock climbing. The play days are appropriate for children ages four and older, and kids as young as seven have climbed to the summit.

Outfitters supply all the necessary equipment, including sticky-soled rubber climbing shoes. After an initial lesson, visitors start out on the less challenging north end of the tower. It's not uncommon for a novice climber to ascend between 50 and 200 feet on the first attempt. Families that wish to keep climbing can take follow-up instruction where they learn the skills that will help them make it to the top.

Mysterious and mesmerizing, Devils Tower was famous even before Close Encounters of the Third Kind, *but the movie helped popularize it as an icon of the West. Climbers can choose among 220 routes to its top.*

ARCHES NATIONAL PARK

Sculpted by wind and weather over millions of years, Arches National Park in Utah is a garden of geological formations. The park contains the largest concentration of natural sandstone arches in the world, including balanced rocks, towers, domes, fins, and pinnacles that preside over a dramatic desert landscape. Water and ice, extreme temperatures, the movement of underground salt deposits, and 100 million years of erosion are the combined forces that brought about the amazing sculptures of Arches National Park.

Children love the unusual names of some of the formations, such as Paul Bunyan's Potty, the Fiery Furnace, and the Parade of Elephants. Although some of the names may invite giggles from youngsters, once they see the grandeur and size of the many arches, they'll be amazed. The park's scenic drive, a paved road that runs 40 miles round-trip through the park, offers the easiest access to its major sights, with plenty of places to stop to get a closer look at the distinctive geological wonders.

Arches is also a great park for hiking and exploring, with many easy trails that are just right for most children. To see

More than 2,000 natural sandstone arches— the greatest concentration in the world—are located in Arches National Park. Kids are awed by the spectacle of the many formations, which include Delicate Arch, the park's signature formation.

Above: *The hike along Devils Garden Trail will take you to the Double O Arch, just one of the many sandstone formations you'll find in Arches National Park.* Right: *Hiking through Arches National Park will provide a close-up look at some of nature's most creative work. Children are fascinated the gravity-defying Balanced Rock and other practically unbelievable formations.*

Delicate Arch, the formation that is most associated with the park, you can take a marked hiking trail that originates at Wolfe Ranch. Here kids can view where the first settlers in this area made their home in 1888. Young children may find the three-mile hike difficult, but families who make the trip are rewarded with a close-up view of the breathtaking formation. Families can also tour the park by mountain bike on Moab Slickrock Bike Trail—it's one of the country's best bike trails,

and it will take you to the park's more remote sights.

Although Arches National Park is a desert, it's a cool, high-altitude desert that supports a diverse ecosystem. Children will be amazed at the assortment of wildlife they'll see while hiking. Reptiles rule in the desert terrain, and lizards and snakes are often spotted sunning themselves on rocks alongside the trails. Try to

catch a glimpse of the leopard lizard, which measures about 12 inches long. Other animals you might see include coyotes, porcupines, and gray foxes.

Visitors are encouraged to learn more about Arches National Park at the visitor center near the park entrance. You'll find information about hiking and guided tours throughout the park. Camping in the park is limited to Devils Garden Campground.

UTAH OLYMPIC PARK

Visitors to this Park City attraction can test their mettle in some of the Olympic sports the venue hosted in 2002, including luge, bobsled, and ski jumping. They can also watch Olympic hopefuls train for the next winter games. The park is also a favorite with freestyle aerialist skiers, who train in the summer by landing from their flips, twists, and jumps in a 750,000-gallon splash pool. The 389-acre facility includes Nordic jumps of six different lengths; a 1,335-meter track with five start areas for bobsled, luge, and skeleton; freestyle aerials training areas; and a lodge, a ski museum, and an Olympic Winter Games Museum.

During the summer, kids ages 6 through 12 can participate in a day camp to learn ski jumping. Other camps are available for kids ages 8 through 14 who want to test their skills at ice hockey, speed skating, luge, bobsled, ski jumping, freestyle skiing,

biathlon, curling, and skeleton. Every Saturday during the summer, the Flying Ace All-Stars skiers and snowboarders present a 25-minute show, soaring

Above: *This display in Utah's Olympic Park features some of the highlights of the winter games.* Left: *Ice and snow are helpful but not necessary. Kids love the high-speed twists and turns on the luge and skeleton tracks at Olympic Park.*

up to 60 feet in the air and performing acrobatic feats before landing in the splash pool.

In winter, intermediate skiers can take a half-day Nordic ski-jumping lesson. By the end of the session, visitors will be soaring off the ten-kilometer jump—quick learners can attempt an even longer one. Half-day slopeside ski-jumping lessons are also available for kids. There are luge and skeleton lessons for those 13 and older. Tours of the facility and the two museums are offered in summer and winter.

If you're just visiting for the day, there's still plenty to do. Try out the Quicksilver Alpine Slide, a state-of-the-art metal track that duplicates the narrow, twisting, downhill plummet of a bobsled run. Or you can ride on two different zip lines: The steel cables are set at the top of the 90- and 120-meter ski jumps, and a pulley system whisks riders down the steepest zip line track in the world. The lines run parallel to the ski jumping tracks—and your trip may even take you alongside a ski jumper soaring through the air.

Ski jumping takes nerves of steel, as this perspective demonstrates.

Best Friends Animal Sanctuary

The largest no-kill animal sanctuary in the United States, Best Friends is located in Kanab, Utah, at the heart of the famous Golden Circle of national parks: Zion, the Grand Canyon, Bryce Canyon, and Lake Powell. It houses about 1,500 dogs, cats, horses, donkeys, rabbits, birds, goats, and other animals. Each animal is named, fed, and housed in clean and comfortable surroundings, and a lucky 75 percent of them are adopted into happy homes.

Visitors are welcome year-round, and free, guided tours are offered daily. After the tour, visitors can volunteer to help out with the canine residents of Dogtown or play with the felines in Cat World. There are pigs aplenty and an abundance of bunnies just waiting to be petted.

Guests who want to spend the night can reserve a cottage overlooking the horse pastures, and they are encouraged to take a dog home for a sleepover in their cabins. It's a good way for the sanctuary to determine the dog's socialization skills, and many visitors fall in love with their animal guests and make arrangements to adopt them.

It's difficult to leave empty-handed. Every year some 20,000 people visit Best Friends Animal Sanctuary, and about 3,500 of them stay a few days to help feed, exercise, and play with the animals.

GLACIER NATIONAL PARK

This magnificent expanse of glacier-capped mountain peaks, forests, alpine meadows, and lakes in Montana is home to more than 70 species of mammals, including grizzly bears, mountain lions, and wolves.

The park extends into Canada and connects with Waterton Lakes National Park to create one large protected area, which is officially called Waterton–Glacier International Peace Park. Both have been designated Biosphere Reserve and World Heritage Sites.

Glacier has 13 campgrounds and many short, self-guided nature hikes that make it easy for families to enjoy the true beauty of the park. A variety of ranger programs operate year-round, and an expanded program is offered during the summer, when special guided hikes, evening slide presentations, campfire programs, and other family activities are available.

Glacier National Park, named for the rivers of ice that sculpted its dramatic alpine landscape, is the national park many people say they would most like to revisit.

Little Bighorn Battlefield National Monument

The wide-open prairie and rolling hills are quiet now, and the green and golden hues of the landscape give it an air of tranquility. However, the Little Bighorn Battlefield National Monument in Montana commemorates the military disaster of 1876 known as Custer's Last Stand. It was here that U.S. Army Colonel George Armstrong Custer and his 7th Cavalry battled bands of Lakota Sioux, Cheyenne, and Arapaho. The monument memorializes those who died. It also acknowledges the battle as one of the last efforts of the Northern Plains Indians to preserve their ancestral way of life.

Park rangers are on duty year-round to explain the history of the site. During the summer, they relate the legend of the famous colonel, his adversaries Sitting Bull and Crazy Horse, and the battle that took the lives of Custer, several hundred soldiers, and a number of Native American warriors. A museum features exhibits of the battle, a biography of Custer, the weapons used by both sides, and some background information on the events leading up to the battle. Interpretive markers guide visitors to Custer Hill, a common grave marked by a monument bearing the names of all the soldiers who died in the battle, and the American Indian Memorial that recognizes and honors the Native Americans who were killed at Little Bighorn.

These tombstones each mark the location of a fallen participant—whether U.S. soldier or Native American warrior—at the Battle of Little Bighorn. It was made a national cemetery in 1879 to commemorate all who gave their lives here.

VIRGINIA CITY

Virginia City is a Gold Rush boom-town that is remarkably well preserved. It was built and settled in the rough-and-ready days of the Old West when about $30 million in gold was panned from the area's rivers and streams in three years. The town grew quickly as prospectors flooded the area seeking their fortunes. When gold fever died down, Virginia City fell into decline. The residents who stayed could not afford to remodel or rebuild. The town attracted the early interest of the preservation-minded Bovey family in the early 1940s. After decades of restoration, Virginia City was named a National Historic Landmark.

At its peak, Virginia City was populated by vigilantes, villains, and desperadoes. Visitors today can walk the same wooden boardwalks these colorful characters strolled in the town's heyday. More than 100 historic buildings replete with artifacts and furnishings are open to the public. Visitors can poke into 1860s barbershops and saloons or take a stagecoach ride around town. They can also see a gunfight reenactment or an old-fashioned melodrama. Children can even try their hand at panning gold, just as the prospectors once did.

High in the Rocky Mountains you'll find Virginia City. This remnant of the Gold Rush days once had a population of more than 10,000.

THE LEWIS AND CLARK NATIONAL HISTORIC TRAIL INTERPRETIVE CENTER

Meriwether Lewis and William Clark looped through Montana several times on their cross-continental journey, traveling across mountains and prairies and navigating huge sections of the Missouri River. Appropriately, the Interpretive Center is situated in Great Falls on the bluffs overlooking the very river they so often canoed and portaged. The center is the largest museum dedicated to the Lewis and Clark expedition and provides a wealth of information and exhibits about their famous journey.

Before beginning the tour of the museum, visitors can watch a reenactment of the meeting between President Thomas Jefferson and the two explorers. Then they follow the route the adventurers took all the way to the coast of Oregon. Along the way, children can crawl inside a miniature Native American lodge, where they listen to the sound of drums, inspect items made by Native Americans, and pull a rope as if they're portaging the falls.

In the summer, a day camp is offered along the river, where kids learn how to decorate clothing with beads, set up a wedge tent, and prepare the kind of campfire meal the explorers might have eaten.

The life-size display of Lewis and Clark's portage around the falls of the Missouri River shows how members of the expedition painstakingly hauled canoes and supplies around waterfalls that were between 70 and 80 feet high.

CRATERS OF THE MOON NATIONAL MONUMENT AND PRESERVE

Called by an early visitor the strangest 75 square miles on the North American continent, Craters of the Moon National Monument and Preserve is a remarkable volcanic landscape pockmarked with cinder cones, lava tubes, deep fissures, and lava fields. Rather than one large volcano cone, there are many small craters and fissures through which lava flowed at one time. In some places, the molten lava encased standing trees and then hardened. Eventually, the wood rotted, resulting in bizarre tree-shape lava molds. The landscape is so strange and lunarlike that American astronauts have actually trained at the site.

Drive the seven-mile road that loops through the preserve to discover the spatter and cinder cones, lava flows and

fields, and craters.

The park also has a network of fairly easy trails that provide access to its odd geological features. Plants and wildlife have adapted to the unusual environment and are present in surprising numbers, including several hundred species of plants and about 2,000 insect species. Mammals, reptiles, and two varieties of amphibians

Welcome to the strange, lunarlike country of Craters of the Moon National Monument and Preserve. The park was formed by volcanic eruptions.

make their homes in the stark setting as well.

River Rafting on the Salmon River

The longest undammed river in the lower 48 states, the legendary Salmon River is considered one of the continent's premier rafting destinations. It's too rough and dangerous for families with small children to run early in the season. But beginning about mid-July, the water warms up and calms down, and it settles into an excellent river for family rafting trips through one of nature's most breathtaking wilderness areas.

A number of outfitters offer special trips in both the main and the middle forks of the river that focus on family fun. Year round, the Main Fork of the Salmon River is best for children ages seven and older. Its spacious sandy beaches are perfect for making camp, and it features great swimming holes and glimpses of abandoned mines and pioneer homesteads. The river has just enough white-water thrills to entertain the kids without being intimidating. The Middle Fork of the Salmon River is usually a bit more challenging, but during mid- to late summer, lower water levels make it ideal for families with kids younger than seven years old.

In many places, this powerful waterway slices a path through steep canyon walls that are completely inaccessible except by water—it's the second deepest river gorge on the continent. The Salmon River has more than 100 sets of rapids over a distance of about 105 miles, and its varied elevation and terrain keep kids delighted. The wildlife viewing on both river trips is legendary, and you're likely to see bighorn sheep perched high on the canyon walls, mule deer grazing in soft meadows, and river otters playing in the foaming waters.

On all trips, the river guides set up camp and prepare dinner, including child-friendly fare. Most family trips are four to six days long and include plenty of stops to get out and play, explore historical sites, take short hikes, fish, and swim—even in the mild rapids.

Sometimes glassy smooth and sometimes turbulent, the Salmon River features rapids such as the Bodacious Bounce and the Slide, perfect for families who love a splashing good time.

SAWTOOTH NATIONAL FOREST

Located in south-central Idaho, Sawtooth National Forest is named for its sharp serrated peaks that can be seen silhouetted against the sky like the teeth of a saw. These jagged mountains and forests feature some of the wildest country in North America. Some 1,100 lakes and more than 3,000 miles of rivers famous for their salmon, steelhead, and native trout run through Sawtooth National Forest and make it a perfect spot for young fishing enthusiasts. Numerous hiking trails wind through its rugged terrain. During the winter months, downhill skiing is a favorite pastime, particularly in Sun Valley. There are also plenty of trails for cross-country skiing, snowshoeing, and snowmobiling.

Families will find the best of both worlds at Sawtooth National Forest—camping and hiking in the mountains and fishing in Redfish Lake.

REDFISH LAKE

Gorgeous glacier-fed Redfish Lake, located in Sawtooth National Forest, has a sandy beach, a lodge, and excellent camping. A variety of family-oriented activities begin at the visitor center, such as guided animal tracking walks and lectures on a variety of subjects. Boaters can rent paddleboats, kayaks, canoes, and motorboats from the marina. Horseback riding is offered at a nearby ranch.

THE PACIFIC

Welcome to the Pacific, a land of sublime beauty and extreme contrasts. Tour the majestic towering redwood forests in northern California or enjoy the non-stop excitement of a state-of-the-art amusement park. Lounge on the tropical beaches of Hawaii or roam the icy enchantments of Alaska's glacier-cut landscape. Vibrant cities such as San Francisco and Seattle offer many attractions and cultural events. The far western reaches of the United States are packed with natural wonders and city pleasures.

Iditarod Sled Dog Race, Alaska

DISNEYLAND

Walt Disney envisioned a place where parents could recapture childhood memories and enjoy a magical world of fantasy with their children. Disneyland in Anaheim brought this vision to life. Many of its early rides and attractions are still in place and are as popular as ever, attesting to the power and longevity of Disney's imagination. The Mad Tea Party and Jungle Cruise rides continue to thrill young visitors, and

Mickey and Minnie, in updated attire, still wander the park greeting their young fans.

But that's not to say that Disneyland hasn't kept up with the times. New shows, rides, and themed areas have been added to the park over the years. Visitors enjoy a selection that now includes Main Street USA, Tomorrowland, Frontierland, Fantasyland,

Adventureland, Critter Country, Mickey's Toontown, and New Orleans Square. An adjacent park, Disney's California Adventure, features rides and attractions inspired by the Golden State, including the California Screamin' roller coaster and Soarin' Over California, which takes you on a virtual hang-gliding ride over the state, enhanced by the aromas of orange groves and saltwater. Downtown Disney, located in the middle of the resort complex, is a shopping and dining hub of activity that will keep all ages entertained.

Something old, something new, and everything to delight the family can be found at Disneyland. An old favorite, the Mad Tea Party ride, has been taking families for a spin since the park opened in 1955.

SANTA CATALINA ISLAND

Only 22 miles from Los Angeles, quiet Santa Catalina seems a world apart from the hustle and bustle of the city across the water. It's a traffic-free, clean-air vacation spot for any active family that likes to hike, snorkel, kayak, and explore.

Visitors take ferries from San Pedro, Long Beach, or Dana Point to one of Catalina's two principal towns: Avalon, with its famous casino, or the more isolated Two Harbors. Both towns have picturesque harbors, which kids can explore in easy-to-use ocean kayaks and pedal boats that are rented on the island.

Most of the island's beaches are rather rocky, but there's plenty to do besides lounge in the sand. Lover's Cove, a protected marine preserve, is a short walk from Avalon and is an excellent spot for snorkeling. The fish are plentiful and used to people, thanks to frequent feedings from passengers on the glass-bottom boats that tour the area. Much of the interior of the island is protected by the Catalina Island Conservancy. It oversees the diverse island habitat that is home to plant and animal species found nowhere else in the world. The organization also sponsors a nature center at Avalon Canyon and conducts nature walks every evening. Kids will enjoy the center's hands-

on exhibits that feature information about the island's native wildlife and hiking its many trails. *It should be noted that there was a major fire on Santa Catalina in 2007; most recreational facilities were unaffected, but the wilderness interior suffered significant damage.*

Above: *Where you'll find islands, you'll find water, and where you'll find water— boats! Santa Catalina Island is one place where there are more boats than cars. The island attracts about one million tourists each year.* Right: *Beautiful Avalon Bay was named after the paradise described in the legend of King Arthur.*

SEQUOIA AND KINGS CANYON NATIONAL PARKS

General Sherman is the leader among trees. This huge sequoia tops off at 275 feet—as tall as a 26-story building. It is Sequoia's most famous resident and the largest living organism in the world. A gargantuan 36 feet in diameter, at approximately 2,500 years old, it's the oldest of its species. Thousands of General Sherman's relatives fill the pristine forests of these two spectacular national parks.

The best place to see these breathtaking giants is suitably named the Giant Forest, home to four of the five tallest trees in the park. Visitors also enjoy the park's diverse landscape, which includes deep canyons, granite cliffs, wildflower-filled meadows, and a wild river. An easy 1.7-mile hike starts near the Giant Forest and leads to a 1,200-foot waterfall that is especially dramatic in early summer when run-off from the melting snowpack is at its peak.

Below: *The drive-through in Sequoia National Park is open 24 hours! Before this sequoia fell in 1937, it stood 275 feet high. Rather than attempt its removal, the park service carved a tunnel through it that measures 17 feet wide and 8 feet high.* Inset: *They grow 'em big in Kings Canyon National Park. The largest and oldest trees in the United States are located here, so prepare your kids to be amazed.*

YOSEMITE NATIONAL PARK

The awesome sights of Yosemite's towering granite peaks, cascading waterfalls, glacial lakes, and giant trees attract families year after year. At the park's center is half-mile-deep Yosemite Valley, carved by glaciers during the last ice age. Sights like the soaring El Capitán, the majestic Half Dome, and the thundering waterfall of Bridal Veil are not to be missed.

It's no wonder American nature photographer Ansel Adams found much of his inspiration here, popularizing many of Yosemite Valley's granite landmarks in his black-and-white photographs.

The Ahwahnee Hotel, a grand hotel in a grand setting, is a popular stop for weary travelers. The hotel houses a collection of priceless Native American baskets as well as a display of unique Persian rugs.

A number of bike trails crisscross Yosemite Valley, and the park also uses a fleet of shuttle buses to help control the flow of traffic during peak vacation months. To get a real sense of the park's majesty and the diversity of its terrain, explore the less visited parts of the valley by heading into its higher reaches, such as idyllic Tuolumne Meadows. This picturesque sierra meadow features clear mountain streams and stark granite outcroppings surrounded by snow-capped peaks. It serves as a trailhead for some of the park's most spectacular hikes.

Left: *Half Dome, located at the eastern end of Yosemite Valley, is a breathtaking sight. The granite formation is an estimated 87 million years old. Geologists believe the other "half" of Half Dome broke off when glaciers began to recede in the valley.*
Below: *The largest granite rock in the world, El Capitán, stands 3,600 feet high. It's a popular destination for mountain climbers.*

MONTEREY BAY AQUARIUM

Just off the coast of Monterey, in the deepwater canyons of the Pacific, lies a world of mysterious marine life. Monterey Bay Aquarium brings this world to its visitors with extraordinary exhibits that are sure to captivate families.

Hands-on experiences are its hallmark, from touch pools to steerable underwater cameras. Divers communicate with visitors from huge tanks where fish reside among three-story stalks of kelp, and staff members who feed the mischievous sea otters tell tales about their adorable charges. A special petting pool lets children touch rubbery bat rays and nubby sea stars.

The aquarium's Splash Zone is a special exhibit and play area where children can crawl through, climb on, and pop up in displays as they visit nearly 60 different sea creatures in their coral reef and rocky shore homes. Just about everyone's favorite are the comical black-footed penguins. Their antics are great fun to watch, especially at mealtime.

Other not-to-miss aquarium exhibits include the giant octopus exhibit and Outer Bay, full of sea turtles, barracuda, and other creatures that inhabit the open ocean. White sharks are even on exhibit in this area at times; if they are accidentally caught in commercial fishing gear the aquarium houses and cares for them until they are ready to return to the wild.

It's easy to see why the Monterey Bay Aquarium attracts more than one million visitors a year. The facility offers fascinating exhibits that capture children's imaginations and inspire their awareness of the ocean's fragile ecosystem.

Let's see—if it's black and white, swims, and eats fish, it must be Shamu? Not so, according to the penguins that also inhabit SeaWorld. They make up a waddling welcome crew that is quite an entertaining sight.

SeaWorld

Beware the Soak Zone, or at least wear quick-drying clothing when you visit SeaWorld in San Diego. When everyone's favorite killer whale sends up its signature greeting, those closest to the tank will be deluged by a wall of water as Shamu leaps out of the air and belly smacks back into the pool. The acrobatic mammal is a SeaWorld favorite—indeed, its main attraction. But Shamu gets some serious competition in the cuteness department from some of SeaWorld's other creatures, especially the gentle, sweet-faced manatees and the waddling penguins. A number of shows besides Shamu's feature animal acts.

The park has a collection of rides that include water coasters, raft rides, and the Wild Arctic experience, where guests find themselves on a stomach-twirling simulated helicopter ride to a remote Arctic research station. If you care to take a stroll through shark-infested waters, check out the 280,000-gallon shark exhibit that features a 57-foot-long acrylic tunnel that allows you to walk right through a school of pointy-toothed predators.

SAN DIEGO ZOO

From the tiny shrew to the mighty elephant, the San Diego Zoo offers visitors some of the world's most exceptional animals. Located in Balboa Park and one of the finest zoos on the continent, it is home to more than 3,800 creatures representing 800 species.

The Monkey Trails and Forest Tales exhibit spans three acres and features more than 30 species of African and Asian forest creatures. Visitors can observe animals from a walkway at treetop level or along paths on the ground. You'll encounter a rare pygmy hippopotamus,

Opposite: *Since the giant pandas arrived at the San Diego Zoo in 1987, the photogenic residents have been delighting children with their antics. You can see them at the Giant Panda Research Station.* Right: *The Indian rhinoceros and her calf are among the many residents of the San Diego Wild Animal Park. Thanks to the park's breeding program, dozens of species have been saved from extinction.*

mandrills, and clouded leopards. You'll even travel through a bog garden and see carnivorous plants along its pathways. In Tiger River, a simulated Asian rainforest, mist-shrouded trails wind down a canyon into Tiger River Pass, where tigers, tapirs, and other creatures wander among exotic trees and plants. At the base of the river is a four-acre African rainforest where hippos swim and monkeys play.

Many of the animals at the Children's Zoo, such as wombats, spider monkeys, and owls, are trained as animal ambassadors and accept being observed and touched by children. And what mouse wouldn't feel at home at the San Diego Zoo? The Mouse House is made from a large loaf of bread, which is replaced each week as its residents gnaw and nibble their way through the walls. Children love visiting the nurseries to see the baby animals as they are fed and cuddled by their keepers. Don't be disappointed if the nurseries are empty; it simply means that the zoo's animal mothers are doing their jobs and caring for their babies.

SAN DIEGO WILD ANIMAL PARK

A visit to the 1,800-acre San Diego Wild Animal Park is as close as many families get to an African safari. In the park's vast enclosure, exotic animals roam freely as they would in their native Asia or Africa. You'll see thousands of animals—giraffes, oryx, zebras, antelopes, and elephants—wandering through rolling plains and grassy savannas. Lions and other big predators are separated from their prey in spacious environments. Visitors can select from several different tours, which each include motorized transport. The park was originally established as a breeding facility for the San Diego Zoo and now holds about 3,500 animals representing more than 400 species. The fact that about 650 animals are born each year attests to its success.

TOURNAMENT OF ROSES PARADE

The residents of Pasadena celebrated the first Tournament of Roses Parade on January 1, 1890. Horse-drawn carriages adorned with flowers paraded through the city streets. This event began the annual New Year's tradition that draws about one million people to Pasadena to watch the parade. Millions more watch the televised event from their homes.

The lavishly decorated floats are a labor of love, and some builders spend all year on their elaborate creations. The parade, consisting of floats, a Rose Queen, spirited marching bands, equestrian units, and celebrity Grand Marshals, travels a 5.5-mile route through town.

Before the parade, families can watch float makers decorate their projects with thousands of blossoms, see award-winning marching bands, get up close to the horses that will prance in the parade, and sample barbeque delights. After the parade, the floats are on display for several days.

You'll never see the Tournament of Roses Parade take place on a Sunday. An agreement with Los Angeles churches states that the parade will be held on January 2 if the traditional date falls on a Sunday.

CALIFORNIA STATE RAILROAD MUSEUM

The impact of the railroad and how it shaped the history, culture, and economy of California and the West is told through the various exhibits in this vast Sacramento museum. You'll find 21 meticulously restored railroad cars and locomotives on display here. On the main floor, check out the Governor Stanford steam locomotive, the first engine used by the Central Pacific, and then get a close-up view of a huge diesel engine.

Several displays invite visitors to climb aboard for a closer look. Children can sit in the engineer's cab of a Santa Fe steam locomotive and experience the sounds and the rocking motion of a sleeping car on a pretend rail trip. Little ones can play with Thomas the Tank Engine trains and wooden Brio trains and tracks. A display entitled Small Wonders: The Magic of Toy Trains features some 1,000 vintage toy trains and an elaborate toy train layout. Between April and September, steam train excursions take visitors for a six-mile round-trip ride along the banks of the Sacramento River.

The cavernous exhibit rooms of the California State Railroad Museum house the mighty engines and lavish coaches that once traveled the rails. It is one of North America's most visited railroad museums.

ALCATRAZ ISLAND

Atop Alcatraz Island sits the infamous prison that Al Capone once called home. Kids will love their visit to the country's most noted lockup. Audio tours discuss some of the various escape attempts that have become a part of the island's history. Even though Alcatraz is only about one mile off San Francisco's shore, most would-be escapees were swept out to sea by the treacherous currents of the San Francisco Bay or died of exposure in the icy Pacific Ocean.

The boat trip to Alcatraz Island is just part of the entertainment. You'll find tour boats docked between Fisherman's Wharf and Pier 39. This area offers a hodgepodge of tourist delights, and your kids will love browsing the souvenir shops and watching the street performers as you wait to board your boat. As you travel across the bay you'll be treated to breathtaking views of the San Francisco skyline and the Golden Gate Bridge.

Right: *Kids will love the tour of Alcatraz, the country's infamous federal prison whose gloomy confines once housed Al Capone and George "Machine Gun" Kelly.* Below: *Isolation and solitude come to mind when you first see Alcatraz Island. This prison was designated for criminals who were the worst of the worst.*

EXPLORATORIUM

You'll never hear the words "hands off" or "don't touch" at this San Francisco family favorite. On the contrary, this wonderful museum teaches children about the world and the way it works through the hands-on, touch-and-tinker experiences of more than 650 permanent exhibits.

One crowd pleaser is Shadow Box, a darkened room with phosphorescent vinyl wallpaper that freezes your shadow on the wall when a strobe light flashes. In another favorite exhibit, a ten-foot-tall tornado alters its shape when you place your hands in it. Make reservations to experience the Tactile Dome, an interactive excursion through total darkness where your sense of touch becomes your only guide.

Don't miss the museum's wave-activated acoustic sculpture titled The Wave Organ. It's located a short walk from the Exploratorium on a jetty in San Francisco Bay. The intensity and complexity of the music made by the waves is directly related to the tides and weather.

Above: *Music at high tide? The Wave Organ, an environmental sculpture located near the Exploratorium, is activated by the waves of the Pacific Ocean.* Right: *Amazing! A tornado you can touch is just one of the many exhibits kids love at San Francisco's Exploratorium.*

HEARST CASTLE

Hollywood celebrities, business tycoons, and political heavy-weights of the 1920s and 1930s were all entertained by William Randolph Hearst at Hearst Castle, an opulent 165-room hilltop hideaway above the California coastline in San Simeon. Hearst was not one to live the simple life, and his home overflows with unbelievable treasures and priceless art from all over the world. He spent millions building his estate and, in its heyday, he entertained lavishly.

Hearst's heirs presented this grandiose Shangri-la and its treasures to the state in 1958 for public exhibition. Some of the home's many rooms can be viewed in the five different tours offered to visitors. First-timers should opt for Tour One through the gardens and into the cavernous main entry hall. Other parts of the mansion, including the billiard room, the dining hall with its king-size trestle table and bannerlike flags, the private theater, and the indoor Roman Pool lined with actual gold-leaf glass mosaic tiles, are a part of this tour. Nighttime tours include a living-history program, when the castle

William Randolph
Hearst's hilltop castle will amaze kids with its grandeur. The Neptune Pool and its 17 grand dressing rooms are favorite stops along the tour.

comes alive with docents dressed in elegant 1930s clothing playing poker in the sitting rooms or lounging about in the ornate library.

SANTA BARBARA

Blessed with a mild Mediterranean climate, this Spanish-style beach town is beautiful year-round. You can spend lazy days at the beach or visit the town's many parks and playgrounds. Other Santa Barbara favorites include a zoo and a stunning botanical garden. Rent bikes or skates or hire a surrey and cruise the three-mile paved beachfront path, kayak along the shore, or meander along the mile-long boardwalk, one of the state's oldest working piers.

The pier in Santa Barbara has weathered fires and earthquakes during its 130-year history. Once a hub of activity for cargo and passenger ships, the pier now serves as a docking area for pleasure boats and whale-watching tours.

I MADONNARI STREET PAINTING FESTIVAL

Each Memorial Day weekend, professional and student street painting artists transform Old Mission, Santa Barbara's historic plaza, into a brilliantly colored art gallery. Using chalk and the plaza sidewalk, these artists create exquisite reproductions of old masters as well as modern works ablaze with color and fine detail. Music on the mission lawn and food vendors selling Italian favorites make for a festive day. If your child's inner artist is inspired, you can purchase a square of pavement and a box of chalk and let the creating begin.

LEGOLAND

The popular building blocks that have amused so many young builders are the inspiration behind this Carlsbad amusement park. It's one of four Legoland parks around the world, and the only one located in North America.

Many of the rides in the park use a super-size version of the signature design and colors of the bricks, while other attractions are actually made out of Lego pieces. Don't miss the amazing Miniland, USA, which displays seven regions of the United States, all animated and constructed completely out of 20 million Lego bricks. You'll see Cape Canaveral, window washers scaling a New York City skyscraper, and a busy San Francisco pier, complete with little Lego sea lions basking in the sun. Other marvels in the park include a fiery red,

9-foot-tall, 34-foot-long Lego dinosaur and a carefully constructed scene of a woman on a balcony watering her petunias.

Many displays are geared to toddlers and preschoolers. A favorite is the Fairy Tale Brook, where guests can take a boat ride through enchantingly constructed versions of their favorite fairy tales. At the Musical Fountain they can step on colored circles surrounding a huge fountain to make instruments play a lively tune.

Kids love the 120 acres of fun rides, entertaining shows, and imaginative buildings that make up Legoland. The Coast Cruise is one of the park's 50 rides.

Older kids will enjoy the roller coasters and the funny Royal Joust, where they ride galloping Lego hobbyhorses. They'll also enjoy driving cars on a grid of streets complete with traffic lights and stop signs—after they learn the rules of the road, of course. An unusual Knights' Tournament ride turns and twists in the air and lets guests choose the ride's thrill factor and intensity level.

It just wouldn't be a full day without some hands-on Lego activity. A trip to the Imagination Zone will let the kids try their hands at construction, with an endless

You can take a trip around the country and never leave California! Kids love visiting the miniature version of the nation's capital created from Lego bricks.

supply of Legos and Duplos. At the model shop, kids can see master builders create new and exciting Lego models for the park right before their eyes.

BIG SUR COASTLINE

This scenic stretch of coastline has a breathtaking beauty that invites many stops for family pictures. One minute you're standing atop a high cliff looking down at a crashing sapphire sea, and the next you're hiking through a misty redwood forest. The Big Sur coastline begins just south of Monterey, where Point Lobos Reserve encompasses a group of headlands, coves, and rolling meadows. Hiking trails follow the shoreline, where you'll probably catch a glimpse of sea otters floating on their backs and snacking on abalone. Between the months of December and May, migrating gray whales are a common sight.

On your drive you'll come to Garrapata State Park, which features two miles of beaches, dense redwood groves, and a fun hike up to a beautiful view of the Pacific. Another must-see is Jade Cove, accessible by a rugged, rocky pathway to the beach. Here pieces of jade litter the pebbly shoreline, and visitors are allowed to take home what they can carry. Be sure to stop in at Nepenthe, a legendary restaurant perched on high cliffs whose outdoor seating area looks out across the vast Pacific and down the Big Sur coastline.

You'll find rustic campsites as well as luxury hotels as you drive along Big Sur coastline. The scenery is fantastic—its dramatic, rocky beaches are quite a departure from those found in southern California.

THE GETTY CENTER

Collections of world-class European paintings and sculpture may not sound appealing to many children at first, but the Getty Center's spacious layout invites exploring. Kids love roaming the center's gardens and patios and snacking at its outdoor café.

The museum is located atop a hill. Kids enjoy the tram ride to the top, where they'll find a stunning view of Los Angeles and a courtyard with fountains, benches, and snack bars.

On your way into the galleries, pick up a copy of the Art Detective Cards or the brochure titled "Family Fun at the Getty" to help guide your visit.

Each exhibit features descriptions to engage children. The collections are housed in separate buildings.

When your kids have finished viewing the treasures in one building, you'll head outside to get to the next gallery—a perfect way to explore the Getty's gardens, plazas, and pools.

After you take in the exhibits at the Getty Center, enjoy the view that overlooks the Los Angeles area.

OREGON DUNES
NATIONAL RECREATION AREA

This glorious national recreation area is filled with wind-sculpted dunes that tower nearly 500 feet above sea level and stretch 40 miles along the Oregon coast. It's a popular spot for families who enjoy hiking, fishing, canoeing, horseback riding, and camping.

A major lure that attracts many families is the chance to go roaring across the dunes in all-terrain vehicles (ATVs). Oregon Dunes National Recreation Area contains some of the best ATV and dune buggy areas in the United States. A number of rental locations can be found along the coast, from Florence to North Bend.

Since ATVs and hiking don't mix, three ATV areas for riders of all experience levels have been designated in locations separate from the areas for camping and other outdoor activities. The area also has several large lakes that are perfect for waterskiing and swimming.

Like a vast ocean of sand, the Oregon Dunes are constantly shifting and changing. Widely known for its ATV trails, the recreation area also has more than 30 lakes and ponds and a variety of hiking trails for active families.

SEASIDE

Seaside is a family favorite first discovered by vacationers in the mid-1800s. This coastal town in Oregon offers a wide, smooth beach dotted with playgrounds and volleyball nets. Its boardwalk has an aquarium and a classic amusement park with bumper cars and saltwater taffy. Seaside is a national landmark and marks the end of the Lewis and Clark National Historic Trail. The town has a statue commemorating the explorers.

Many find the ocean water a little too cold for swimming. Because the average temperature of the water is about 55 degrees, a wet suit is a practical idea. Many children amuse themselves by splashing at the water's edge, collecting driftwood, and playing in the sand. The ocean waves are excellent for surfing and boogie boarding. Rentals are available.

Kite flying and bike riding are popular pastimes here as well, and a number of shops rent bikes, in-line skates, four-wheeled surreys, and three-wheeled FunCycles designed for pedaling on the packed sand during low tide. The quaint village is filled with intriguing shops, cafés, a carousel, and movie theaters.

Above: *You'll find many reminders that Lewis and Clark ended their journey in what is now the town of Seaside.* Left: *Kids love the wide beaches and a busy boardwalk in Seaside. Romping on its three miles of powdery sand and exploring the oceanfront activities make for an enjoyable family vacation.*

CRATER LAKE NATIONAL PARK

Your first glimpse of Crater Lake in Oregon will be memorable. The caldera in which the sapphire blue lake sits was formed after a series of volcanic explosions; consequently, the landscape is quite rugged and varied. It's the deepest lake in the United States and the seventh deepest in the world.

Rim Drive runs the 33-mile circumference of the lake and features more than 20 scenic overlooks with spectacular views. You can access the shoreline at Cleetwood Cove. At the bottom of a steep trail you'll find tour boats that take visitors around the lake and out to Wizard Island, a small volcanic cone rising from the crystalline water. Camping and hiking through the old-growth forests are also popular, and cross-country skiing is excellent during the eight-month-long winters.

The deep, blue beauty that is Crater Lake results from its great depth and the clarity and purity of its water. Wizard Island was created during a volcanic eruption 7,000 years ago.

In addition to camping, visitors can stay at the historic Crater Lake Lodge. Built in 1915, the lodge is located on the edge of the caldera and offers views of the lake.

THE COLUMBIA RIVER GORGE AND MULTNOMAH FALLS

The Columbia River Gorge is an impressive river canyon carved by the Columbia as it flows into the Pacific Ocean. The gorge features dramatic cliffs and has the highest concentration of waterfalls in the Pacific Northwest. The combination of climate and location creates a wind tunnel effect in the gorge. As a result, it's a favorite location of windsurfers and kite surfers. A drive through the gorge is frequently enhanced by the sight of the colorful sails and kites pulling surfers through the water at speeds up to 35 miles per hour.

It's an easy hike to see the grand Multnomah Falls, the second highest continuous waterfall in the United States. The trail is paved and crosses a bridge before continuing to a viewpoint at the top.

Kids love the narrated tour on Mount Hood Railroad's excursion train. During the tour's layover in the town of Parkdale they can browse through shops or visit a museum. An old-fashioned stern-wheeler riverboat makes frequent runs up and down the scenic river and provides a relaxing way to take in the sights.

An awesome sight as it cascades 620 feet down Larch Mountain in the Columbia River Gorge, Multnomah Falls attracts about two million visitors each year.

PORTLAND ROSE FESTIVAL AND ROSE GARDENS

After a busy day of sightseeing and traveling, there's no better place to stop and smell the roses. Portland's climate is perfect for growing the popular plant, and in 1889 local rose enthusiasts created the Portland Rose Society to encourage amateurs to cultivate the aromatic flower. A few years later, society members organized the festival and floral parade that has become an annual June tradition.

In its early years, the Rose Festival was highlighted by horse-drawn floats and fireworks. The present-day event includes the flower-festooned Grand Floral Parade. Other favorites are the evening Starlight Parade and the kids-only Junior Parade. The festival's program of events now has hundreds of family-friendly activities and performances, which include a children's stage complete with clowns, jugglers, magicians, and musicians. Dragon boat and milk-carton boat races and tours of naval ships are big attractions for children. Auto races, air shows, a carnival, a Wild West area, food booths, an art show, and musical performances round out the experience. In between the non-stop fun, drop by Portland's famous Rose Gardens and enjoy the abundant colors and heavenly fragrances.

Portland has three separate rose gardens, each featuring hundreds of varieties of the fragrant flower and thousands of plants to peruse.

OLYMPIC NATIONAL PARK

For most people, the term "rain forest" conjures up an image of a hot, steamy jungle located in the tropics. However, Olympic National Park in the northwest corner of Washington contains a temperate rain forest populated by ferns, lichens, salamanders, and stands of old-growth trees adorned with moss. The park embraces three distinctly different ecosystems: snowcapped mountains with alpine meadows that rise at its eastern flank; the rugged wilderness of the Pacific coast that sits at its western edge; and the emerald-colored rain forest between the two.

Booklets that describe many of the park's shorter hiking trails are available at any nature center in the park. The Hall of Mosses Trail in the Hoh Rain Forest is an easy hike and provides an excellent look at the varied plant life. The Marymere Falls Trail at Lake Crescent is a longer hike across wooden bridges to a 90-foot-high waterfall.

The coastline at the Olympic Park's western border offers dramatic cliffs and rocky beaches dotted by tide pools teeming with life. Park naturalists conduct regular tide-pool discovery walks at Rialto and Kalaloch beaches, which kids are sure to find fascinating.

Top: *The view from this pristine mountain meadow in Olympic National Park takes in the majestic peaks. Rugged beaches and lush forests also make up the park, 95 percent of which is designated wilderness area.* Bottom: *You can explore the coastline of Olympic National Park on your own, or take a guided tour that will allow kids a hands-on look at tide pools.*

SEATTLE CENTER

Seattle Center, home of the futuristic Space Needle, is the cultural heart of the city. Its 74 acres are filled with enough high-quality entertainment to keep a family happy for days.

For a view of Seattle Center and beyond, board the Space Needle's glass-enclosed elevator for the 41-second journey to its top. It will bring you 520 feet aboveground, where you can dine in a rotating restaurant or walk around the viewing station for a fabulous panorama of downtown Seattle, Puget Sound, Lake Union, and Mount Rainier.

The Pacific Science Center has attractions for every member of the family. You can learn how an animatronic dinosaur works and walk through a warm, humid tropical butterfly house. The antics of East African naked mole rats, some of the most unusual animals you'll ever see,

are endlessly entertaining. Head to the technology exhibit to play virtual soccer or compete against a robot in a game of tic-tac-toe, or settle into your seat and enjoy some stargazing by way of a live presentation at the planetarium.

The Seattle Children's Museum is filled with hands-on adventure. Visitors of all ages enjoy sending balls through a busy cityscape of pulleys, pipes, mazes, and levers to learn about cause and effect in Cog City. In the Mindscape technology studio, your kids can record a song or

become part of a virtual reality video game. An artist-in-residence is always on hand to guide kids through art projects that relate to various exhibits in the drop-in art studio. Younger children will enjoy the activities in Discovery Bay.

Seattle Center is home to one of the best children's theaters in the country. The Seattle Children's Theatre stages top-notch performances of classic children's literature and new works as well. At the end of every performance, members of the cast return to the stage to conduct a question-

The focal point of the Seattle skyline, the Space Needle overlooks Seattle Center, a mecca of amusement park activity, museums, and restaurants in the heart of the city.

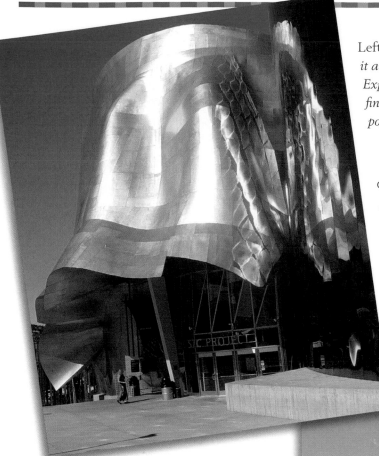

Left: *Its eye-catching design makes it an instant landmark—explore the Experience Music Project and you'll find exciting exhibits that bring popular music to life.*

clothing, musical instruments, and handwritten lyrics.

Children of all ages will enjoy a visit to the Sound Lab, where they can strap on a guitar, climb behind a drum set, or sit at the keyboards in a soundproof studio and play along with their selection of recorded music.

Ready for some outdoor fun? Visit the Center's International Fountain, which attracts children like a magnet during warm, sunny days. A number of grassy knolls and gardens offer ideal locations for a family picnic, and the Fun Forest Amusement Park features a variety of children's rides and games.

Below: *Cool! Seattle Center's International Fountain is a favorite gathering spot for kids on a hot day. The unique attraction was built to resemble the form of a sea urchin.*

and-answer period with members of the young audience.

The Experience Music Project, housed in a gleaming, freeform building designed by Frank Gehry, celebrates musical innovation. The museum is a delight for the senses and uses interactive technology and hands-on exhibits to delve into the influences of various types of music. The city's vibrant musical history is featured in an exhibit about famous rock bands that originated in Seattle, including The Jimi Hendrix Experience, Nirvana, and Pearl Jam. There's an exhibit on the evolution of the guitar, and another in which artists tell their own stories. The museum houses an extensive display of artifacts, including

NORTHWEST FOLKLIFE FESTIVAL

Under the Space Needle, the Northwest Folklife Festival sprawls across the 74 acres of Seattle Center every Memorial Day weekend. The event is a four-day extravaganza of ethnic music, dance, crafts, food, and folklore from more than 100 countries. Eighteen stages offer nonstop performances, demonstrations, and workshops for every imaginable cultural tradition, including gospel music, hula dancing, and barbershop singing. There are also gypsy bands and a hilarious liar's contest. Street performers and artists are everywhere—you can find a musical saw player, a kilt-clad highland piper, and a punked-out preteen virtuoso on the violin.

Programs featuring circus acts, music, storytelling, and crafts are headquartered in the Discovery Zone. Here kids can perform various activities, from creating Chinese dragon masks to building their own harmonica and learning how to play it. The large stages showcase the most popular acts, which might be a group of bluegrass fiddlers, a Brazilian carnival band, or a West African drum corps. The food village offers regional favorites such as berry shortcake and Pacific Northwest salmon; more exotic fare from around the world is also available.

Left: *A colorful celebration since 1972, the Folklife Festival attracts performers from all over the world as well as from the Pacific Northwest.* Below: *Celebrating cultural history, the Northwest Folklife Festival inspires children through ethnic dance, music, and crafts.*

PIKE PLACE MARKET

The fishmongers at Pike Place Market in Seattle put on one of the best shows in town. They toss the catch of the day through the air like a football as they engage the customers in all kinds of banter. They often pick up the largest fish they can shoulder and invite a visitor to pucker up for a kiss.

Other vendors at the market aren't quite as entertaining, but their wares are just as fresh and enticing. Since Washington is the apple state, every apple product imaginable can be found at a variety of shops, including at least 20 kinds of apple butter, cinnamon apples, candy apples, and, in the fall, fresh apples of all varieties.

The market is one of Seattle's most famous landmarks and tourist attractions. More than 100 farmers and 200 artists and craftspeople occupy the market. You'll also find an assortment of retail shops. Spanning three levels, the market offers the best of Washington's seasonal flowers and produce. Visitors can shop among the vivid colors of exquisite tulips and daffodils in early spring and enjoy juicy golden Rainier cherries in early summer, blueberries in August, and all kinds of high-quality, locally grown produce year-round. Amusing street performers are regulars at the market, and you can choose from a wide assortment of restaurants and cafés, including the world's first Starbucks.

Called the soul of Seattle, Pike Place Market began in 1907 as a public market for consumers to buy directly from growers. It's grown into a major tourist destination with hundreds of shops and restaurants. Kids love its bustling activity.

SAN JUAN ISLANDS

North of Seattle in Puget Sound sits the San Juan Archipelago, a collection of 172 named islands and another several hundred rocky island outcroppings that appear at low tide. Although about 40 of these idyllic islands are inhabited, most people living here reside on the four that have ferry service: San Juan, Orcas, Lopez, and Shaw. Many families take bicycles aboard the ferry to explore the islands at a leisurely pace.

The islands' sheltered waters are home to harbor seals, sea lions, sea otters, dolphins, and orcas. Whale watching is a popular pastime, particularly around Friday Harbor on San Juan Island (the largest island of the group). This area is home to three resident pods of orcas and was the backdrop for the *Free Willy* movie series.

You can learn more about the orcas that populate the waters near the San Juan Islands with a visit to the Whale Museum, located near historic Friday Harbor on San Juan Island.

Take a whale-watching boat tour or head to Lime Kiln Point State Park to play in the sand and watch orcas feed just 30 feet from shore.

WASHINGTON STATE INTERNATIONAL KITE FESTIVAL

The ornate and intricate kites featured in this weeklong festival are worlds away from the diamond-shape structures you used to make out of newspaper, string, and old rags. The festival takes place every August in Long Beach in the southwestern corner of Washington. The event attracts kite fanatics who come to show off their impressive flying skills and stunningly beautiful kites, as well as families looking for a novel way to enjoy a day at the beach.

The festival takes on an international theme with traditional kites from places such as Bali, China, Japan, India, Malaysia, and Thailand. You'll see flying trains made of multiple kites on one string. The aerial dodges, swoops, and twists of stunt kites are great fun to watch, as are the fierce battles of the fighter kites. Kite sizes range from miniscule (there's even a prize for

the smallest) to very large. Some are three-dimensional.

Children have their own section of the beach for flying kites, and there are kite-making workshops and all kinds of competitions. And if you just can't get enough of these flying creations at the festival, a kite museum in town has some fascinating displays and a gift shop.

At the Washington State International Kite Festival you'll see kites of all shapes and sizes representing countries from the far reaches of the world. On the final day of the festival, the crowd is invited to join in the fun and fly their own kites.

First established as Mount McKinley National Park in 1917, Denali has been termed North America's last frontier. Adventure-seeking families will find plenty of opportunities to fish, hike, and camp during the summer months. Winter activities include cross-country skiing and dogsledding.

DENALI NATIONAL PARK & PRESERVE

Denali's rugged, subarctic Alaskan wilderness area encompasses glaciers, tundra, and North America's highest mountain: 20,320-foot-tall Mount McKinley. The park's six million acres are home to grizzly bears, wolves, caribou, and moose, all living in relatively undisturbed isolation. To maintain the stability of the environment, the park has been set up to minimize visitors' impact on the delicate ecosystem, and traffic is strictly controlled. Only the first 14 miles are open to cars; beyond this point, visitors take a shuttle bus or a train to travel deeper into the park.

Most tourists visit in summer, when they can hike, climb, and camp, but the park is also open in winter for dogsledding and ice climbing. Skijoring, a sport where the skier is pulled along the ground on cross-country skis by sled dogs, is also popular. Rangers patrol the park during the winter months on dogsleds, a tradition that began with the first rangers in the 1920s. Families touring in summer can visit the dogs in their kennels. Children will enjoy watching these remarkable dogs and their speed and enthusiasm when they are hitched to a wheeled sled for a short run on a track that circles the kennels.

GLACIER BAY NATIONAL PARK & PRESERVE

The bay and its tidewater glaciers and deep fjords are major attractions at Glacier Bay National Park & Preserve. Nearly one-fifth of this marine wilderness is made up of water, and it features the largest nonpolar ice field in the world. The park is best toured by boat, which allows you to see huge chunks of ice breaking off of glaciers and crashing into the sea. Touring by boat also affords the best chances to catch sight of the many animals that live in the water and along the shore.

Each summer, humpback whales return to the bay from their warm winter homes near Hawaii to feed on shrimp, krill, and schools of small fish. They are a common sight as they leap out of the water and slap back down with a resounding thunder. Minke whales, orcas, and porpoises also feed in the waters just offshore. Steller sea lions congregate on rocky islands, and harbor seals breed and nurture their pups on the floating ice in the park's waters.

Dwarfed by the icy formations that give Glacier Bay National Park & Preserve its name, the tour boat offers the best vantage point to observe the abundance of wildlife found there.

WORLD ICE ART CHAMPIONSHIPS AND KID'S PARK

The world's best ice sculptors convene in Fairbanks in late February or early March to create dozens of frozen sculptures near the center of town. The ice in Fairbanks is considered some of the best in the business, and is so crystal clear that you can read a newspaper through a block that is four feet thick.

For children, the best part of the festival is a captivating four-acre ice playground with an imaginatively carved entrance that may take the form of a fairyland castle or an icy fortress with ice-cream-cone turrets. Inside, kids will find an amazing world of slides, rides, mazes, and houses—all made of ice. A favorite of many younger

children is a ride known as "the twirly," made of giant ice-carved Easter baskets that hold the child as you spin them across the ice.

The imaginative ice slides take all forms, from giant roller skates to the slippery tentacles of a two-story octopus. The *Brontosaurus* slide is a favorite, as children

glide down its frozen curving tail. Mazes carved into the ice are perfect for crawling kiddies, and cabins and carved ice trains complete the frozen playground. At night, the sculptures are illuminated with colored lights, giving the appearance of a stained glass landscape.

After the children enjoy the icy playground, take in the amazing sights of the ice art championship, which features three ice-sculpting events. The Single Block Classic consists of two-person teams that carve their magic from a 7,200-pound block of ice. In the Multi-Block Classic, four-person teams use 12 huge blocks of ice. The teams use everything from chainsaws to dental drills to shape their icy monoliths into works of art. Their efforts often require them to climb atop high scaffolding. The final event, the Fairbanks Open, is for anyone interested in trying their hand at ice carving (it is not a competition). Visit the park while the sculptors are at work to fully appreciate the labor and imagination that goes into each creation.

Opposite: *You can only imagine what the artist will create from these blocks of ice. If you return the next day to the World Ice Art Championships, you'll no doubt find an imaginative, intricate sculpture.* Above: *The championship began in 1988, when established artists were invited to Alaska to teach their craft to local ice carvers.* Right: *Beautiful, but only for a short time, the amazing sculptures created at the World Ice Art Championships will last until the first thaw.*

IDITAROD SLED DOG RACE

The longest dogsled race in the world covers 1,150 miles from Anchorage to Nome along an old mail route known as the Iditarod Trail. Many children know of its beginnings from the story of Balto, the famous sled dog. In 1925, an epidemic struck Nome and the hospital needed medicine as soon as possible. The city had few roads and no railroads, frequent snowstorms had grounded airplanes, and boats couldn't navigate the frozen Bering Sea. Sled dogs saved the day, relaying the medicine from Anchorage across the snow and ice to Nome, and Balto was the lead dog of the final leg of the trip.

The present-day Iditarod kicks off on the first Saturday in March, when mushers and their teams of 12 to 16 dogs take off from Anchorage. Kids love watching the teams of eager barking dogs dash from their starting positions. Volunteers and non-mushers get involved in the race in a number of ways. Some people bid for the chance to ride with a musher for the first 11 miles of the race, while others make booties for the dogs to wear to protect their feet from the ice and snow.

… And here's a pat on the head before you go. These sled dogs will cover more than 1,000 miles across Alaska during the Iditarod.

HAWAII VOLCANOES NATIONAL PARK

Not many national parks offer a daily lava flow update so you know where to go—or not go—to view these molten masses. Updates are available via phone, on the park's Web site, and at the Kilauea Visitor Center at the entrance to Hawaii Volcanoes National Park. Rangers at the center will help you plan your visit. Older children will enjoy the spectacle of a live lava flow, but families with young children should proceed with caution through the park, where a number of areas are closed to the public.

The park sets the standard for volcanoes, as it is home to the world's most massive volcano, Mauna Loa, as well as Kilauea, the world's most active volcano. Kilauea has been spewing lava constantly since 1983 and has added more than 500 acres of land to the Big Island. You can drive the Chain of Craters Road throughout the park, but exploring the area on foot is an exciting experience. The Halema'uma'u Overlook is about a ten-minute walk from the road and offers views of a bubbling crater that is 3,000

feet across and almost 300 feet deep. Another favorite hike for families is the 20-minute walk through a rain forest to the giant Thurston Lava Tube, a cavelike formation that was created hundreds of years ago during an eruption on Kilauea's summit.

Below: *A moving mass of molten lava meets the ocean water in a release of steam—just one of the incredible sights at Hawaii Volcanoes National Park. Informational programs at this fascinating destination will give children insight into how the islands were formed.*

Inset: *Kilauea Volcano is known as the "drive-up volcano" because of its many roads and paths that afford easy access to its active areas.*

The USS Arizona Memorial

The USS *Arizona* Memorial in Oahu stretches across the water above the sunken midsection of the battleship on which 1,177 crewmembers died during the attack on Pearl Harbor in 1941. It's a poignant and moving reminder of the tragic event that led to America's involvement in World War II. Children will learn about the attack in a 23-minute film that precedes a short boat ride on a Navy launch to the memorial.

The memorial is divided into three main sections: the entry and assembly rooms; a central area designed for ceremonies and general observation; and the shrine room, where the names of those killed on the *Arizona* are engraved on a marble wall. Be sure to ask for the informative booklet specifically designed to help children understand what the monument represents. It guides young visitors through the events of the attack and explains the importance of remembering those who died.

Top: *The unique design of the USS Arizona Memorial was intended by its architect to reflect the mood of the country immediately following Pearl Harbor. Sagging at the center, the structure stands strong at both ends, indicating initial defeat but ultimate victory.* Bottom: *Visible just below the surface of the water, the battleship lies beneath the memorial that bears its name.*

WAIKIKI BEACH

This famous two-mile stretch of sand in Oahu is home to scores of family-friendly beach hotels and all kinds of action-packed excitement. Waikiki Beach is the perfect place to go if you're looking for warm ocean water and golden beaches. Kids will enjoy strolling along the beachfront promenade, stopping for shaved ice or an ice-cream cone, taking a dip in the ocean, and checking out the parade of people passing by.

Be sure to take an exhilarating ride in an outrigger canoe, where you paddle out beyond the breakers and are carried back to shore by the ocean's cresting waves. Waikiki is an excellent place to learn to surf, and lessons are available at just about every hotel or water sports center on the beach.

If you can tear yourself away from the water, hike the landmark volcanic crater Diamond Head, visit the indigenous animals of Honolulu Zoo, or tour the Bishop Museum to view an interesting collection of Polyncsian artifacts.

Paradise at the end of a rainbow, the famous stretch of sand known as Waikiki Beach is a natural playground for vacationing families who enjoy swimming, snorkeling, and surfing.

OAHU'S NORTH SHORE BIG SURF COMPETITION

Some of the tallest ocean waves in the world are found at Oahu's acclaimed North Shore coastline during the winter months. These crashing walls of water are perfect for surfing and offer one of the best free shows on the islands. The North Shore is home to world-renowned surf contests such as the Vans Triple Crown, which is held here from early November to late December and attracts the world's top surfers. Another contest, the impromptu Eddie Aikau Big Wave Invitational, is never scheduled in advance. This event is put together at the last minute anytime the waves reach heights of 20 feet or more.

There are a number of locations around the island to watch intrepid surfers catch the big waves. Some of the preferred locations are Sunset Beach, Waimea Bay, Ali'i Beach Park, and Ehukai Beach Park, home of the famed Banzai Pipeline. The waves may be larger at Sunset and Waimea, but at Ehukai, when the waves surge from deep water onto a shallow coral reef, a perfect, treacherous tube, or pipeline, is formed. Families can settle in with a picnic lunch and watch the action from the beach.

Oahu's North Shore is the perfect place to "hang ten." In the winter months, it's a surfer's paradise thanks to the monster waves that roll in from Alaska, 2,000 miles away. During the summer, the calm waters are perfect for diving and snorkeling.

The festive Canoe Pageant presents a colorful interpretation of Pacific history presented in song and dance at the Polynesian Cultural Center.

POLYNESIAN CULTURAL CENTER

The colorful costumes, lively songs, and intricate dances of a number of Pacific region cultures are presented at the Polynesian Cultural Center in Oahu. You'll see Fiji, New Zealand, Marquesas, Samoa, Tahiti, Tonga, and Hawaii all represented in these authentically re-created island villages scattered about the 42-acre property decorated with palm trees and tropical gardens. You can travel to each village on foot over a series of bridges or by canoe along the freshwater lagoon that links each village.

Every stop has something for children to enjoy. They can fish, bowl, play shuffleboard, take hula lessons, and try their hand at many more activities. Natives in each village demonstrate crafts and skills such as creating clothing from bark, sparking a fire by rubbing sticks together, and climbing a coconut tree. Each day ends with a lavish luau and Polynesian revue that features more than 100 native performers from all corners of the Pacific.

WAIMEA CANYON

Dubbed "The Grand Canyon of the Pacific" by Mark Twain, Waimea Canyon's sharply eroded cliffs reveal layers of vivid colors that seem to change in the sun. Unlike the Grand Canyon, plentiful rainfall keeps this canyon and its surrounding area thick with vegetation, and visitors are frequently treated to the sight of vivid rainbows. At ten miles long, one mile wide, and more than 3,500 feet deep, this Kauai landmark is the largest canyon in the Pacific.

Hiking is one way to see this breathtaking natural wonder. Numerous lookouts are provided along the trails. In Waimea Canyon State Park, try the Kukui/Iliau Loop Trail, an easy 15-minute quarter-mile nature walk with markers that identify the forest plants. It offers a great canyon view and a covered picnic area. A more rigorous hike that older children may enjoy is the Canyon Trail to Waipo'o Falls.

Another popular way to see Waimea is from the air. Helicopter excursions give passengers an excellent perspective as they circle the canyon and soar along the Na Pali Coast, where high mountain cliffs rise from the ocean floor.

Above: *The verdant green beauty of Waimea Canyon can be appreciated by helicopter, from a car, or on foot along its 45 miles of hiking trails that crisscross the valley and outlying areas.* Left: *The lines visible in the canyon walls in Waimea indicate different volcanic eruptions and lava flows that have occurred over the centuries.*

KAPALUA BEACH

Hawaii is home to hundreds of gorgeous sandy beaches, and the sunny island of Maui certainly has its fair share. But many consider the golden sand of Maui's Kapalua Beach to be the best of all the Hawaiian Islands.

Kapalua is especially well suited for families with small children. It is situated on a sheltered stretch of a crescent-shape bay that protects it from any rough surf. Coral reefs and rocky peninsulas further protect the shore. The calm water and an easily accessible reef make it an excellent place for children to learn to snorkel. They'll love the colorful tropical fish and vivid coral formations.

In early spring, humpback whales are a common sight just offshore. The whales give birth to their calves in the warm island waters and remain until both mother and calf are strong enough to swim back to their feeding grounds in the Arctic.

In a part of the country known for beautiful beaches, Kapalua ranks as one of the most family-friendly. Volcanic rocks at both ends of the stretch of beach protect it from the swells of winter storms and make it safe for swimming year-round.

CANADA AND MEXICO

Located at opposite ends of the continent, Canada and Mexico offer unique vacations with different cultures for families to experience. Canadian attractions include the Hockey Hall of Fame and the breathtaking beauty of Banff National Park and Lake Louise. Mexico's beaches beckon with white sand and warm water, and its lively, unusual festivals are a treat for the entire family. Many popular destinations feature tours of the country's archaeological treasures and provide a fascinating look at Mexico's history.

Niagara Falls, Canada–United States Border

OLD QUEBEC

Canada's walled city, Old Quebec, is the only fortified city in North America. A three-mile-long wall of ancient stone surrounds Old Quebec, a designated World Heritage Site, and separates it from Quebec City. Historic Old Quebec features an abundance of 17th- and 18th-century buildings and is located on a steep hill, overlooking the St. Lawrence River.

Old Quebec is divided into Upper Town and Lower Town. The two sections are connected by a tram railway, or funicular, that travels between them. Another way to get from Upper to Lower Town is to use the old-fashioned route and climb the sharply angled Breakneck Stairs.

Lower Town is a captivating maze of winding streets, many of which have been restored to their romantic 18th-century appearance. The pedestrian-only Rue du Petit-Champlain is lined with quaint shops, cafés, and restaurants. In Place Royale, the restored main square, costumed fencers stage mock sword fights, blacksmiths pound at forges, and street performers entertain the crowds.

Within the thick ramparts of Upper Town are old stone houses, famous churches, and majestic historic buildings. Each structure is made of gray stone, a building material used widely throughout

The regal Château Frontenac has been a familiar sight in Old Quebec since the late 19th century. The legendary landmark has welcomed a wide variety of guests, including world leaders, royalty, and celebrities.

THE ICE HOTEL

If you're looking for some unusual accommodations for the night, check out the Ice Hotel. Located about 30 minutes from Quebec City on beautiful Lake St. Joseph, this hotel is constructed of ice, and each year its architecture is unique. The seasonal structure takes about five weeks to build and requires 4,500 tons of snow and 250 tons of ice. It opens during the winter months, shutting down in late March as the warmer weather returns.

Its icy interior doesn't seem cozy, but Quebec's Ice Hotel is a popular tourist attraction. Overnight guests sleep on illuminated blocks of ice while tucked in warm sleeping bags on beds of deer pelts. All eating and drinking utensils are likewise made of ice. You don't have to be an overnight guest at the hotel to tour its frozen rooms and ice sculpture galleries. Dogsledding, cross-country skiing, and other activities are available nearby.

the old city. Above Old Quebec rises the distinctive Château Frontenac, a spire-topped hotel that is one of the signature buildings of the skyline.

Set aside some time to visit the Museum of Civilization and its Canadian Children's Museum. The International Village exhibit has numerous interactive displays, and during the summer children can play in Adventure World, an outdoor exhibit. Canada Hall has life-size displays from the daily life of Quebec's residents through the generations. Performers often interact with visitors in this area.

THE CARNAVAL DE QUEBEC

Just because much of the region is in the grips of winter is no reason not to have a party. The 17-day Carnaval de Quebec traditionally takes place from late January to early February. The event's cheerful snowman mascot, Bonhomme, is a common sight among its more than 300 activities—many taking place at the 268-acre Place Desjardins. Portions of the site are transformed into an ice palace, complete with a children's area with games and an ice maze. A remarkable human foosball game (left) features players who are actually linked on metal poles and shuffle together to try to kick a ball. Maple sugar shacks offer sweet treats, and vendors also sell hot drinks and deep-fried snacks called beaver tails. Participants can enjoy live entertainment or climb a 30-foot ice tower that features slides to the bottom. Other activities include skating, snow rafting, sledding, and skijoring (a cross between cross-country skiing and dogsledding).

PRINCE EDWARD ISLAND

Pastoral Prince Edward Island is Canada's smallest province. Ringed by sandy beaches, the island's quiet countryside features gently rolling hills and scenic farms. It was home to author Lucy Maud Montgomery and served as the setting for her popular *Anne of Green Gables* book series.

Many tourists to the island are fans of the books, and local businesses have embraced this fan base by creating tourist attractions that are charming and fun and maintain the innocent appeal of the series.

First, pay a visit to Avonlea Village, which creates a turn-of-the-century island setting. The Anne of Green Gables Museum is a popular attraction, as is the musical based on the book. In August, the L. M. Montgomery Festival sponsors writing workshops for children ages 12 through 16. Ice-cream socials, horse-and-buggy rides, Victorian games, and a family barn dance are also part of the summer fun.

Even if you haven't read *Anne of Green Gables,* you'll still enjoy a trip to the island. Visitors seeking outdoor adventures can take harbor tours or go seal watching, kayaking, deep-sea fishing, or canoeing. There are trails to hike, clams to dig, lighthouses to climb, and beaches to explore.

Author L. M. Montgomery based much of Anne of Green Gables on her own experiences. Both the author and the fictional heroine of the series grew up as orphans on Prince Edward Island in the early 1900s. The Green Gables House, pictured below, is open to visitors.

NIAGARA FALLS

This famous wall of water at the Canadian and U.S. border is the most powerful waterfall in North America. Once a popular honeymoon destination, Niagara Falls now attracts tourists and families from all over the world.

There are several exciting ways to get as close as possible to its thundering spray. In Ontario, on the Canadian side, don a raincoat and visit the Journey Behind the Falls observation deck. As you peer out, the river explodes in front of you after it free-falls more than 13 stories. The sound of the crashing water is deafening. Or take a boat ride on *The Maid of the Mist* tour, which has been in operation since 1846. These powerful boats take you through the churning waters around the American Falls to the foot of Horseshoe Falls, where millions of gallons of water plummet into a frothy, turbulent pool. The tour provides raingear, but you're still likely to get wet.

Don't miss seeing Niagara Falls after dark, when powerful spotlights bathe the water in ever-changing colors. The light catches the mist, giving the entire area an otherworldly glow. In summer, fireworks displays enhance the splendor of the setting.

Right: *The thundering majesty of Niagara Falls never fails to amaze those who visit. The natural wonder is the second largest waterfall in the world.* Inset: *More than 12 million people visit Niagara Falls each year, and many board* The Maid of the Mist *to get a soggy perspective of the falls.*

Hockey Hall of Fame

You'll need quick reflexes at the Hockey Hall of Fame in Toronto, Ontario—that way, you can block the shots from a virtual Wayne Gretzky and Mark Messier. Put on the pads and step into the action as the two legends launch lightning-fast foam pucks in your direction. Next, grab a stick, step onto the plastic "ice," and go up against a video version of goalie Ed Belfour. A machine records your reaction time, accuracy, and speed.

Kids are certain to enjoy the many interactive exhibits at the Hall of Fame, but don't overlook the other interesting hockey displays. You'll see videos of big games and their highlights, goalie masks, skate and stick collections, jerseys that belonged to some of hockey's greatest stars, and a replica of the Montreal Canadiens' locker room. The original 1893 Stanley Cup resides at the Hall of Fame, along with other legendary hockey memorabilia.

Most visitors to the Hockey Hall of Fame stop at the Stanley Cup display as part of their tour. The cup, first presented in 1893, bears the names of more than 2,000 hockey champions.

CALGARY STAMPEDE

The Calgary Stampede in Alberta is Canada's largest annual event. It's also the world's richest rodeo, awarding one million dollars in prize money to the winners of such daring competitions as bareback and bull riding, barrel racing, steer wrestling, roping, and chuck wagon racing. The event draws rodeo champions from all over the world.

During Stampede Week, everyone in the city of Calgary gets into the rodeo mood: Storefronts are decorated in a Western theme, and Calgary residents swap their regular clothes for boots, jeans, and ten-gallon hats. Most of the events take place in Stampede Park, a fairground that was specially built to accommodate the Stampede. Some of the attractions you'll find there are an amusement park, a pet-

Be careful taking those corners! The Chuck Wagon Race is the signature event at the Calgary Stampede. Some say the event originated during the land rush days when settlers raced to stake their claims.

ting zoo, a number of livestock barns, and musical entertainment on multiple stages. A Kid's Midway features rides and rodeo events for children ages 4 through 12.

But the main attractions are the rodeo events. Some of the best riders compete during Stampede Week. The world-famous Chuck Wagon Race is exactly that—a race of old-fashioned wagons pulled by teams of horses thundering around the track. A nightly Grandstand Show features an extravaganza of entertainers.

BANFF NATIONAL PARK

Banff National Park in Alberta is an extraordinary landscape of craggy, snowcapped peaks that make up the Alberta Rocky Mountains. The park is known for its year-round recreational activities. During the summer, the most scenic areas can be reached on day hikes. Banff has more than 80 maintained trails that cover about 1,000 miles of park land, and they range from leisurely strolls to arduous long-distance treks. One especially lovely short hike from the town of

Banff will take you past dramatic Bow Falls and along the scenic Bow River on easy-to-follow trails. You can also enjoy the scenery on bicycle, on horseback, or in a horse-drawn carriage.

Take a gondola ride to the top of Sulphur Mountain for a beautiful view of Banff's landscape. At the top, several hiking trails fan out along the mountain ridges; whichever you choose, you can't go wrong. If you're looking for something less strenuous than a mountain hike, you

Azure lakes and rivers, dramatic mountain peaks, and dense forests are part of the scenic wonders of Banff National Park. You can hike, bike, or drive through the many different areas of the park.

can find picturesque views from the lovely boardwalk trail.

Banff is a world-class ski resort and offers a wide variety of winter sports, including downhill skiing, cross-country skiing, snowshoe treks, toboggan rides, and dogsledding.

LAKE LOUISE

Snowcapped mountain peaks and formidable glaciers cradle Lake Louise's emerald depths in a natural, icy amphitheater. Situated in Banff National Park in Alberta, it offers one of the most breathtaking views in the world and is a popular vacation site. Lake Louise is a diamond in the wilderness, and its crystal clear waters, glaciers, and waterfalls make it Canada's most famous lake.

The Lake Louise area is known as one of Canada's premier hiking spots. The landscape is crisscrossed by trails that you can take through wooded areas and into high meadows, with stops at overlooks that offer breathtaking views. You can also rent horses for a leisurely ride around the lake or rent a rowboat or canoe to enjoy its mirrored waters.

Teatime amid the splendor of Banff National Park awaits those who hike the 4.5-mile round-trip along Lake Agnes Trail, which begins at the shores of Lake Louise. The trail leads you through a magnificent old-growth forest past Mirror Lake and Bridal Veil Falls before reaching the Lake Agnes Teahouse, where you can stop for refreshments. Farther up the trail, a longer and more arduous hike better suited for older children will take you to yet another teahouse, The Plain of Six Glaciers.

Canoeing in the calm waters of Lake Louise is a great family outing. Don't forget the binoculars—you'll see a variety of wildlife along the lake's edge and in the surrounding mountains.

WEST EDMONTON MALL

Even though this mall in Alberta contains 800 retail stores and businesses, it's more reminiscent of a theme park than a shopping center. It features the world's largest indoor amusement park, a lagoon with a sea lion show, a professional-size ice rink, and 21 movie theaters—and that's just for starters. The huge mall offers electric scooters for rent to help visitors get around.

Even in the dead of Canadian winter, kids can spend the day in their swimsuits at World Waterpark, which boasts North America's biggest wave pool. It has water-slides, rapids rides, play areas for young children, and all kinds of traditional water park fun. Galaxyland Amusement Park's 25 rides include Mindbender—a 14-story, triple-loop roller coaster—and Space Shot, a 120-foot, heart-pounding free fall.

The mall aquarium houses a shark exhibit as well as an assortment of other interesting creatures. Another popular attraction is an indoor lake where you can take scuba-diving lessons, go on a tour by self-propelled submarine, or rent a canoe.

Compared to all these glitzy and elaborate entertainments, some of the mall's other amusements—a 25-lane bowling alley, a miniature golf course, numerous video game arcades, a casino, and an exact replica of Christopher Columbus's ship the *Santa Maria*—may seem like small change but are actually great fun.

It's easy to forget all about shopping at the West Edmonton Mall. Kids love the variety of entertainment, including an invading ship.

VICTORIA AND VANCOUVER ISLAND

Most visitors travel to the friendly capital of British Columbia by ferry, and as they approach the town they see its beautiful Inner Harbour and the peaked roofline of the famous Empress Hotel. After leaving the ferry you may enjoy a spot of tea at the grand old Empress, where the dance scenes for the 1994 movie *Little Women* were filmed. The menu features tiny tea sandwiches, scones with fresh Jersey cream, ripe strawberries, and miniature pastries.

Victoria is also famous for its Butchart Gardens, 55 acres of internationally acclaimed botanical gardens.

A favorite section for children is the Sunken Garden, where they descend a set of stairs into a valley of blooming flowers. On summer evenings, the gardens are alive with music, and their beauty is enhanced by the dramatic lighting that bathes each section.

Bicycling around the island is a popular family pastime and an ideal way to take in its many sights. During your excursion, stop at Miniature World, where younger children will enjoy the tiny landscapes. The British Columbia Museum has many fascinating exhibits and houses a world-renowned collection of totem poles carved by native peoples.

Above: The most photographed attraction on Vancouver Island, the Empress Hotel is famous for its afternoon teas, elegant affairs that attract 75,000 visitors each year. What better time for kids to show off their very proper manners? Right: Named a National Historic Site in 2004, Butchart Gardens is a 55-acre display of floral wonders. On Saturday nights during the summer months, the gardens are illuminated by a fireworks display.

CHICHÉN ITZÁ

When you come upon the ancient city of Chichén Itzá, located on the Yucatán Peninsula, its role as the seat of power in the Mayan world is vividly clear. Massive pyramids, huge stone courts, dozens of temples, and wide plazas are spread out across a vast grassy plain. Bas-relief carvings on the walls of many of the structures include scenes of daily life and depictions of fierce warriors, serpents, jaguars, eagles, and various other animals.

As you tour the area, it's quite easy to imagine life in the city during the Mayan Classic Period of A.D. 300 to 900. It is the most completely restored archaeological site in the Yucatán, and its scale is tremendous.

There are many engrossing sites to visit, but three in particular will prove fascinating to older children. At 75 feet tall, the great stone pyramid known as El Castillo is the tallest structure on the site. Climbing it is a highlight for most children, and from its peak they can survey the great city of Chichén Itzá and the jungles beyond.

Northwest of El Castillo is Chichén Itzá's ancient stone court, where Mayan men played a game called *pok ta pok*. Balls made of rubber harvested from native trees have been discovered in ancient tombs and

Scaling the heights of ancient El Castillo is quite a feat for kids. Chichén Itzá was the scene of many ancient athletic events and rituals that represented Mayan religious beliefs.

are believed to have been used in the game, which involved hurling a ball through one of two stone rings located on either wall of the court. The captain of the losing team was decapitated as a sacrifice to the gods. Carved scenes on the court walls show Mayan ballplayers dressed in heavy protective padding. The carving further details a headless player kneeling while another player holding the head looks on. Be sure to test the acoustics of the court—

a whisper at one end can be heard at the opposite side, and if you clap or whistle, the echo reverberates throughout the court.

A short distance from the main section of Chichén Itzá is the Sacred Cenote, a deep, steep-sided pool used for ceremonial purposes, where sacrificial victims were drowned. Archaelologists explored the cenote in the 20th century, and divers retrieved human remains and a fortune in gold and jade.

Kids will be amazed at what the Mayans accomplished without modern machines and construction equipment. Slaves carried and dragged huge blocks of stone to construct ancient Mayan temples.

Exploring the many other fascinating archaeological treasures from this ancient civilization can take at least a full day. Plan your visit so you can see the evening sound-and-light show, a delightful spectacle of pomp and artistry.

XCARET AND XEL-HA

Xcaret and Xel-Ha in Cancún's Riviera Maya represent the latest innovation in theme parks: They incorporate the assets of their tropical surroundings into exciting activities that introduce the heritage and history of Mexico to park visitors.

Xcaret is noted for its unusual underground river passages. These passages were originally used by the Mayans for stealth warfare. The coral-and-limestone ceilings of the passageways have been chiseled a bit higher and wider to allow for the easy passage of visitors bobbing through with life jackets. You can also snorkel in a lagoon, swim with the dolphins, see animal exhibits, and visit Mayan ruins and a re-created Mayan village. Xcaret presents an extravagant evening show that begins with an exhibition of traditional Mayan games. The show also features a cast of 200, performing folk dances and folk songs.

Although smaller in acreage, Xel-Ha offers a full day's activities.

It features a large lagoon for snorkeling, ruins to explore, hidden beaches with hammocks for relaxing, and a Mayan cave. If you're looking for an authentic lazy river ride, you'll find it here in a spring-fed river that has just enough current to take you on an easy trip downstream. You can investigate Xel-Ha's deep limestone cenotes. Xel-Ha is home to more than 100 species of birds and 350 species of plants, and its surrounding jungle offers a variety of hiking trails.

Below: *Mayan statues remain in the archaeological sites at Xcaret, a destination that provides adventure and insight into the ancient people who once lived there.* Bottom: *The inviting lagoon at Xel-Ha is home to thousands of colorful fish and beautiful coral formations. It's a perfect spot for adventurous snorkelers.*

DAY OF THE DEAD AND NIGHT OF THE RADISHES FESTIVALS

Located in the state of Oaxaca on the Pacific coast, the city of Oaxaca is known for its artistically carved wood figurines, its coffee, and its enthusiastic celebration of two very unusual festivals: Day of the Dead and Night of the Radishes.

Day of the Dead may sound like a somber affair, but in Mexico it's a joyful and cherished celebration that honors the spirits of deceased family members and friends. This tradition is celebrated with great enthusiasm, artistry, and spirituality in Oaxaca. The town's marketplace comes alive on October 31 with handcrafted decorations and homemade treats that are used to decorate the graves of loved ones. On that night, families head to the cemetery to clean and decorate the graves; they then stay up all night to welcome the souls. Elaborate, multicolor sand paintings are fashioned on top of, or next to, the graves, and the cemetery glows with candlelight throughout the night.

The festival known as Night of the Radishes began about 100 years ago during the Christmas season. Vegetable growers attempting to attract customers seized the idea of carving designs into their produce. The large variety of radishes grown in Mexico proved to be

easy to carve. The practice became an annual tradition, and with it grew a friendly competition that has evolved into the annual Night of the Radishes Festival.

Beginning at midday on December 23, Oaxaca's town square is turned into a fantasyland of intricately carved radishes. The creativity that goes into the displays is amazing. Depictions of the Nativity, elaborate market scenes, and lively mariachi bands are just a few of the finished products on display. Help for novice radish carvers is available in a designated beginner's area. The evening concludes with a fireworks celebration.

Top: *In Oaxaca, Day of the Dead is a joyful celebration where cemeteries are awash in candlelight all night.*
Bottom: *Many kids will believe it's just one more reason not to eat their vegetables—the celebration known as Night of the Radishes features some wonderful creations.*

WHALE WATCHING IN THE SEA OF CORTEZ

Every year, thousands of gray whales migrate to the warm coastal waters of Mexico's Baja Peninsula to mate and give birth. They migrate from their summer homes in the Bering and Chukchi seas between Alaska and Siberia, a journey of more than 6,000 miles. While other types of whales also winter in the Sea of Cortez, the gray whales provide the most rewarding experience for whale watchers because they surface about every four or five minutes.

Three locations on Baja's Pacific coast offer particularly good vantage points for watching grays. They include Scammon's Lagoon, about 430 miles south of the U.S.–Mexico border; San Ignacio Lagoon, about 525 miles south of the border; and Magdalena Bay, about 800 miles south of the border. These areas are government-protected marine parks, and whale watching is restricted to boats operated by trained guides.

A number of travel companies specialize in whale-watching trips to the lagoons and other areas of Baja's Pacific coast from mid-December to mid-March, when the numerous gray whales migrate to the area. It's not uncommon to actually pet a whale or see babies just a few days old swimming alongside their mothers.

The warm waters of the Sea of Cortez are home to gray whales and are an excellent whale-watching destination. Kids will be thrilled by a close-up look at these giants.

COZUMEL AND ISLA MUJERES

These two islands offer a quiet departure from nearby Cancún's fast-paced activities and busy beaches. Both islands offer plenty of amenities and are worth a visit in order to combine a relaxing, warm-weather beach vacation with a destination that has true Mexican character.

Cozumel is Mexico's biggest island and can be reached by a 40-minute ferry ride from the mainland's Playa del Carmen, or via air, since the island has an international airport. It's famous for idyllic soft white sand beaches and calm turquoise waters on its western shore. The island is surrounded by three massive reef systems, the Santa Rosa, Colombia, and Palancar, making it a mecca for snorkelers and divers. The eastern, Caribbean side of the island has rockier beaches and rougher waters.

Cozumel's inviting warm waters and spectacular reef system make it a haven for divers. Kids love snorkeling in its calm waters and exploring its beautiful coral reefs.

Two favorite stops are Chankanaab National Park and Chankanaab Lagoon, both located within Isla Cozumel's Reefs National Marine Park. The crystal clear waters of the sheltered lagoon are home to more than 60 species of fish. Its calm water makes it a perfect site for beginning snorkeling.

For a history lesson on the island's Mayan culture, visit the Museum of the Island of Cozumel, located in downtown San Miguel. Its exhibits include a scale model of the island and information about the reef and its inhabitants.

Isla Mujeres is just seven miles from Cancún, and despite the day-trippers who come to play on its beautiful beaches, it remains a serene and peaceful retreat. Most of its hotels are located at Playa del Norte, a large expanse of beach on the northern tip of the island. Isla Mujeres is a popular spot for divers and snorkelers. It is bordered by two reef systems that create a natural aquarium. You cannot rent a car here, but mopeds, bicycles, and golf carts are available, as are taxis.

RESOURCE DIRECTORY

Alabama
Gulf Shores
800-745-7263
www.gulfshores.com

U.S. Space and Rocket Center
800-637-7223
www.spacecamp.com/museum

Alaska
Denali National Park & Preserve
National Park Service
907-683-2294
www.nps.gov/dena

Glacier Bay National Park & Preserve
National Park Service
907-697-2230
www.nps.gov/glba

Iditarod Sled Dog Race
907-248-6874
www.iditarod.com

World Ice Art Championships
  and Kid's Park
Ice Alaska
907-451-8250
www.icealaska.com

Arizona
The Grand Canyon
National Park Service
928-638-7888
www.nps.gov/grca

The Petrified Forest National Park and
  Painted Desert
National Park Service
928-524-6228
www.nps.gov/pefo

Sedona
Sedona Chamber of Commerce
800-288-7336
www.visitsedona.com

Slide Rock State Park
928-282-3034
www.pr.state.az.us/Parks/parkhtml/
  sliderock.html

Arkansas
Arkansas Department of Parks & Tourism
800-628-8725
www.arkansas.com

Blanchard Springs Caverns
USDA Forest Service
888-757-2246
www.fs.fed.us/oonf/ozark/recreation/
  caverns.html

Hot Springs National Park
National Park Service
501-620-6715
www.nps.gov/hosp

Ozark Folk Center State Park
870-269-3851
www.ozarkfolkcenter.com

Ozark–St. Francis National Forests
479-964-7200
www.fs.fed.us/oonf/ozark

California
Alcatraz Island
National Park Service
415-561-4900
www.nps.gov/alcatraz

Big Sur Coastline
Big Sur Chamber of Commerce
831-667-2100
www.bigsurcalifornia.org

California State Railroad Museum
916-445-6645
www.csrmf.org

Disneyland
714-781-4565
disneyland.disney.go.com

Exploratorium
415-397-5673
www.exploratorium.edu

The Getty Center
310-440-7300
www.getty.edu/museum

Hearst Castle
California State Parks
805-927-2020
www.hearstcastle.com

I Madonnari Street Painting Festival
Santa Barbara Festival Office
805-964-4710
www.imadonnarifestival.com

Legoland
760-918-5346
www.legoland.com/california

Monterey Bay Aquarium
831-648-4800
www.mbayaq.org

San Diego Zoo and
  San Diego Wild Animal Park
Zoological Society of San Diego
619-231-1515
www.sandiegozoo.org

Santa Barbara
805-965-3023
www.sbchamber.org

Santa Catalina Island
310-510-1520
www.catalina.com

SeaWorld
800-257-4268
www.seaworld.com/sandiego

Sequoia and Kings Canyon
  National Parks
National Park Service
559-565-3341
www.nps.gov/seki

Tournament of Roses Parade
626-449-4100
www.tournamentofroses.com

Yosemite National Park
National Park Service
209-372-0200
www.nps.gov/yose

Colorado
Glenwood Hot Springs Pool
800-537-7946
www.hotspringspool.com

Great Sand Dunes National Park
National Park Service
719-378-6300
www.nps.gov/grsa

The Manitou and Pikes Peak Cog Railway
719-685-5401
www.cograilway.com

Mesa Verde National Park
National Park Service
970-529-4465
www.nps.gov/meve

Rocky Mountain National Park
National Park Service
970-586-1206
www.nps.gov/romo

Connecticut
Barker Character, Comic &
  Cartoon Museum
203-699-3822
www.barkermuseum.com

Mystic Seaport
860-572-5315
www.mysticseaport.org

Yale Peabody Museum of Natural History
203-432-5050
www.peabody.yale.edu

Delaware
Lewes
Lewes Chamber of Commerce and
  Visitors Bureau, Inc.
877-465-3937
www.leweschamber.com

Winterthur Gardens and
  Enchanted Woods
Winterthur Museum & Country Estate
800-448-3883
www.winterthur.org

Florida
Blizzard Beach
Typhoon Lagoon
407-939-7812
disneyworld.disney.go.com

Busch Gardens, Tampa Bay
888-800-5447
www.buschgardens.com

Destin
Destin Area Chamber of Commerce
850-837-6241
www.destinchamber.com

Everglades National Park
National Park Service
305-242-7700
www.nps.gov/ever

Kennedy Space Center
NASA
321-449-4444
www.kennedyspacecenter.com

St. Augustine
904-825-5033
www.ci.st-augustine.fl.us

Sanibel Island
239-472-1080
www.sanibel-captiva.org

Universal Studios Islands of Adventure
Universal Orlando Resort
407-363-8000
www.universalorlando.com

Venetian Pool
305-460-5306
www.venetianpool.com

Walt Disney World
407-939-6244
disneyworld.disney.go.com

Georgia
Fernbank Museum of Natural History
404-929-6300
www.fernbank.edu/museum

Georgia Aquarium
404-581-4000
www.georgiaaquarium.org

The Golden Isles
Convention and Visitors Bureau
800-809-1790
www.bgivb.com

Savannah
Georgia Department of Economic
  Development
800-847-4842
www.georgia.org

Jekyll Island
Jekyll Island Foundation
912-635-3636
www.jekyllisland.com

The Okefenokee National Wildlife Refuge
U.S. Fish and Wildlife Service
912-496-7836
www.fws.gov/okefenokee

Savannah
Savannah Convention & Visitors Bureau
www.savannah-visit.com

Hawaii
Hawaii Volcanoes National Park
National Park Service
808-985-6000
www.nps.gov/havo

Kapalua Beach
Maui Visitors Bureau
800-525-6284
www.mauichamber.com

Oahu's North Shore Big Surf Competition
North Shore Marketplace
808-637-4558
www.gonorthshore.org

Polynesian Cultural Center
800-367-7060
www.polynesia.com

The USS *Arizona* Memorial
National Park Service
808-422-0561
www.nps.gov/usar

Waikiki Beach
Oahu, Hawaii
800-464-2924
www.gohawaii.com/oahu

Waimea Canyon
800-262-1400
www.kauai-hawaii.com

Idaho
Craters of the Moon National Monument
  and Preserve
National Park Service
208-527-3257
www.nps.gov/crmo

Redfish Lake
800-847-4843
www.visitidaho.org

Sawtooth National Forest
208-737-3200
www.fs.fed.us/r4/sawtooth

Illinois
The Art Institute of Chicago
312-443-3600
www.artic.edu

Chicago International Children's
  Film Festival
Facets Multi-Media
773-281-9075
www.cicff.org

Millennium Park
Chicago Department of Cultural Affairs
312-742-1168
www.millenniumpark.org

Museum of Science and Industry
773-684-1414
www.msichicago.org

Navy Pier
800-595-7437
www.navypier.com

Shedd Aquarium
312-939-2438
www.sheddaquarium.org

Zoolights at Lincoln Park Zoo
312-742-2000
www.lpzoo.com/events/zoolights.html

Indiana
Children's Museum of Indianapolis
317-334-3322
www.childrensmuseum.org

Conner Prairie
800-966-1836
www.connerprairie.org

Holiday World & Splashin' Safari
877-463-2645
www.holidayworld.com

Indianapolis 500 and the 500 Festival
317-927-3378
www.500festival.com

Iowa
Iowa State Fair
800-545-3247
www.iowastatefair.com

Kansas
Dodge City
Dodge City Convention & Visitors Bureau
800-653-9378
www.visitdodgecity.org

The Oz Museum
866-458-8686
www.ozmuseum.com

Kentucky
Kentucky Derby Festival
502-584-6383
www.kdf.org

Louisville Slugger Museum and
  Factory Tour
877-775-8443
www.sluggermuseum.org

Mammoth Cave
National Park Service
270-758-2180
www.nps.gov/maca

National Corvette Museum and
  Factory Tour
800-538-3883
www.corvettemuseum.com

Louisiana
Mardi Gras World
800-362-8213
www.mardigrasworld.com

National World War II Museum
504-527-6012
www.ddaymuseum.org

New Orleans Jazz and Heritage Festival
504-410-4100
www.nojazzfest.com

Spooky Cemeteries and
  Haunted House Tours
866-369-1224
www.neworleanstours.net

Maine
Acadia National Park
National Park Service
207-288-3338
www.nps.gov/acad

Bar Harbor
Bar Harbor Chamber of Commerce
207-288-5103
www.barharborinfo.com

Ogunquit
Ogunquit Chamber of Commerce
207-646-2939
www.ogunquit.org

Maryland
Annapolis
410-266-3960
www.annapolischamber.com

Baltimore & Ohio Railroad Museum
410-752-2490
www.borail.org

Baltimore's Inner Harbor
Baltimore Area Convention and
  Visitors Association
877-225-8466
www.baltimore.org/baltimore_inner_
  harbor.htm

Maryland Science Center
410-685-5225
www.mdsci.org

Massachusetts
Boston Children's Museum
617-426-6500
www.bostonchildrensmuseum.org

Boston's Public Garden
Friends of the Public Garden, Inc.
617-723-8144
www.friendsofthepublicgarden.org

Eric Carle Museum of Picture Book Art
413-658-1100
www.picturebookart.org

Fenway Park
The Boston Red Sox
boston.redsox.mlb.com

Freedom Trail
The Freedom Trail Foundation
617-357-8300
www.thefreedomtrail.org

Martha's Vineyard
508-696-7400
www.mvol.com

Old Sturbridge Village
508-347-3362
www.osv.org

Plimoth Plantation
508-746-1622
www.plimoth.org

Salem
Salem Office of Tourism and
  Cultural Affairs
877-725-3662
www.salem.org

Michigan
Bronner's CHRISTmas Wonderland
989-652-9931
www.bronners.com

Frankenmuth
Frankenmuth Chamber of Commerce and
  Convention & Visitors Bureau
800-386-8696
www.frankenmuth.org

Henry Ford Museum and
  Greenfield Village
Ford Rouge Factory Tour
313-982-6001
www.hfmgv.org

Mackinac Island
Mackinac Island Tourism Bureau
800-454-5227
www.mackinacisland.org

Sleeping Bear Dunes National Lakeshore
National Park Service
231-326-5134
www.nps.gov/slbe

Minnesota
Boundary Waters Canoe Area Wilderness
877-550-6777
www.bwcaw.org

Children's Theatre Company
612-874-0400
www.childrenstheatre.org

Mall of America
952-883-8800
www.mallofamerica.com

Minneapolis Sculpture Garden
Walker Art Center
612-375-7600
www.walkerart.org

St. Paul Winter Carnival
St. Paul Festival and Heritage Foundation
651-223-4700
www.winter-carnival.com

Mississippi
Gulf Islands National Seashore
National Park Service
228-875-9057 (Mississippi)
850-934-2600 (Florida)
www.nps.gov/guis

Missouri
Branson
Branson/Lakes Area Chamber of
    Commerce
800-296-0463
www.explorebranson.com

The Gateway Arch
St. Louis Riverfront
877-982-1410
www.gatewayarch.com

Kaleidoscope
816-274-8300
www.hallmarkkaleidoscope.com

The Magic House
314-822-8900
www.magichouse.com

St. Louis Zoo
800-966-8877
www.stlzoo.org

Silver Dollar City
800-475-9370
www.silverdollarcity.com

Montana
Glacier National Park
National Park Service
406-888-7800
www.nps.gov/glac

The Lewis and Clark National Historic
    Trail Interpretive Center
406-727-8733
www.fs.fed.us/r1/lewisclark/lcic

Little Bighorn Battlefield National
    Monument
National Park Service
406-638-3204
www.nps.gov/libi

Virginia City
406-843-5300
www.virginiacity.com

Nebraska
Buffalo Bill Ranch State Historical Park
Nebraska Game and Parks Commission
308-535-8035

Fort Cody Trading Post
308-532-8081
www.fortcody.com

Fort Robinson State Park
308-665-2919
www.stateparks.com/fort_robinson.html

Henry Doorly Zoo
402-733-8401
www.omahazoo.com

Nevada
City of Reno
775-786-4340
www.cityofreno.com

Hoover Dam
702-494-2517
www.usbr.gov/lc/hooverdam

Las Vegas
702-641-5822
www.lvchamber.com

Whitewater Park and
    Kayak Slalom Racing Course
775-787-5000
www.gowhitewater.com

New Hampshire
Keene Pumpkin Festival
Center Stage Cheshire County
603-358-5344
www.pumpkinfestival.org

Lake Winnipesaukee
www.lakewinnipesaukee.net

Odiorne Point State Park
New Hampshire State Parks
603-436-7406
www.nhstateparks.com/odiorne.html

White Mountain National Forest
USDA Forest Service
603-528-8721
www.fs.fed.us/r9/forests/white_mountain

New Jersey
Seaside Heights
www.seasideheights.net

Six Flags Great Adventure
732-928-1821
www.sixflags.com/parks/greatadventure

New Mexico
Albuquerque International Balloon Fiesta
888-422-7277
www.balloonfiesta.com

Carlsbad Caverns National Park
National Park Service
505-785-2232
www.nps.gov/cave

Santa Fe
Santa Fe Convention & Visitors Bureau
800-777-2489
www.santafe.org

Taos Pueblo
Taos County Chamber of Commerce
800-732-8267
www.taoschamber.com

New York
Adirondack Park
NYS Adirondack Park Agency
518-891-4050
www.apa.state.ny.us

American Museum of Natural History
212-769-5100
www.amnh.org

Ausable Chasm
866-782-4276
www.ausablechasm.com

Broadway
800-276-2392
www.broadway.com

Bronx Zoo
The Wildlife Conservation Society
718-367-1010
www.bronxzoo.com

Central Park
The Central Park Conservancy
212-310-6600
www.centralparknyc.org

Circle Line Tours
Harbor Cruises Information
866-782-8834
www.circlelinedowntown.com

Cooperstown
National Baseball Hall of Fame and
    Museum
888-425-5633
www.baseballhalloffame.org

Ellis Island
The Statue of Liberty–Ellis Island
    Foundation, Inc.
212-561-4588
www.ellisisland.org

Empire State Building
212-736-3100
www.esbnyc.com

Lake Placid/Essex County Visitors Bureau
518-523-2445
www.lakeplacid.com

Macy's Thanksgiving Day Parade
212-494-4495
www.macys.com/campaign/parade/
    parade.jsp

Metropolitan Museum of Art
212-535-7710
www.metmuseum.org

Radio City Music Hall
212-307-7171
www.radiocity.com

Statue of Liberty
National Park Service
212-363-3200
www.nps.gov/stli

Times Square
Times Square Alliance
212-768-1560
www.timessquarenyc.org

Village Halloween Parade
www.halloween-nyc.com

North Carolina
Great Smoky Mountains National Park
National Park Service
865-436-1200
www.nps.gov/grsm

Outer Banks
252-441-8144
www.outerbankschamber.com

Wrightsville Beach
Cape Fear Coast Convention &
    Visitors Bureau
877-406-2356
www.cape-fear.nc.us

North Dakota
International Peace Garden
888-432-6733
www.peacegarden.com

Theodore Roosevelt National Park
National Park Service
701-842-2333 (North Unit)
701-623-4466 (South Unit)
www.nps.gov/thro

Ohio
Cedar Point Amusement Park/Resort
419-627-2350
www.cedarpoint.com

Kings Island
800-288-0808
www1.cedarfair.com/kingsisland

The National Underground Railroad
   Freedom Center
877-648-4838
www.freedomcenter.org

Pro Football Hall of Fame Festival
800-533-4302
www.profootballhoffestival.com

Rock and Roll Hall of Fame and Museum
216-781-7625
www.rockhall.com

Oklahoma
National Cowboy &
   Western Heritage Museum
405-478-2250
www.nationalcowboymuseum.org

Red Earth Native American Cultural
   Festival
405-427-5228
www.redearth.org/festival.php

Oregon
The Columbia River Gorge and
   Multnomah Falls
541-308-1700
www.fs.fed.us/r6/columbia/forest/

Crater Lake National Park
National Park Service
541-594-3000
www.nps.gov/crla

Oregon Dunes National Recreation Area
541-750-7000
www.fs.fed.us/r6/siuslaw/recreation/
   tripplanning/oregondunes/

Portland Rose Festival and Rose Gardens
Portland Rose Festival Association
503-227-2681
www.rosefestival.org

Seaside
Seaside Oregon
503-738-3097
www.seasideor.com

Pennsylvania
Crayola FACTORY®
610-515-8000
www.crayola.com/factory

Carnegie Science Center
412-237-3400
www.carnegiesciencecenter.org

Franklin Institute Science Museum
215-448-1200
www.fi.edu

Gettysburg National Military Park
717-334-1124 x431
www.nps.gov/gett

Hersheypark
800-437-7439
www.hersheypa.com

Independence Hall
National Park Service
215-965-2305
www.nps.gov/inde/indep-hall.html

Kennywood Amusement Park
412-461-0500
www.kennywood.com

Mummers Museum
www.mummersmuseum.com

Mummers Parade
215-336-3050
www.mummers.com

Pennsylvania Dutch Country
Pennsylvania Dutch Convention &
   Visitors Bureau
800-723-8824
www.padutchcountry.com

Please Touch Museum®
215-963-0667
www.pleasetouchmuseum.org

Sesame Place
215-752-7070
www.sesameplace.com

Rhode Island
Block Island
Block Island Chamber of Commerce
800-383-2474
www.blockislandchamber.com

Green Animals Topiary Garden
Newport Mansions
The Preservation Society of Newport
   County
401-847-1000
www.newportmansions.org

South Carolina
Charleston
CACVB Executive Offices
800-774-0006
www.charlestoncvb.com

Edisto Island
Edisto Chamber of Commerce
888-333-2781
www.edistochamber.com

Fort Sumter National Monument
National Park Service
843-883-3123
www.nps.gov/fosu

Kiawah Island
ResortQuest Kiawah Island Reservations
800-861-1624
www.kiawah.com

South Dakota
Crazy Horse Memorial
605-673-4681
www.crazyhorse.org

Mammoth Site
605-745-6017
www.mammothsite.com

Mount Rushmore
National Park Service
605-574-3171
www.nps.gov/moru

Wind Cave National Park
National Park Service
605-745-4600
www.nps.gov/wica

Tennessee
Dollywood
800-365-5996
www.dollywood.com

Graceland
Elvis Presley Enterprises
800-238-2000
www.elvis.com/graceland

National Civil Rights Museum
901-521-9699
www.civilrightsmuseum.org

National Storytelling Festival
International Storytelling Center
800-952-8392
www.storytellingcenter.com/festival/
   festival.htm

Pigeon Forge
800-251-9100
www.mypigeonforge.com

Tennessee Aquarium
800-262-0695
www.tnaqua.org

Texas
AIA Sandcastle Competition
713-520-0155
www.aiasandcastle.com

Bat Watching at the Congress Avenue
   Bridge
800-538-2287
www.batcon.org

Big Bend National Park
National Park Service
432-477-2251
www.nps.gov/bibe

Everyone's Art Car Parade and Festival
713-926-6368
www.orangeshow.org/artcar.html

Fiesta San Antonio
The Fiesta San Antonio Commission
877-723-4378
www.fiesta-sa.org

Houston Livestock Show and Rodeo
832-667-1000
www.hlsr.com

Padre Island National Seashore
361-949-8068
www.nps.gov/pais

San Antonio
800-447-3372
www.sanantoniocvb.com

Schlitterbahn Waterparks
830-625-2351
www.schlitterbahn.com

SeaWorld
800-700-7786
www.seaworld.com/sanantonio

Space Center Houston
281-244-2100
www.spacecenter.org

Utah
Arches National Park
National Park Service
435-719-2299
www.nps.gov/arch

Best Friends Animal Sanctuary
435-644-2001
www.bestfriends.org

Utah Olympic Park
435-658-4200
www.olyparks.com

Vermont
Ben & Jerry's Ice Cream Factory Tour
866-258-6877
www.benjerry.com

Sand Bar State Park
802-893-2825
www.vtstateparks.com/htm/sandbar.cfm

Shelburne Museum
802-985-3346
www.shelburnemuseum.org

Virginia

Assateague Island National Seashore
National Park Service
410-641-1441 (Maryland district)
757-336-6577 (Virginia district)
www.nps.gov/asis

Busch Gardens, Williamsburg
800-343-7946
www.buschgardens.com

Chincoteague Pony Swim
Chincoteague Chamber of Commerce
757-336-6161
www.chincoteaguechamber.com

Colonial Williamsburg
Colonial Williamsburg Foundation
757-229-1000
www.colonialwilliamsburg.org

Historic Jamestowne and
    Jamestown Settlement
Jamestown–Yorktown Foundation
888-593-4682
www.historyisfun.org

Mount Vernon
Historic Mount Vernon
703-780-2000
www.mountvernon.org

Shenandoah National Park
National Park Service
540-999-3500
www.nps.gov/shen

Steven F. Udvar-Hazy Center
202-633-1000
www.nasm.si.edu/udvarhazy

Virginia Aquarium
757-385-3474
www.virginiaaquarium.com

Virginia Beach
Virginia Beach Tourism
800-822-3224
www.vbfun.com

Washington

Northwest Folklife Festival
206-684-7300
www.nwfolklife.org

Olympic National Park
National Park Service
360-565-3130
www.nps.gov/olym

Pike Place Market
Pike Place Market Preservation &
    Development Authority
206-682-7453
www.pikeplacemarket.org

San Juan Islands
360-378-5240
www.sanjuanisland.org

Seattle Center
206-684-7200
www.seattlecenter.com

Washington State International
    Kite Festival
360-642-4020`
www.kitefestival.com

Washington, D.C.

America's Independence Day Parade
800-215-6405
www.july4thparade.com

Bureau of Engraving and Printing
Department of the Treasury
877-874-4114
www.bep.treas.gov

International Spy Museum
866-779-6873
www.spymuseum.org

National Air and Space Museum
The Smithsonian Institution
202-633-1000
www.nasm.si.edu

The National Cherry Blossom Festival
202-547-1500
www.nationalcherryblossomfestival.org

The National Mall
National Park Service
202-426-6841
www.nps.gov/nacc

National Museum of the American Indian
Smithsonian Institution
202-633-1000
www.nmai.si.edu

National Zoo
Smithsonian Institution
202-633-4800
www.nationalzoo.si.edu

West Virginia

Harpers Ferry National Historical Park
National Park Service
304-535-6029
www.nps.gov/hafe

Winter Festival of Lights
Oglebay Resort
800-624-6988
www.oglebay-resort.com

Wisconsin

Door County Chamber of
    Commerce/Visitor & Convention
    Bureau
800-527-3529
www.doorcounty.com

Jelly Belly Candy Co. Tour Center
800-522-3267
www.jellybelly.com

Noah's Ark Waterpark
608-254-6351
www.noahsarkwaterpark.com

Washington Island
www.washingtonisland.com

The Wisconsin Dells
800-223-3557
www.wisdells.com

Wyoming

Buffalo Bill Historical Center
307-587-4771
www.bbhc.org

Cody Nite Rodeo
Buffalo Bill Cody Stampede Board
800-207-0744
www.codystampederodeo.com

Devils Tower National Monument
National Park Service
307-467-5283
www.nps.gov/deto

Grand Teton National Park
National Park Service
307-739-3300
www.nps.gov/grte

Yellowstone National Park
National Park Service
307-344-7381
www.nps.gov/yell

Canada

Banff National Park and Lake Louise
Banff Lake Louise Tourism
403-762-8421
www.bannflakelouise.com

Calgary Stampede
800-661-1260
calgarystampede.com

Carnaval de Québec
866-422-7628
www.carnaval.qc.ca

Hockey Hall of Fame
416-360-7765
www.hhof.com

The Ice Hotel
877-505-0423
www.icehotel-canada.com

Niagara Falls
Niagara Falls Tourism Authority
800-563-2557
www.niagarafallstourism.com

Old Quebec
Quebec City Tourism
877-783-1608
www.quebecregion.com

Prince Edward Island
800-463-4734
www.gov.pe.ca

Vancouver
Greater Vancouver Visitors and
    Convention Bureau
604-682-2222
www.tourismvancouver.com

Victoria
800-663-3883
www.tourismvictoria.com

West Edmonton Mall
800-661-8890
www.westedmall.com

Mexico

Chichén Itzá
Mexico Tourism Board
800-446-3942
www.visitmexico.com

Cozumel
www.islacozumel.com.mx

Day of the Dead
011 52 951 63443
www.day-of-the-dead.org

Isla Mujeres
isla-mujeres-mexico.com

Xcaret
011-52-998-883-0470
www.xcaret.com

Xel-Ha
011-52-998-884-9422
www.xel-ha.com

INDEX

TRADEMARK ACKNOWLEDGMENTS

The brand-name products mentioned in this publication are trademarks or service marks of their respective companies. The mention of any product in this publication does not constitute an endorsement by the respective proprietors of Publications International, Ltd., nor does it constitute an endorsement by any of these companies that their products should be used in the manner represented in this publication.

500 Festival® is a registered service mark of Brickyard Trademarks, Inc.; ABC® is a registered service mark of American Broadcasting Companies, Inc.; Adventureland® is a registered service mark of Walt Disney Productions; AFC® is a registered service mark of The National Football League; AIA® is a registered trademark, service mark and collective membership mark of The American Institute of Architects; Al Capone® is a registered service mark of Dillinger, LLC; Amazon Rising® is a registered service mark of Shedd Aquarium Society; American Girl Place® is a registered trademark and service mark of Pleasant Company; American Girl® is a registered trademark and service mark of Pleasant Company; American Institute of Architects® is a registered collective membership mark of The American Institute of Architects; American Museum of Natural History® is a registered service mark of the American Museum of Natural History; Angelina Ballerina® is a registered trademark and service mark of Helen Craig, Katharine Holabird, and HIT Entertainment, PLC; Anne of Green Gables® is a registered trademark and service mark of Anne of Green Gables Licensing Authority, Inc.; Ansel Adams® is a registered trademark of the Trustees of The Ansel Adams Publishing Rights Trust, John P. Schaefer, William A. Turnage, and David H. Vena; B.B. King® is a registered service mark of King Road Shows, Inc.; Baltimore & Ohio Railroad Museum® is a registered service mark of the Baltimore & Ohio Railroad Museum; Barbie® is a registered trademark and service mark of Mattel, Inc.; Beach Street USA® is a registered service mark of the Resort Leadership Council; Beanie Babies® is a registered trademark of Ty, Inc.; Bear Mountain Fire Tower® is a registered service mark of The Dollywood Company; Bellagio® is a registered trademark and service mark of Bellagio, LLC; Belly Flops® is a registered trademark of Herman Goelitz Candy Co., Inc.; Ben & Bill's® is a registered service mark of Ben & Bill's Chocolate Emporium; Ben & Jerry's® is a registered trademark and service mark of Ben & Jerry's Homemade Holdings, Inc.; Bert® is a registered trademark of Muppets, Inc.; Best Friends® is a registered trademark and service mark of Best Friends Animal Sanctuary; Big Bear Plunge® is a registered service mark of The Dollywood Company; Big Bird® is a registered trademark of Muppets, Inc.; Blizzard Beach® is a registered service mark of The Walt Disney Company; Bob Hope® is a registered trademark and service mark of Hope Enterprises, Inc.; Bonhomme Carnaval® is a registered trademark and service mark of Carnaval de Quebec Inc.; Bronner's® is a registered service mark of Bronner Display & Sign Advertising, Inc.; Bronx Zoo® is a registered trademark of the Wildlife Conservation Society; Budweiser® is a registered trademark and service mark of Anheuser-Busch, Inc.; Build-A-Bear Workshop® is a registered trademark and service mark of Build-A-Bear Workshop, Inc.; Busch Gardens® is a registered service mark of Anheuser-Busch, Inc.; Cadillac® is a registered trademark of the General Motors Corporation; Calgary Stampede® is a registered trademark of Calgary Exhibition and Stampede; California Screamin'® is a registered service mark of Disney Enterprises, Inc.; Camp Snoopy® is a registered service mark of United Feature Syndicate, Inc.; Canadian Museum of Civilization® is a registered trademark of Musee Canadien des Civilisations/Canadian Museum of Civilization; Castaway Bay® is a registered trademark and service mark of Cedar Fair, LP, Cedar Fair Management Company; Cedar Point® is a registered service mark of Cedar Fair LP; Celebration City® is a registered service mark of Herschend Family Entertainment Corporation; Christmas Spectacular® is a registered service mark of Radio City Trademarks, LLC; Churchill Downs® is a registered service mark of CDIP, LLC, CDIP Holdings, LLC; Circus Circus® is a registered service mark of Circus Circus Hotels, Inc.; Cirque du Soleil® is a registered trademark and service mark of Creations Meandres, Inc.; Clyde and Seamore® is a registered service mark of Sea World, Inc.; Clyde Sea Lion® is a registered service mark of Sea World, Inc.; Colonial Williamsburg® is a registered service mark of Colonial Williamsburg Foundation; Conga Gorilla Forest® is a registered trademark and service mark of the Wildlife Conservation Society; Conner Prairie® is a registered service mark of Earlham College; Corvette® is a registered trademark of General Motors Corporation; Crawfish Monica® is a registered trademark of Kajun Kettle Foods, Inc.; Crayola® is a registered service mark of Binney & Smith Properties, Inc.; Crazy Horse Memorial® is a registered service mark of The Crazy Horse Memorial Foundation; Critter Country® is a registered service mark of Disney Enterprises, Inc.; Crystal Pier® is a registered service mark of Crystal Pier Hotel, Inc.; Curious George® is a registered trademark and service mark of Houghton Mifflin Company; Dairy Queen® is a registered trademark and service mark of American Dairy Queen Corporation; Dennis the Menace® is a registered trademark of Post-Hall Syndicate, Inc.; Derby Festival® is a registered service mark of Kentucky Derby Festival, Inc.; Diana Ross® is a registered trademark and service mark of Image Equity Management, Inc.; Dinosphere® is a registered service mark of The Children's Museum of Indianapolis, Inc.; Disney® is a registered trademark of Disney Enterprises, Inc.; Disney World® is a registered service mark of Disney Enterprises, Inc.; Disneyland® is a registered trademark and service mark of Disney Enterprises, Inc.; Disney's Animal Kingdom® is a registered service mark of Disney Enterprises, Inc.; Disney's Beauty and the Beast® is a registered trademark and service mark of Disney Enterprises, Inc.; Disney's California Adventure® is a registered service mark of Disney Enterprises, Inc.; Dixie Stampede® is a registered service mark of Dixie Stampede, Inc.; Dolly Parton® is a registered service mark of Dolly Parton; Dollywood® is a registered trademark and service mark of Dolly Parton Productions, Inc.; Donald Duck® is a registered service mark of Disney Enterprises, Inc.; Dora the Explorer® is a registered trademark and service mark of Viacom International Inc.; Dorothy® is a registered trademark of Turner Entertainment Co.; Downtown Disney® is a registered service mark of Disney Enterprises, Inc.; Dr. Seuss® is a registered trademark of Dr. Seuss Enterprises, LP; Dr. Seuss' How the Grinch Stole Christmas!® is a registered trademark of Dr. Seuss Enterprises, LP Geisel-Seuss Enterprises, Inc.; DUPLO® is a registered trademark of Interlego A.G.; Eddie Aikau® is a registered trademark of Clyde Aikau; Edge of Africa® is a registered trademark and service mark of Busch Entertainment Corporation; Edsel® is a registered trademark of Ford Motor Company; El Toro® is a registered service mark of Six Flags Theme Parks, Inc.; Ellis Island: The National Museum of Immigration® is a registered service mark of The Statute of Liberty-Ellis Island Foundation; Elvis Presley Automobile Museum® is a registered service mark of Elvis Presley Enterprises, Inc.; Elvis Presley® is a registered trademark and service mark of Elvis Presley Enterprises, Inc.; Elvis® is a registered trademark and service mark of Elvis Presley Enterprises, Inc.; Empire State Building® is a registered service mark of the Empire State Building Company; Enchanted Woods® is a registered service mark of Henry Francis Du Pont Winterthur Museum, Inc.; Epcot® is a registered service mark of Disney Enterprises, Inc.; Epcot® is a registered trademark of Walt Disney Productions; Eric Carle® is a registered trademark of Eric Carle; Ernie® is a registered trademark of Muppets, Inc.; Escape from Pompeii® is a registered service mark of Busch Entertainment Corporation; ESPN Zone® is a registered service mark of ESPN, Inc.; Experience Music Project® is a registered trademark and service mark of Experience Learning Community; Exploration Station® is a registered service mark of the Bourbonnais Township Park District; Exploratorium® is a registered service mark of The Palace of Arts and Science; Exploratorium® is a registered trademark of The Exploratorium; F-150® is a registered trademark of Ford Motor Company; FamilyFun® is a registered trademark of Disney Enterprises, Inc.; Fantasyland® is a registered service mark of The Walt Disney Company; Felicity® is a registered trademark and service mark of Pleasant Company; Fenway Park® is a registered trademark of the Boston Red Sox Baseball Club LP; Fernbank Museum of Natural History® is a registered trademark and service mark of Fernbank, Inc.; Five & Dime General Store® is a registered service mark of UTBW, LLC; Flintstones® is a registered trademark and service mark of Hanna-Barbera Productions, Inc.; Ford® is a registered trademark and service mark of Ford Motor Company; Fountains of Bellagio® is a registered trademark of Bellagio, LLC; Frankenmuth Bavarian Inn® is a registered service mark of Zehnder's, Inc.; Frankenmuth® is a registered service mark of Frankenmuth Chamber of Commerce; Free Willy® is a registered trademark of Time Warner Entertainment Company, LP; Freedom Center® is a registered trademark and service mark of National Underground Railroad Freedom Center, Inc.; Freer Gallery of Art® is a registered trademark of the Smithsonian Institution; Fritos Chili Pie® is a registered trademark of Recot, Inc.; Frontierland® is a registered service mark of Walt Disney Productions; Froot Loops® is a registered trademark of the Kellogg Company; Galaxyland® is a registered trademark and service mark of West Edmonton Mall Property, Inc.; Girl Scouts® is a registered trademark of Girl Scouts of the United States of America, Inc.; Good Morning America® is a registered service mark of American Broadcasting Companies, Inc.; Graceland® is a registered trademark and service mark of Elvis Presley Enterprises, Inc.; Grand Floral Parade® is a registered service mark of the Portland Rose Festival Association; Great Balloon Race® is a registered service mark of Kentucky Derby Festival, Inc.; Green Gables House® is a registered trademark of the Province of Prince Edward Island; Green Monster® is a registered service mark of Boston Red Sox Baseball Club Limited Partnership New England Sports Ventures, LLC; Greenfield Village® is a registered service mark of The Edison Institute; Greyhound® is a registered trademark and service mark of The Greyhound Corporation; Guinness World Records® is a registered trademark and service mark of Guinness World Records Limited; Hallmark® is a registered service mark of Hallmark Cards, Inc.; Hanna-Barbera® is a registered trademark of Hanna-Barbera Productions, Inc.; Haunted Happenings® is a registered service mark of BPM Productions, Inc.; Haunted Mansion® is a registered service mark of Disney Enterprises, Inc.; Hearst Castle® is a registered trademark of the State of California Department of Parks and Recreation; Hemisfair Park® is a registered service mark of City of San Antonio; Henry Doorly Zoo® is a registered service mark of Omaha Zoological Society; Henry Ford Museum® is a registered service mark of The Edison Institute; Henry Moore® is a registered trademark and service mark of The Henry Moore Foundation; Herbie Hancock® is a registered service mark of Hancock, Herbert J.; HERSHEYPARK® is a registered service mark of Hershey Foods Corporation; HERSHEY'S KISSES® is a registered trademark of the Hershey Chocolate & Confectionery Corporation; HERSHEY'S® is a registered trademark of the Hershey Chocolate & Confectionery Corporation; Historic Jamestowne® is a registered trademark and service mark of The Association for the Preservation of Virginia Antiquities; Hockey Hall of Fame® is a registered trademark of the Hockey Hall of Fame and Museum; Holiday World® is a registered service mark of Santa Claus Land, Inc.; Hood® is a registered trademark of H.P. Hood Inc.; Hurricane Harbor® is a registered service mark of Six Flags Theme Parks, Inc.; Iditarod® is a registered service mark of Iditarod Trail Committee, Inc.; If I Ran the Zoo® is a registered service mark of Dr. Seuss Enterprises, LP Geisel-Seuss Enterprises, Inc.; IMAX® is a registered trademark and service mark of Imax Corporation; Indian Museum of North America® is a registered service mark of The Crazy Horse Memorial Foundation; Indianapolis 500® is a registered trademark and service mark of the Indianapolis Motor Speedway Corporation; Indy® is a registered trademark and service mark of the Indianapolis Motor Speedway Corporation; International Peace Garden® is a registered service mark of the State of North Dakota; International Spy Museum® is a registered trademark and service mark of The House On F Street, LLC; Jackalope® is a registered service mark of Charles H. McQuade; Jamestown Settlement® is a registered trademark of Jamestown-Yorktown Foundation; Jelly Belly® is a registered trademark and service mark of Jelly Belly Candy Company; Jim Henson® is a registered service mark of Jim Henson Productions, Inc.; Jimi Hendrix® is a registered trademark and service mark of Experience Hendrix, LLC; John Philip Sousa® is a registered trademark of The Instrumentalist Co.; Josefina Montoya® is a registered trademark of Pleasant Company; Josefina® is a registered trademark and service mark of Pleasant Company; Journey Behind the Falls® is a registered trademark of The Niagara Parks Commission; Jungle Cruise® is a registered service mark of Disney Enterprises, Inc.; JVC® is a registered trademark of Victory Company of Japan, Limited; Kalahari® is a registered service mark of Kalahari Development LLC; Kaleidoscope® is a registered service mark of Hallmark Cards, Inc.; Kentucky Derby® is a registered trademark of Churchill Downs, Inc.; Kermit the Frog® is a registered trademark of Henson Associates, Inc.; King Kong® is a registered trademark of MGA Entertainment, Inc.; Kingdoms of the Night® is a registered service mark of Omaha Zoological Society; Kings Island® is a registered service mark of Paramount Parks, Inc.; L.M. Montgomery® is a registered trademark and service mark of Heirs of L.M. Montgomery Inc.; Land Rover® is a registered trademark and service mark of Land Rover; Le Château Frontenac® is a registered service mark of Legacy EF Inc.; LEGO® is a registered trademark of Kirkbi AG; LEGO® is a registered trademark and service mark of Interlego A.G.; LEGOLAND® is a registered service mark of Kirkbi AG; LEGOLAND® is a registered trademark of Interlego A.G.; LIFE® is a registered trademark of Time Incorporated; Li'l Abner® is a registered trademark of Capp Enterprises, Inc.; Lone Ranger® is a registered trademark of Golden Books Publishing Company, Inc.; Looney Tunes® is a registered trademark of Time Warner Entertainment Company, LP; Lou Gehrig® is a registered service mark of CMG Worldwide, Inc.; Louisville Slugger Museum & Factory® is a registered service mark of Hillerich & Bradsby Co.; Louisville Slugger® is a registered trademark of Hillerich & Bradsby Co.; M&M's World® is a registered service mark of Mars, Incorporated; Macy's Thanksgiving Day Parade® is a registered service mark of Federated Department Stores, Inc.; Madame Tussaud's®